365 Ultimate Dessert Recipes

(365 Ultimate Dessert Recipes - Volume 1)

Michele Sova

Copyright: Published in the United States by Michele Sova/ © MICHELE SOVA

Published on November, 19 2020

All rights reserved. No part of this publication may be reproduced, stored in retrieval system, copied in any form or by any means, electronic, mechanical, photocopying, recording or otherwise transmitted without written permission from the publisher. Please do not participate in or encourage piracy of this material in any way. You must not circulate this book in any format. MICHELE SOVA does not control or direct users' actions and is not responsible for the information or content shared, harm and/or actions of the book readers.

In accordance with the U.S. Copyright Act of 1976, the scanning, uploading and electronic sharing of any part of this book without the permission of the publisher constitute unlawful piracy and theft of the author's intellectual property. If you would like to use material from the book (other than just simply for reviewing the book), prior permission must be obtained by contacting the author at author@chardrecipes.com

Thank you for your support of the author's rights.

Content

365 AWESOME DESSERT RECIPES 8

1. 3 Ingredient Cake Mix Balls Recipe 8
2. 3 Ingredient Oreo Slice Recipe 8
3. 3 Layered Ice Cream Cake Recipe................ 8
4. ANZAC Pudding Recipe 9
5. ANZAC Slice With Passionfruit Icing Recipe 9
6. Aero Bar Ice Cream Slice Recipe 9
7. Aero Bar Mint Slice Recipe 10
8. Apple Pie Recipe 10
9. Apple And Almond Croissant Custard Pudding Recipe 10
10. Australia Day Lamington Ice Cream Cake Recipe 11
11. Baileys Cheesecake Recipe 12
12. Baileys Cookies And Cream Parfaits Recipe 12
13. Baileys Custard Slice Recipe 13
14. Baked Pears With Cinnamon And Walnut Recipe 13
15. Baked Pineapple Cheesecake Recipe 13
16. Baked Raspberry Cheesecake 14
17. Banana Bread Supreme Recipe 14
18. Banana Caramel Pie 15
19. Banana Fritters Easy Recipe 15
20. Banana And Walnut Cake Recipe 15
21. Banoffee Pavlova Recipe 16
22. Basic Baked Cheesecake Recipe 16
23. Basic Biscuit Dough Recipe 16
24. Basic Butter Cake Recipe 17
25. Basic Muffin Base Recipe 17
26. Basic No Bake Cheesecake 17
27. Basic Pancakes Recipe 18
28. Best Eggnog Christmas Wreath Recipe 18
29. Best Eggnog Recipe 19
30. Best Homemade Custard Recipe 19
31. Best Mango Mousse Recipe 19
32. Best Mini Cheesecakes Recipe 20
33. Best No Bake Cheesecake Recipe 20
34. Best Strawberry Tiramisu Recipe 20
35. Best Weet Bix Slice Recipe 21
36. Best Ever Banana Cake Recipe 21
37. Best Ever Cupcakes Recipe 22
38. Betty's Rum Balls Recipe 22
39. Black Forest Trifle Recipe............................. 22
40. Blueberry Flower Twist 23
41. Boiled Cherry Fruit Cake Recipe 23
42. Boiled Pineapple Fruit Cake Recipe 23
43. Brulee Style Strawberry Cheesecake Pizza Recipe 24
44. Butterscotch Pudding Recipe 24
45. Cadbury Clinkers Rocky Road Recipe 25
46. Cafe Choc Chip Cookies Recipe 25
47. Caramel Hedgehog Slice Recipe 25
48. Cheat's Christmas Shortbread Recipe 26
49. Cheesecake Log... 26
50. Cherry Cake 26
51. Cherry Ripe Balls Recipe 27
52. Cherry Ripe Trifle Recipe 27
53. Choc Chip Muffins Recipe 28
54. Choc Salted Caramel Tart Recipe 28
55. Choc Banana Cookies 28
56. Choc Top Freckle Cookies Recipe 29
57. Chocolate Brownies Recipe 29
58. Chocolate Cheesecake Recipe 30
59. Chocolate Christmas Balls Recipe 30
60. Chocolate Crackles Recipe............................ 30
61. Chocolate Fruit Mince Puddings With Custard And Strawberries Recipe 31
62. Chocolate Hot Cross Bun Bread And Butter Pudding Recipe 31
63. Chocolate Mint Slice Christmas Balls Recipe 32
64. Chocolate Orange No Bake Cheesecake ... 32
65. Chocolate Raspberry Trifle Cake 33
66. Chocolate Rum Balls Recipe 33
67. Chocolate Slice Recipe 34
68. Chocolate Spiders Recipe 34
69. Chocolate And Salted Caramel Cookie Sandwiches Recipe 34
70. Christmas Cake Balls Recipe 34
71. Christmas Carrot Balls Recipe..................... 35
72. Christmas Choux Pastry Wreath With Cream Filling Recipe 35
73. Christmas Cookie Strips 36
74. Christmas Cookies Recipe 36
75. Christmas Cookies With Walnut Filling Recipe 37
76. Christmas Fruit Punch Recipe 37
77. Christmas Funfetti Popcorn With Honey

Butter Toffee Recipe 38
78. Christmas Honey Biscuits Recipe 38
79. Christmas Jelly Slice Recipe 38
80. Christmas Kourampiedes Recipe 39
81. Christmas Muffins Recipe 39
82. Christmas Muffins Recipe 40
83. Christmas Pudding Popsicles Recipe 40
84. Christmas Sago Plum Pudding 40
85. Christmas Squares Recipe 41
86. Christmas Trifle Recipe 41
87. Cinnamon Rolls Recipe 41
88. Classic Pavlova Recipe 42
89. Coconut Mango Cake Recipe 42
90. Condensed Milk Custard Cake Recipe 43
91. Condensed Milk Slice 43
92. Cookie Monster Pancakes Recipe 43
93. Cookies And Cream Cheesecake 44
94. Cookies And Cream Cheesecake Recipe ... 44
95. Cranberry Cheesecake Dream Slice Recipe 45
96. Cranberry, Pistachio And White Chocolate Hedgehog Recipe 45
97. Cream Cheese Lattice Slice 46
98. Creamed Rice Recipe 46
99. Crustless No Bake Cheesecake Recipe 46
100. Cupcakes Quick And Easy Recipe 47
101. Custard Cake Recipe 47
102. Custard Tart Recipe 47
103. Czech Christmas Cookies 48
104. Dark Chocolate And Strawberry Galette Recipe 48
105. Dark Chocolate, Fig And Orange Parfait Recipe 49
106. Delicious Spotty Dotty Cookies Recipe 49
107. Dessert Cob Loaf Recipe 50
108. Divine Vanilla Slice Recipe 50
109. Double Choc Ripple Cake Log Recipe 50
110. Easiest Jam Drops Recipe 51
111. Easter Bunny Cookies 51
112. Easy Apple Cake Recipe 52
113. Easy Banana Cake Recipe 52
114. Easy Banana Muffins Recipe 52
115. Easy Banana And Chocolate Bread And Butter Pudding Recipe 52
116. Easy Bread And Butter Pudding Recipe ... 53
117. Easy Caramel Sauce Recipe 53
118. Easy Chocolate And Condensed Milk Truffles Recipe 53
119. Easy Christmas Fruit Cake Recipe 54
120. Easy Cut Out Sugar Biscuits Recipe 54
121. Easy Festive Slice 55
122. Easy Lemon Self Saucing Pudding Recipe 55
123. Easy Mango Fruit Cake Recipe 55
124. Easy No Bake Caramel Slice 56
125. Easy No Bake Caramel Slice Recipe 56
126. Easy No Bake Cheesecake Recipe 56
127. Easy No Bake Nut Slice 57
128. Easy No Bake Slice 57
129. Easy Orange Cake With Orange Icing Recipe 57
130. Easy Pavlova Recipe 58
131. Easy Pikelets Recipe 58
132. Easy Mix Butter Cake Recipe 58
133. Eggless Chocolate Cake Recipe 59
134. Endive Tart Recipe 59
135. Fig And Craisin Fruit Cake 60
136. Flake Baked Bananas Recipe 60
137. Flor's Leche Flan Recipe 60
138. Flourless Peanut Butter And Choc Chip Cookies Recipe 61
139. Frozen Lemon Cream Pie Recipe 61
140. Frozen Mango Bars Recipe 62
141. Fruit Mince Cigars Recipe 62
142. Fruit Mince Crumble Slice Recipe 62
143. Fruit Tart 63
144. German Snowballs Recipe 63
145. Gingerbread Cookies Recipe 64
146. Gluten Free Rum Balls Recipe 64
147. Golden Gaytime Frozen Cheesecake Recipe 64
148. Gran's Christmas Fruit Balls Recipe 65
149. Guilt Free Choc Chip Peanut Butter Cookie For One Recipe 65
150. Healthier Chocolate Tart Recipe 65
151. Hidden Orange Pudding Recipe 66
152. Honey Joys Recipe 67
153. Impossible Pudding Recipe 67
154. Individual Banoffee Pies Recipe 68
155. Individual Sticky Date Puddings Recipe ... 68
156. Jelly Cheesecake Recipe 68
157. Lamington Cheesecake Recipe 69
158. Lemon Baked Cheesecake Recipe 69
159. Lemon Coconut Cake Recipe 70
160. Lemon Curd Cheesecake With Lemon Jelly

Topping Recipe 70
161. Lemon Meringue Cheesecake Recipe 71
162. Lemon Meringue Pie Recipe 71
163. Lemon Slice Recipe 71
164. Lemon Yoghurt Cake Recipe 72
165. Lemonade Scones Recipe 72
166. Limoncello Christmas Cake Recipe 72
167. Limoncello Tiramisu Recipe 73
168. Little Dutch Pancakes Recipe 73
169. Macadamia Christmas Cake Recipe 74
170. Macadamia And Fruit Mince Truffles Recipe 74
171. Magic Cake Recipe 75
172. Magic Peanut Butter Biscuits Recipe 75
173. Malteser Layer Cake Recipe 75
174. Malteser And Banana Cake Recipe 76
175. Mango Brulee With Passionfruit Cream Recipe 76
176. Mango Cake With Curd Recipe 76
177. Mango Cheesecake Slice Recipe 77
178. Mango Cheesecake Recipe 77
179. Mango Fruit Cake Recipe 78
180. Mango Granita Recipe 78
181. Mango Ice Cream 78
182. Mango Ice Cream Recipe 79
183. Mango Log Recipe 79
184. Mango Mousse 80
185. Mango Mousse Recipe 80
186. Mango Popsicles Recipe 80
187. Mango Rosé Jelly Jars Recipe 81
188. Mango Slice 81
189. Mango Tart 81
190. Mango And Coconut Muffins Recipe 82
191. Mango And Coconut Parfait Recipe 82
192. Mango And Raspberry Tiramisu Recipe ... 83
193. Mango And Salted Caramel Ice Cream Cake Recipe 83
194. Mars Bar Slice Recipe 84
195. Mars Bar Slice With A Twist Recipe 84
196. Marshmallow Easter Bunnies 85
197. Marshmallow And Weet Bix Slice Recipe . 85
198. Melt And Mix Christmas Cake Recipe 85
199. Merry Mango Trifle Recipe 86
200. Mini Christmas Pudding Recipe 86
201. Mini Christmas Puddings 86
202. Mini Christmas Tree Cupcakes 87
203. Mini Mango Cakes 87

204. Mixed Berries Dessert Recipe 88
205. Mixed Berry Trifle Recipe 88
206. Mixed Fruit Pie Pops Recipe 88
207. Moist Orange Poppy Seed Cake Recipe ... 89
208. Monica's Lemon Cake Recipe 89
209. Mum's Wine Trifle 89
210. Neenish Tart Slice Recipe 90
211. Neenish Tarts 91
212. New York Baked Cheesecake 91
213. No Spread Lemon Sugar Cookies Recipe . 92
214. No Bake Bliss Cake Recipe 92
215. No Bake Brownies Recipe 93
216. No Bake Caramel Cheesecake Recipe 93
217. No Bake Carrot Cake Bliss Balls Recipe ... 93
218. No Bake Cheesecake Recipe 94
219. No Bake Cheesecake Recipe 94
220. No Bake Choc Orange Fudge Cake Recipe 95
221. No Bake Choc Raisin Slice Recipe 95
222. No Bake Chocolate Almond Slice Recipe . 96
223. No Bake Chocolate Biscuit Cake 96
224. No Bake Chocolate Hazelnut Slice 96
225. No Bake Chocolate Log 97
226. No Bake Chocolate Rum Slice 97
227. No Bake Chocolate Slice Recipe 97
228. No Bake Christmas Cakes 98
229. No Bake Coconut Snowballs Recipe 98
230. No Bake Coconut And Date Balls Recipe . 98
231. No Bake Cookies 99
232. No Bake Creamy Cheesecake Recipe 99
233. No Bake Creamy Rice Pudding Recipe 99
234. No Bake Dream Slice Recipe 100
235. No Bake Fruit Tart Recipe 100
236. No Bake Ginger Caramel Slice Recipe ... 100
237. No Bake Hazelnut Slice Recipe 101
238. No Bake Lattice Lemon Cheesecake Slice Recipe 101
239. No Bake Lemon Cheesecake Recipe 101
240. No Bake Lemon Cheesecake Slice 102
241. No Bake Lemon Cheesecake Recipe 102
242. No Bake Lemon Coconut Slice Recipe .. 103
243. No Bake Licorice Allsorts Slice Recipe .. 103
244. No Bake Lindt Ball Cheesecake Recipe .. 103
245. No Bake Marshmallow Slice Recipe 104
246. No Bake Mock Cheesecake Recipe 104
247. No Bake Muesli Bars Recipe 105
248. No Bake Muesli Slice Recipe 105

249. No Bake Neapolitan Coconut Ice Slice Recipe 106
250. No Bake Nutella Bars Recipe 106
251. No Bake Pavlova Recipe 106
252. No Bake Pineapple Pudding Recipe 107
253. No Bake Strawberry Cheesecake Recipe. 107
254. No Bake Strawberry Milkshake Cheesecake Recipe 107
255. No Bake Strawberry Slice Recipe 108
256. No Bake Trail Mix Cookies Recipe 108
257. No Bake Walnut Cookie Recipe 108
258. No Bake Weet Bix Slice 109
259. No Bake White Chocolate Cheesecake Recipe 109
260. No Bake Fruit Tart Recipe 109
261. No Bake Mini Cheesecakes Recipe 110
262. No Bake Peach Tart 110
263. Nut Free Chocolate Bliss Slice Recipe 111
264. Old Fashioned Slow Cooker Rice Pudding Recipe 111
265. Oma's Gingerbread Recipe 111
266. Oreo Cheesecake 112
267. Pancakes Recipe 112
268. Passionfruit Cheese Lova Recipe 113
269. Passionfruit Delicious Pudding Recipe ... 113
270. Passionfruit Summer Snowcake Recipe .. 114
271. Passionfruit Vanilla Yoghurt Bars Recipe 114
272. Pavlova 114
273. Pavlova Recipe 115
274. Peanut Butter Cookies Recipe 115
275. Peanut Butter And Papaya Cream Protein Bars Recipe 116
276. Peppermint Chocolate Shapes 116
277. Peppermint Crisp Cheesecake Recipe 116
278. Peppermint No Bake Cheesecake 117
279. Pie Maker Vanilla Slices Recipe 117
280. Pineapple Lumps Cheesecake Recipe 118
281. Pineapple And Banana Loaf Recipe 118
282. Pink Lemonade Jelly Slice Recipe 119
283. Poached Pear And Pomegranate Sponge Cake Recipe 119
284. Portuguese Custard Tarts Recipe 120
285. Pumpkin Scones Recipe 121
286. Queenslander Truffles Recipe 121
287. Quick And Easy Anzac Biscuits Recipe .. 121
288. Quick And Easy Mango Fruit Cake Recipe 122
289. Raspberry Jam Heart Palmiers Recipe 122
290. Raspberry Meringue Trifle Recipe 122
291. Raspberry And White Chocolate Muffins Recipe 123
292. Raspberry, Orange And Almond Simnel Cake Recipe 123
293. Raw Blueberry And Hemp Tarts Recipe 124
294. Raw Muddled Raspberry Cheesecakes.... 124
295. Reindeer Poop Recipe 125
296. Rhubarb, Pear And Almond Cake Recipe 125
297. Ricotta Tiramisu Recipe 125
298. Rocky Road Christmas Pudding Recipe . 126
299. Rocky Road Recipe 126
300. Rocky Road Skillet Cookie 126
301. Rocky Road White Christmas Recipe 127
302. Rum Balls Recipe 127
303. Sam Wood's Choc Mint Slice Recipe 128
304. Self Saucing Chocolate Pudding 128
305. Shortbread Biscuits Recipe 128
306. Shortbread Simple Recipe 129
307. Shortbread Recipe 129
308. Simple Banana Muffins Recipe 129
309. Simple Chocolate Cupcakes Recipe 130
310. Slab Lova With Strawberry Curd Recipe 130
311. Slow Cooker Christmas Cake Recipe 131
312. Snickers Slice: No Bake Recipe 131
313. Snowballs Recipe 132
314. Soft Caramel Fudge Recipe 132
315. Sour Cream Apple Slice Recipe 133
316. Speculaas And Coconut No Bake Cheesecake Recipe 133
317. Sponge Flan With Cheesecake Cream And Strawberries 134
318. Stay Fresh Scones Recipe 134
319. Stewed Rhubarb Recipe 134
320. Sticky Mixed Fruit Puddings Recipe 134
321. Strawberries 'n' Cream Recipe 135
322. Strawberry Cake Recipe 135
323. Strawberry Cheesecake Recipe 136
324. Strawberry Pavlova Roll Recipe 136
325. Strawberry Ripple Cheesecake Recipe 137
326. Strawberry And White Choc Muffins Recipe 137
327. Stuffed Strawberries 137
328. Sugar Free Mango Nice Ice Cream Recipe

138
329. Sugar Free Vanilla Cheesecake With Mango Topping Recipe 138
330. Summer Trifle With Pineapple Recipe 139
331. Super Moist Chocolate Cupcakes Recipe 139
332. Sweet Petite Mince Tarts Recipe 140
333. Sweet Potato Marshmallow Pie Recipe ... 140
334. TIFFXO: Tiffiny Hall's Spelt Chocolate And Zucchini Muffins Recipe 142
335. Tim Tam Cheesecake Balls Recipe 142
336. Tim Tam Cheesecake With Salted Caramel Recipe 142
337. Tim Tam Hedgehog Slice 143
338. Tiramisu Recipe 143
339. Toblerone Cheesecake Slice Recipe 144
340. Toblerone Mousse Recipe 144
341. Traditional Christmas Pudding Recipe 145
342. Tropical Cheesecake Log Recipe 145
343. Tropical Coconut Meringue Torte 146
344. Tuckshop Banana Cake Recipe 146
345. Turkish Delight Fridge Cake Recipe 146
346. Turmeric Mango Smoothie Bowl Recipe 147
347. Vanilla Bean Panna Cotta With Mango And White Chocolate Macadamia Truffle Recipe 147
348. Vanilla Slice Recipe 148
349. Vanilla Slice Recipe 148
350. Very Simple Banana Bread Recipe 149
351. Walnut Christmas Cookies 149
352. Warm Chocolate Brownies With Salted Caramel Sauce And Custard Recipe 149
353. Weet Bix, Honey And Banana Loaf Recipe 150
354. Wendy's Easy Pavlova 151
355. White Chocolate Grand Marnier Truffles Recipe 151
356. White Chocolate Key Lime Pie Recipe ... 151
357. White Chocolate Malteser Cheesecake Recipe 152
358. White Chocolate And Mango Cheesecake Recipe 152
359. White Chocolate And Strawberry Pavlova Recipe 153
360. White Christmas Peppermint Surprise 153
361. White Christmas Pudding Balls Recipe ... 154
362. White Christmas Truffles Recipe 154
363. White Christmas Recipe 154
364. Wholemeal Vegan Blueberry Pancakes Recipe 155
365. Yo Yo Biscuits Recipe 155

INDEX **156**

CONCLUSION **159**

365 Awesome Dessert Recipes

***

1. 3 Ingredient Cake Mix Balls Recipe

Serving: 0 | Prep: 15mins | Cook: 5mins | Ready in: 20mins

Ingredients

- 600g iced white chocolate mud cake
- 400g white chocolate, chopped
- Hundreds & thousands, to sprinkle

Direction

- Line a large baking tray with baking paper. Use your hands to break the mud cake into small pieces (including the icing) until coarsely crumbed. Roll one tbs of the mixture firmly into a ball. Transfer to the prepared tray. Repeat with the remaining mixture to make 24 balls.
- Place the chocolate in a heatproof bowl over a saucepan of simmering water (make sure the base of the bowl doesn't touch the water). Stir until chocolate has melted. Remove the bowl from the pan.
- Spread hundreds and thousands on a plate. Working one at a time, use two forks to dip a ball into the melted chocolate. Allow excess chocolate to drain back into the bowl before rolling in the hundreds and thousands. Return to the tray. Set aside for 20 minutes or until set.

2. 3 Ingredient Oreo Slice Recipe

Serving: 12 | Prep: 255mins | Cook: 0S | Ready in: 255mins

Ingredients

- 4 cups thickened cream whipped
- 1 cup milk
- 3 packets Oreo biscuits

Direction

- Using a large dish (30cm x 22cm), spread one third of the whipped cream on the base of the dish.
- Dip cookies one at a time into the milk and place on the cream layer.
- Top with one third of the cream again and add another layer of milk-dipped cookies.
- Top with the remaining cream and place undipped cookies on top to decorate. Refrigerate for 4 hours.

3. 3 Layered Ice Cream Cake Recipe

Serving: 0 | Prep: 360mins | Cook: 0S | Ready in: 360mins

Ingredients

- 4 L vanilla ice cream softened
- 200 g chocolate honeycomb bar crushed
- 140 g Nestle* Peppermint Crisp chocolate bars crushed
- 150 g Mars mini M&Ms

Direction

- Line a ring tin, loaf tin or cake tin well with plastic wrap, allowing it to overlap the sides.
- Divide ice-cream into three and place into separate bowls.

- In one bowl, add the honeycomb and mix slowly until combined.
- Repeat with the peppermint bars in the next bowl, and then the chocolate covered buttons in the last bowl.
- Layer the tin with the honeycomb ice-cream, smooth out evenly. Repeat for the peppermint and then the m&m layer.
- Cover loosely with plastic wrap and freeze overnight.
- When ready to serve, remove from freezer and stand for a couple of minutes, then turn cake out onto a plate.
- Cut into slices and serve.

4. ANZAC Pudding Recipe

Serving: 6 | Prep: 25mins | Cook: 25mins | Ready in: 50mins

Ingredients

- 1 1/2 cups self-raising flour
- 100g butter
- 1/2 cup rolled oats
- 1/2 cup sugar
- 1/4 cup coconut
- 1 cup milk
- 1 egg
- 1 tsp vanilla essence
- Sauce
- 50g butter
- 1/2 cup golden syrup
- 2 cups boiling water

Direction

- Preheat oven to 160C.
- Sift flour and then rub in butter with fingers.
- Add rolled oats, sugar, coconut and mix.
- In a separate bowl, mix milk, eggs and vanilla, then add to the dry ingredients. Mix well.
- Sauce: For the sauce, mix together butter, syrup and boiling water.
- Pour over mixture and cook for 25 minutes.

5. ANZAC Slice With Passionfruit Icing Recipe

Serving: 10 | Prep: 15mins | Cook: 5mins | Ready in: 20mins

Ingredients

- 1/2 cup coconut
- 75g butter melted
- 1/2 cup condensed milk
- 1 1/4 cups icing sugar
- 2 tbs passionfruit pulp
- 400g ANZAC biscuits

Direction

- Finely crumb the ANZAC biscuits in a food processor or by hand.
- Place the crumbs into a large bowl. Stir in the coconut, butter and condensed milk. Mix well.
- Press the mix firmly into a slice tin 20cm x 30cm.
- Refrigerate for a few hours or until firm.
- Sift the icing sugar into a bowl, then stir in passionfruit pulp to make a firm paste. Microwave on high for 30 seconds, or until it is warm and spreadable, or place over a bowl of simmering water.
- Spread icing over the slice. Return to fridge until the icing is set, then cut into squares.

6. Aero Bar Ice Cream Slice Recipe

Serving: 12 | Prep: 15mins | Cook: 360mins | Ready in: 375mins

Ingredients

- 600 ml cream
- 395 g condensed milk

- 375 g Aero Peppermint Crisp chocolate bars crushed
- 1 packet malt biscuits

Direction

- Line a slice tray with biscuits.
- Whip condensed milk and cream until thick.
- Stir in aero bar and spread over biscuits and top with another layer of biscuits.
- Freeze until firm. When serving cut along biscuit like a giant sandwich.

7. Aero Bar Mint Slice Recipe

Serving: 12 | Prep: 15mins | Cook: 0S | Ready in: 15mins

Ingredients

- 125 g butter melted
- 1 cup caster sugar
- 1 tbs cocoa powder
- 1 tbs condensed milk
- 50 g Nestle* Aero Peppermint Crisp chocolate bars crushed
- 250 g chocolate ripple biscuits crushed

Direction

- Melt butter in microwave for about 45 seconds, then add sugar and mix until sugar has dissolved.
- Add cocoa and condensed milk.
- Add biscuits and Aero bar to other ingredients and mix well.
- Place mixture into a slice tin and ice with chocolate icing.
- Place in the fridge overnight.

8. Apple Pie Recipe

Serving: 8 | Prep: 30mins | Cook: 80mins | Ready in: 110mins

Ingredients

- 6 apples cooked large
- 3/4 cup water
- 1 tbs sugar *to taste
- Pastry
- 2 cups self-raising flour
- 125g unsalted butter
- 2 tbs sugar
- 1 egg
- 2 tbs water

Direction

- Peel and slice apples into a medium-sized pot with sugar and water.
- Bring to boil and simmer until cooked. Drain and cool.
- Sift flour into mixing bowl and add sugar and butter. Rub in with fingers until mixture resembles crumbs.
- Add beaten egg and water.
- Roll out half the mix with rolling pin adding flour as needed. Cover bottom of greased and floured pie dish with rolled out pastry, add apples and repeat with the rest of the pastry on the top.
- Cut around edge of pie dish with a knife and press layers together with a floured fork. Brush with a little milk and sprinkle with caster sugar.
- Bake at 180C (170C fan forced) for approximately 45-60 minutes until brown.

9. Apple And Almond Croissant Custard Pudding Recipe

Serving: 4 | Prep: 100mins | Cook: 60mins | Ready in: 160mins

Ingredients

- 6 croissant
- 900 g thick vanilla custard
- 50 g flaked almonds

- 2 granny smith apple
- 1/2 cup currants
- 2 tbs caster sugar

Direction

- Cut the croissants in half. Peel and slice the apples into very thin slices - so thin you can almost see through!
- Arrange half of the croissants over the base of oven safe dish. Place the apple slices and 1/4 cup of currants over the top and sprinkle with 1 tablespoon of the caster sugar. Pour half of the custard over the top of the mixture.
- Place the remaining croissants on top of the dish and pour over the remaining custard. Let the mixture sit at room temperature for 1.5 hours to allow the custard to soak into the croissants.
- Preheat oven to 170C.
- Sprinkle the remaining currants and flaked almonds over the top of the soaked croissants and sprinkle with the remaining tablespoon of caster sugar.
- Place the dish into your preheated oven and bake for 1 hour or until the top of the pudding begins to turn golden.
- Carefully remove the pudding from the oven and let it sit for 10 minutes before cutting to serve.

10. Australia Day Lamington Ice Cream Cake Recipe

Serving: 8 | Prep: 15mins | Cook: 5mins | Ready in: 20mins

Ingredients

- 225 g double unfilled sponge cake
- 1 1/2 Litres vanilla ice cream
- 125 g fresh raspberries
- 125 g dark chocolate chopped
- 1 tbs coconut oil
- 1/4 cup shredded coconut

Direction

- Lay 2 large sheets of plastic wrap on top of each other and use to line a 1.75L (7-cup) loaf pan, allowing the sides to overhang. Line with a sheet of baking paper, extending over the 2 long sides.
- Break up the sponge cake into a food processor and process briefly to form coarse crumbs. Spoon 500ml of the ice cream into a large mixing bowl and add half the crumbs. Allow ice cream to soften slightly then use a metal spoon to mix in the crumbs until evenly combined (the ice cream should be just soft but not melted). Spoon into the pan and smooth the surface, pressing down firmly to make an even layer. Freeze for 2 hours or until firm.
- Spoon another 500ml of ice cream into a mixing bowl and mash with a large metal spoon until softened. Spread over the first layer in the pan, smoothing the surface. Return to the freezer. Puree the raspberries in a food processor and pour over the ice cream. Freeze for 2 hours or until firm.
- Use the remaining ice cream and crumbs to make another layer (see step 2). Spread into the pan. Fold the paper and overhanging plastic over the surface and freeze for another 2 hours, or overnight, until very firm.
- Melt the chocolate and coconut oil in the microwave until just warm and melted, but not hot. Stir until combined and smooth, then transfer to a jug and cool to room temperature.
- Invert the loaf pan onto a chilled serving platter and remove the plastic and paper. Slowly pour the chocolate mixture over the loaf, allowing it to drizzle down the sides a little. Working quickly before it sets, sprinkle the top with coconut. Return to the freezer until serving time.

11. Baileys Cheesecake Recipe

Serving: 12 | Prep: 20mins | Cook: 5mins | Ready in: 25mins

Ingredients

- Base
- 185 g digestive biscuits
- 100 g butter melted
- 2 tbs caster sugar *optional
- Filling
- 3 tsp gelatine powder
- 2 tbs water
- 500 g cream cheese
- 15 ml Baileys Irish cream liqueur
- 300 g sweetened condensed milk
- 300 ml thickened cream whipped
- 100 g milk chocolate grated *to decorate

Direction

- Base: Crush biscuits and mix with melted butter.
- Press evenly into the base of a springform tin and refrigerate while preparing filling.
- Filling: Sprinkle gelatine over water in a small heatproof bowl. Microwave for 30 seconds and stir until gelatine dissolves. Cool for 5 minutes.
- Beat cream cheese, Irish cream and condensed milk together until smooth.
- Beat cream in small bowl until soft peaks form.
- Stir in warm gelatine mixture into cream cheese mixture.
- Fold in whipped cream and grated chocolate.
- Pour into springform pan and refrigerate for 4-5 hours to set or overnight for a firmer cheesecake.
- Garnish with grated chocolate and whipped cream, if desired.

12. Baileys Cookies And Cream Parfaits Recipe

Serving: 6 | Prep: 30mins | Cook: 0S | Ready in: 30mins

Ingredients

- 1 packet Oreo biscuits
- 115 g milk chocolate melts
- 1/2 cup milk
- 600 ml thickened cream
- 50 ml Baileys liqueur
- 1/4 cup icing sugar
- 6 cherries fresh

Direction

- Chill six short drinking glasses in the fridge, so that they're ready to layer up.
- Remove the white cream filling from all the Oreos, then put the chocolate biscuits into a mini whizz. Whizz them up until they become fine crumbs.
- Put the milk chocolate melts into a bowl and pour the hot milk over them. The heat of the milk should melt the chocolate. Stir it all gently until it's melted together, then set it aside to cool.
- Put the cream, Baileys and icing sugar into the bowl of a mixer. Whip the cream to stiff peaks.
- Divide the cream mixture into two halves. To one half gently and gradually fold in the chocolate mixture.
- Now you should have all the elements: cream, chocolate cream, biscuit crumbs and cherries. Using a spoon, layer them into a glass alternately.
- Start with chocolate cream, then add a large spoonful of biscuit crumbs, followed by chocolate cream and then finish with cream and more biscuit crumbs. Top it with a cherry.
- Layer up six glasses and when it's time for dessert you won't even have to cut anything into pieces. Just serve them with a spoon and your work here is done.

13. Baileys Custard Slice Recipe

Serving: 0 | Prep: 20mins | Cook: 0S | Ready in: 20mins

Ingredients

- 200g Marie biscuits
- 100g butter, melted
- 600ml thickened cream
- 100g pkt instant pudding
- 2 tbs custard powder
- 100ml Baileys Irish Cream
- Icing sugar, for dusting

Direction

- Line a square cake tin with baking paper, allowing plenty to hang over the side. In a food processor, blitz biscuits to form a fine crumb. Add melted butter and blitz again until fully combined. Pour into the prepared tin and use a large spoon or glass to press down into an even layer. Refrigerate for 30 minutes to set.
- Place cream in a large bowl and sprinkle over instant pudding and custard powder. Use electric beaters to whip for 2 - 3 minutes until thick and smooth. Add Baileys and continue beating for a further minute.
- Pour the cream mixture over the biscuit base, smoothing the top. Refrigerate for at least 2 hours or overnight.
- Use the overhanging baking paper to lift the slice from the tin. Place on a board and sprinkle liberally with icing sugar. Slice into squares and serve.

14. Baked Pears With Cinnamon And Walnut Recipe

Serving: 0 | Prep: 5mins | Cook: 30mins | Ready in: 35mins

Ingredients

- 6 pears
- 1 cup sugar
- 1 cup water
- 1 tsp whole cloves
- Filling
- 1/2 cup walnuts crushed
- 1 tsp ground cinnamon

Direction

- Preheat oven to 180C.
- Core pears from the bottom leaving the stem intact. Place the pears in a deep saucepan with sugar and water. Cook for approximately 10 minutes or until they start to get tender. Remove from heat.
- Combine walnut and cinnamon.
- Once the pears are cool enough to handle, fill with the walnut mixture and place upright in an oven proof dish. Drizzle remaining syrup over the pears and place cloves in the syrup. Bake in the preheated oven for approximately 20 minutes or until golden.
- Enjoy warm with ice-cream, cream or custard.

15. Baked Pineapple Cheesecake Recipe

Serving: 10 | Prep: 30mins | Cook: 50mins | Ready in: 80mins

Ingredients

- 125 g butter melted
- 250 g Nice biscuits crushed
- 500 g cream cheese brought to room temperature
- 410 g (crushed) canned pineapple drained reserve liquid
- 1 tbs cornflour
- 3 egg brought to room temperature
- 3/4 cup sugar
- 1 tsp vanilla essence

Direction

- Combine crushed biscuits and melted butter or margarine.
- Press onto base and sides of greased 20-22 cm springform pan.
- Combine reserved syrup and cornflour and heat gently in a medium saucepan, until thick.
- Add pineapple and mix well.
- Pour thickened pineapple over biscuit base.
- Beat cream cheese until smooth.
- Add sugar, eggs and vanilla and continue beating until mixture is thick and smooth.
- Pour over pineapple in pan.
- Place pan on baking tray, place in centre of oven and bake at 180C for 25 minutes.
- Turn oven off and leave cheesecake in oven with door ajar until at room temperature.
- Refrigerate, then serve with whipped cream.

16. Baked Raspberry Cheesecake

Serving: 10 | Prep: 45mins | Cook: 180mins | Ready in: 225mins

Ingredients

- 350 g cream cheese
- 530 g ricotta
- 4 egg
- 1 lime juiced zested
- 300 g caster sugar
- 1/2 tsp vanilla extract
- 1 1/2 tbs cornflour
- 3 tbs water
- Raspberry Sauce
- 150 g frozen raspberries
- 1/2 cup caster sugar
- 2 tsp cornflour
- 2 tbs water
- Base
- 50 g almond meal
- 100 g plain flour
- 50 g caster sugar
- 100 g butter

Direction

- Base: Process all ingredients, combine into a soft crumb.
- Line the base of a 24 cm springform cake tin with cooking paper. Press crumb mix onto base forming an even, compact base.
- Bake at 150C for approximately 20 minutes or until light brown. Set aside to cool.
- Filling: Mix cornflour and water into a runny paste.
- Combine all other ingredients in a food processor and mix to smooth paste. Then add the cornflour mix and combine to create a creamy texture. Set aside.
- Raspberry Sauce: Add frozen raspberries and sugar to a saucepan over medium heat and bring to a simmer, reduce heat and simmer for 5 minutes. Add cornflour mixed with water slowly to make a thick sauce. Stop adding the cornflour mix if the raspberries thicken too much. Set aside and cool.
- Line the sides of tin with baking paper.
- Carefully spoon the raspberry sauce around the top of the base evenly.
- Add the cheesecake filling over the raspberry sauce. The cake tin should be about ¾ full.
- Bake for 1 hour at 150C, turn off oven and leave in hot oven for another hour with door closed. Refrigerate until cool.

17. Banana Bread Supreme Recipe

Serving: 12 | Prep: 15mins | Cook: 30mins | Ready in: 45mins

Ingredients

- 3 bananas mashed medium ripe
- 2 tbs golden syrup
- 1/4 cup caster sugar
- 1 egg
- 1 cup self-raising flour

- 1 pinch salt
- 1 tbs cinnamon sugar *to taste

Direction

- Heat oven to 180C and grease and line the base of a loaf tin.
- Mash bananas in a medium-sized bowl, then add golden syrup.
- Add caster sugar and mix well.
- Add egg, sifted flour and salt, and lightly mix until just combined.
- Pour mixture into loaf tin and lightly sprinkle with cinnamon sugar.
- Bake for 30 minutes or until a skewer inserted into the middle comes out clean.

18. Banana Caramel Pie

Serving: 8 | Prep: 20mins | Cook: 0S | Ready in: 20mins

Ingredients

- 200 g Nice biscuits
- 75 g unsalted butter
- Filling
- 380 g NESTLE Top n Fill Caramel
- 3 banana
- 300 ml thickened cream
- 30 g milk chocolate

Direction

- For base, crush biscuits with rolling pin or in food processor. Melt butter and add to crushed biscuits.
- Lightly grease a 25cm pie dish. Add biscuit crumbs and press firmly on base and around sides with a glass. Refrigerate for 15 minutes.
- Gently heat caramel top 'n' fill and pour into chilled biscuit base. Slice 3 bananas (around 1cm thickness) and place on caramel.
- Whip thickened cream and spoon onto the bananas. Grate or curl milk chocolate and sprinkle on top of cream. Refrigerate or serve straight away.

19. Banana Fritters Easy Recipe

Serving: 4 | Prep: 15mins | Cook: 25mins | Ready in: 40mins

Ingredients

- 2 cups self-raising flour
- 1/2 tsp bicarbonate of soda
- 1 1/2 cup water
- 4 bananas
- 1 cup plain flour
- 1/2 cup oil

Direction

- Sift flour and bicarbonate of soda into a bowl. Add water and mix to a smooth batter.
- Peel bananas, cut into three and roll lightly in flour.
- Drop banana pieces into batter and drain off excess batter.
- Deep fry in hot oil until golden brown.
- Remove, drain on absorbent paper. Serve hot with ice-cream.

20. Banana And Walnut Cake Recipe

Serving: 12 | Prep: 15mins | Cook: 75mins | Ready in: 90mins

Ingredients

- 125 g butter
- 3/4 cup sugar
- 1/2 cup walnuts chopped
- 1 3/4 cup self-raising flour
- 2 egg beaten
- 3 banana mashed

- 1 tsp bicarbonate of soda
- 3 tbs milk
- 1 tbs boiling water

Direction

- Cream butter, sugar and water together.
- Gradually add eggs, then the mashed bananas.
- Dissolve bicarbonate of soda in milk and add flour alternately with milk to banana mixture.
- Add chopped walnuts.
- Bake at 180C for about an hour or until knife comes out clean.

21. Banoffee Pavlova Recipe

Serving: 10 | Prep: 25mins | Cook: 90mins | Ready in: 115mins

Ingredients

- 6 egg whites
- 350 g caster sugar
- 400 g NESTLE Top n Fill Caramel chilled
- 300 g thickened cream whipped
- 2 bananas sliced
- 1 block milk chocolate grated *to decorate

Direction

- Beat eggs whites until soft peaks form.
- Add the sugar gradually until dissolved, approximately 10 minutes.
- Mark 25 cm circle on two pieces of baking paper and line 2 trays.
- Place mix evenly into two circles and bake at 100C for 1½ hours. Allow to cool in oven.
- When cool place one meringue disc onto serving plate, spread with half the Top 'n' Fill then place 1 sliced banana evenly on disc.
- Spread with half the beaten cream, then repeat, finishing with flake or grated chocolate.

22. Basic Baked Cheesecake Recipe

Serving: 18 | Prep: 20mins | Cook: 85mins | Ready in: 105mins

Ingredients

- 250g biscuits
- 1 tsp mixed spice
- 100g butter melted
- Filling
- 500g cream cheese
- 2/3 cup caster sugar
- 4 eggs
- 1 tsp vanilla essence
- 1 tbs lemon juice

Direction

- Grease a 20cm springform tin.
- Crush biscuits in food processor and add mixed spice and butter.
- Line base of tin with foil and brush sides with oil. Press crumbs over base and sides of tin. Place in fridge for 20 minutes.
- Meanwhile, to make the filling, preheat oven to 180C.
- Beat cream cheese until smooth. Add sugar, vanilla and lemon juice. Beat until smooth.
- Add eggs, 1 at a time, beating well after each addition.
- Pour mix into tin and bake for 45 minutes or until just firm to the touch.

23. Basic Biscuit Dough Recipe

Serving: 0 | Prep: 15mins | Cook: 25mins | Ready in: 40mins

Ingredients

- 250 g butter softened
- 2/3 cup caster sugar
- 1 tsp vanilla essence

- 1 egg
- 2 1/4 cups plain flour sifted

Direction

- Mix butter, sugar and vanilla in a bowl with electric mixer, until light and creamy.
- Add egg and mix until combined.
- Stir in 2 cups of flour for a soft dough, or 2¼ cups of flour for a firm dough.
- Add flavourings and shape, as desired.
- Bake at 180C for approximately 12-15 minutes.

24. Basic Butter Cake Recipe

Serving: 12 | Prep: 15mins | Cook: 85mins | Ready in: 100mins

Ingredients

- 185 g butter softened
- 1 cup caster sugar
- 1 tsp vanilla essence
- 3 eggs large
- 2 cups self-raising flour
- 1/4 cup milk

Direction

- Preheat oven to 180C and grease a 20 cm cake tin well.
- In a large bowl, beat the butter, sugar and vanilla together with an electric mixer until light and creamy.
- Add the eggs one at a time and beat well after each addition.
- Sift the flour over the mixture alternately with the milk, adding a third at a time. Stir in lightly.
- Spoon batter into prepared tin and bake for 50-60 minutes or until a skewer pulls clean from the middle of the cake.
- Cool cake in tin for a few minutes before turning out onto a wire rack.

- Cake can be iced or dusted with icing sugar if desired.

25. Basic Muffin Base Recipe

Serving: 0 | Prep: 5mins | Cook: 20mins | Ready in: 25mins

Ingredients

- 2 cups self-raising flour
- 1/2 cup sugar
- 1 egg beaten
- 1/4 cup canola oil
- 1 cup milk

Direction

- Preheat oven to 180C. Place all ingredients in a bowl.
- Mix until just combined.
- Scoop the mixture into patty cakes in a muffin pan. Bake for approximately 20 minutes.

26. Basic No Bake Cheesecake

Serving: 12 | Prep: 15mins | Cook: 440mins | Ready in: 455mins

Ingredients

- 250 g biscuits crushed
- 125 g butter melted
- Filling
- 250 g cream cheese softened
- 395 g condensed milk
- 1/3 cup lemon juice fresh

Direction

- Place baking paper into a 25 cm springform tin, extending paper up the sides of the tin.

- Mix biscuits crumbs and butter until well-combined.
- Pack tightly into tin.
- Place in fridge to set.
- Filling: In a bowl, beat cheese until soft.
- Add condensed milk and mix until smooth.
- Add lemon juice. Mix well.
- Pour into biscuit base and smooth over.
- Allow to set in the fridge for 2 hours or overnight.

27. Basic Pancakes Recipe

Serving: 0 | Prep: 15mins | Cook: 15mins | Ready in: 30mins

Ingredients

- 1 cup self-raising flour
- 1 cup milk
- 1 egg

Direction

- Preheat a large, non-stick frypan.
- Place all the ingredients into a bowl and mix until just combined.
- Lightly grease the pan with butter or cooking spray.
- Cook large spoonfuls of batter until bubbles burst on the surface and the edges start to go dry.
- Turn and cook other side until golden brown.

28. Best Eggnog Christmas Wreath Recipe

Serving: 0 | Prep: 90mins | Cook: 20mins | Ready in: 110mins

Ingredients

- 1/4 cup pistachios crushed
- 1/4 cup sugar crystals
- 1/4 cup hard lollies
- Filling
- 2 egg yolks
- 40 g sugar
- 1/2 tbs cornflour
- 120 g cream
- 1 tsp vanilla essence
- 2 tsp nutmeg
- 1 tsp allspice
- Choux pastry
- 3 eggs beaten
- 200 ml water
- 85 g butter
- 110 g plain flour
- 30 g sugar
- Toffee
- 300 g sugar
- 75 ml water

Direction

- Line two baking trays with baking paper and set over to side. Preheat oven to 170C degrees fan-forced.
- To make the pastry - Add water, sugar and butter to a pot and bring to the boil. Once boiling slowly add the flour and mix vigorously until the mixture forms a ball and comes away from the sides of the pot. Allow to cool for about 10 minutes. Then, add back on to a very low heat and mix in egg mix to create a smooth paste like dough. (May not need all of the egg). Fill a piping bag and pipe the mixture into small 3cm round dollops. Cook for about 12 minutes or until they have turned slightly golden. Pierce a small hole into each one and cook again for another 10 minutes or until the outside is golden and the centre is cooked. Allow to cool for 20 minutes. Once the pastry is cool, put filling mix into a piping bag and pipe into each pastry ball. Be sure to fill them up, but not make them explode. After all balls are full, arrange into a circle/ wreath shape, ensuring everyone overlaps another.
- For the filling- In a small pot, bring cream to the boil. In a separate bowl add egg yolks,

sugar, corn flour and spices. Once cream has begun to boil, take off heat and slowly pour into egg mix, stirring constantly to prevent the eggs from scrambling. Then put the mixture back in the pot and onto a low heat. Continue to stir whilst on the heat until mixture thickens and corn flour has been cooked. (Be careful not to let the mixture catch on the bottom. Remove once thick and cool in fridge.
- For the toffee- In a deep saucepan, bring water and sugar to the boil. Try not to stir the liquid too much to prevent the sugar from crystallising. Continue to boil until liquid reaches 150C degrees/hard toffee. To test, drop a small bit onto a plate and see if it sets. Once the temperature reaches 150C, it should begin to turn slightly golden. Remove from heat.
- Assembly the Wreath- Carefully, use a spoon to pour toffee over the choux wreath. Make sure it all gets covered to ensure that the pastrys all stick together. Whilst still hot, put on decorations. I used lemon thyme leaves/flowers, sugar crystals, crushed pistachios and candy balls (however the decorations are completely up to you). Allow to cool. Clean up any excess toffee and serve.

29. Best Eggnog Recipe

Serving: 6 | Prep: 10mins | Cook: 0S | Ready in: 10mins

Ingredients

- 6 egg
- 1 cup sugar
- 1 tbs sugar
- 1/2 tsp vanilla extract
- 1/4 tsp nutmeg
- 3/4 cup brandy
- 1/2 cup rum
- 2 cup milk
- 2 cup cream

Direction

- Beat eggs for 2-3 minutes until very frothy.
- Gradually beat in sugar, vanilla and nutmeg.
- Stir in brandy, rum, milk and cream.
- Pour into jug for serving.

30. Best Homemade Custard Recipe

Serving: 4 | Prep: 10mins | Cook: 15mins | Ready in: 25mins

Ingredients

- 2 whole eggs
- 3 tbs cornflour
- 3 cups milk
- 3 tbs sugar *to taste
- 1 tsp vanilla essence

Direction

- Whisk eggs, cornflour and milk together in a saucepan until smooth.
- Continue whisking on stovetop until custard becomes thick and creamy.
- Remove from heat, then whisk in sugar and vanilla.

31. Best Mango Mousse Recipe

Serving: 4 | Prep: 15mins | Cook: 15mins | Ready in: 30mins

Ingredients

- 2 mango large
- 1 tbs lemon juice
- 1/2 cup pure icing sugar sifted
- 1 tbs gelatine powder
- 1/4 cup hot water
- 300 ml thickened cream whipped

Direction

- Peel and chop mangoes.
- Blend with the lemon juice and icing sugar.
- Pour into glass bowl.
- Dissolve gelatine in the hot water. Add to mango mixture and mix well.
- Fold in the whipped cream mixing well.
- Chill until set.

32. Best Mini Cheesecakes Recipe

Serving: 10 | Prep: 15mins | Cook: 25mins | Ready in: 40mins

Ingredients

- 250 g Arnott's butternut snap biscuits
- 250 g cream cheese softened
- 1/2 cup caster sugar
- 2 eggs
- 1 cup fresh blueberries *to decorate

Direction

- Preheat oven to 140C.
- Arrange patty papers in a muffin tray.
- Place a biscuit in the bottom of each patty paper.
- Beat cream cheese, gradually adding sugar until mix is smooth.
- Add eggs, one at a time, mixing until smooth.
- Spoon mixture into the patty papers.
- Place berries on top and bake for approximately 25 minutes, or until cooked.
- Refrigerate when cool.

33. Best No Bake Cheesecake Recipe

Serving: 10 | Prep: 30mins | Cook: 220mins | Ready in: 250mins

Ingredients

- 600 g vanilla cake mix
- 1 cup coconut
- 125 g butter melted
- 85 g jelly crystals
- 2 x 375 g cream cheese
- 300 ml thickened cream
- 1 mango optional

Direction

- Cake Base: Combine vanilla cake mix and coconut, add melted butter.
- Mix should stay together when pressed, but crumble when touched, if it is dry, add more butter.
- Press into a greased or lined deep slice tin.
- Bake for 20 minutes at 180C. Allow to cool.
- Topping: Mix jelly crystals in 1 cup warm water, allow to cool slightly.
- Whip thickened cream until to form soft peaks.
- Mix cream cheese and jelly until creamy.
- Fold in thickened cream.
- Fold in fruit if using.
- Spread over cooked base,
- Place in freezer to set quickly, or fridge to set slowly.

34. Best Strawberry Tiramisu Recipe

Serving: 4 | Prep: 360mins | Cook: 10mins | Ready in: 370mins

Ingredients

- 250 g fresh strawberries
- 125 g sugar
- 4 tbs strawberry liqueur
- 300 ml thickened cream
- 4 tbs icing sugar
- 1/2 tsp ground cinnamon
- 250 g mascarpone
- 100 g Savoiardi sponge finger biscuits

- 1 pinch cinnamon sugar *to decorate

Direction

- Reserve a few strawberries for garnish.
- Slice the remaining strawberries into small pieces and add to a saucepan with the sugar.
- Stir over low heat until sugar has dissolved. Allow to simmer.
- Meanwhile, whip the thickened cream with the icing sugar and ground cinnamon to a soft peak stage. Then add the mascarpone and half the liqueur, and continue beating for a minute until the mascarpone is blended with the cream.
- Remove strawberry mixture from heat and puree slightly with a stick blender.
- Stir the remaining liqueur into the strawberry sauce. Strain the sauce, reserving both liquid and fruit pulp separately.
- To assemble, dip each savoiardi biscuit quickly into the warm strawberry sauce and arrange in a single layer on the base of a casserole dish. Spread the reserved fruit pulp over the first layer of biscuits.
- Cover with half the mascarpone cream and spread evenly.
- Dip the remaining biscuits into the sauce and arrange over the cream. Spread the rest of the mascarpone cream over the second layer.
- Dust with cinnamon sugar and decorate with reserved berries. Drizzle some of the remaining strawberry syrup over the top.
- Refrigerate for at least 4 hours, or preferably overnight.

35. Best Weet Bix Slice Recipe

Serving: 10 | Prep: 15mins | Cook: 15mins | Ready in: 30mins

Ingredients

- 4 Weet-Bix crushed
- 1 cup plain flour
- 1/2 cup coconut
- 1/2 cup sugar
- 1 tbs cocoa
- 70 g butter
- 1/4 cup water

Direction

- Preheat oven to 180C (160C fan-forced). Melt butter and mix into crushed Weet-Bix.
- Add remaining ingredients and stir to combine.
- Line a square cake tin with baking paper. Press Weet-Bix mixture into the base. Bake for 15 minutes.
- To make icing, sift icing sugar into a bowl. Add milk gradually, stirring, until you have a smooth, spreadable consistency. Pour icing over slice in tin. Spread to cover completely. Allow to set. Slice.

36. Best Ever Banana Cake Recipe

Serving: 10 | Prep: 15mins | Cook: 75mins | Ready in: 90mins

Ingredients

- 1 1/2 cups self-raising flour
- 1 tsp bicarbonate of soda
- 3/4 cup sugar
- 3 bananas mashed
- 1/2 cup oil
- 2 eggs lightly beaten

Direction

- Grease a ring tin and line base with baking paper.
- Sift flour and soda into a bowl. Add sugar.
- Make a well in centre and add bananas, eggs and oil.
- Stir until mixture is smooth.
- Pour into cake tin and bake at 150C for 1 hour.

- Ice with cream cheese or lemon icing if desired.

37. Best Ever Cupcakes Recipe

Serving: 0 | Prep: 10mins | Cook: 20mins | Ready in: 30mins

Ingredients

- 2 eggs
- 200 ml thickened cream
- 1 tsp vanilla extract
- 3/4 cup caster sugar
- 1 cup self-raising flour sifted

Direction

- Crack eggs into a 250 mL measuring cup then fill to the top with thickened cream. Pour into mixing bowl.
- Beat with electric mixer for 1 minute.
- Add vanilla extract and sugar.
- Beat for 3 minutes.
- Fold flour into mixture with wooden spoon until blended.
- Place mixture into a 12-hole muffin pan lined with paper cases.
- Bake at 180C until light golden, approximately 15-20 minutes.

38. Betty's Rum Balls Recipe

Serving: 0 | Prep: 30mins | Cook: 140mins | Ready in: 170mins

Ingredients

- 1 vanilla butter cake
- 3 Sanitarium Weet-Bix
- 1 cup coconut
- 3/4 cup currants
- 3 tbs cocoa powder
- 30 ml rum
- 1 tsp rum essence optional *to taste
- 395 ml condensed milk
- 1 cup coconut to coat

Direction

- Blend cake and Weet Bix in food processor. Place in a large mixing bowl.
- Add coconut, cocoa and currants. Mix well.
- Make a well in the middle, add rum, essence and condensed milk and mix until a sticky rolling consistency.
- Roll into balls and coat in extra coconut.
- Refrigerate until needed.

39. Black Forest Trifle Recipe

Serving: 8 | Prep: 180mins | Cook: 0S | Ready in: 180mins

Ingredients

- 1 chocolate sponge roll
- 680 g morello cherries reserve liquid
- 170 g jelly crystals
- 500 ml thick vanilla custard
- 1 tbs liqueur
- 375 g dark chocolate
- 150 g cherries fresh
- 4 cup water

Direction

- Make jelly with liquid from cherries and water, allow to set.
- Slice sponge roll and line bottom and sides of a large bowl.
- Sprinkle with liqueur.
- Layer half the Morello cherries over the sponge.
- Add a layer of jelly and another layer of Morello cherries.
- Top with custard.

- Grate dark chocolate on top and add fresh cherries.

40. Blueberry Flower Twist

Serving: 8 | Prep: 10mins | Cook: 25mins | Ready in: 35mins

Ingredients

- 2 sheets Pampas puff pastry thawed
- 100 g frozen blueberries
- 160 g raspberry jam
- 1 egg lightly whisked
- 1 tbs demerara sugar

Direction

- Preheat oven to 220°C conventional or 200°C fan-forced. Line a baking tray with baking paper.
- Cut a 24cm circle from each sheet of puff pastry. Place 1 circle on the prepared tray. Combine frozen blueberries and jam in a medium bowl and spread over circle, leaving a 3cm border. Place second circle on top and press edges to seal.
- Place a 4cm glass upside down in the centre. Using kitchen scissors, cut up to the glass to make 16 wedges. Remove glass. Twist each wedge once. Brush with egg. Sprinkle with sugar. Bake for 25 minutes or until golden and puffed.
- Serve while still warm.

41. Boiled Cherry Fruit Cake Recipe

Serving: 10 | Prep: 10mins | Cook: 105mins | Ready in: 115mins

Ingredients

- 200g butter, chopped
- 375g pkt mixed dried fruit
- 200g glace cherries, plus extra to serve
- 1 cup brown sugar
- 1/4 cup dry sherry
- 1 cup self-raising flour
- 1 cup plain flour
- 2 tsp mixed spice
- 1/2 tsp bicarbonate of soda
- 3 eggs, lightly whisked
- Icing sugar, to dust

Direction

- Place the butter, mixed fruit, cherries, brown sugar, sherry and 1 cup water in a saucepan over medium heat. Bring to the boil. Reduce heat to low and simmer for 10 minutes. Set aside to cool.
- Preheat oven to 160C/140C fan forced. Line the base and side of a round 20cm cake pan with baking paper
- Add the flours, mixed spice, bicarbonate of soda and eggs to the fruit mix and stir until well combined. Pour into the prepared pan. Bake for 55 mins or until a skewer inserted into the cake comes out clean. Set aside to cool in the pan.
- Dust with icing sugar and top with extra cherries to serve.

42. Boiled Pineapple Fruit Cake Recipe

Serving: 20 | Prep: 15mins | Cook: 95mins | Ready in: 110mins

Ingredients

- 500 g mixed dried fruit
- 440 g (crushed) canned pineapple
- 1 cup sugar
- 125 g butter chopped
- 1 tsp mixed spice
- 1/2 tsp ground cinnamon
- 1 tsp bicarbonate of soda

- 2 eggs beaten
- 1 cup self-raising flour
- 1 cup plain flour

Direction

- Place fruit, crushed pineapple including juice, butter, sugar and spices in a saucepan. Boil for 5 minutes.
- Add bicarbonate of soda. Turn off heat and allow to cool.
- Add eggs and flour.
- Preheat oven 160C. Pour into a prepared cake tin and bake for 40 minutes or until the top is golden.
- Remove from oven, cover with foil and bake for a further 50 minutes.

43. Brulee Style Strawberry Cheesecake Pizza Recipe

Serving: 8 | Prep: 5mins | Cook: 30mins | Ready in: 35mins

Ingredients

- 1 sheet pie pastry, refrigerated
- 8 ounces cream cheese
- 1/2 cup sugar
- 1/2 tsp vanilla essence
- Strawberry sauce
- 2 cups fresh strawberries sliced
- 1 tbs sugar
- 1/4 tsp corn starch
- 1 pinch salt
- 1 cup whipped cream

Direction

- Preheat the oven to 180C. Beat cream cheese, sugar, and vanilla until smooth for about one minute. Place GLAD Bake cooking paper on a sheet pan and lay pie dough on top. Spread cream cheese mixture onto pie crust. Bake for 30 minutes. Cool.
- Place 1 cup strawberries, sugar, corn starch, and salt in a medium saucepan. Place remaining berries in large bowl, then set aside. Using a potato masher, thoroughly mash berries in saucepan. Cook over a medium heat until sugar is dissolved and mixture is thick and bubbling for about four to seven minutes. Pour over berries in bowl and stir to combine.
- Cut the pizza into eight triangles. Top with 1/4 cup of strawberry sauce. Garnish with whipped cream.

44. Butterscotch Pudding Recipe

Serving: 6 | Prep: 15mins | Cook: 40mins | Ready in: 55mins

Ingredients

- 1 cup self-raising flour
- 3/4 cup sugar
- 1 pinch salt
- 60g butter
- 1/2 cup milk
- Sauce
- 2 tbs golden syrup
- 1 1/2 cups hot water
- 30g butter

Direction

- Sift sugar, salt and flour into a bowl.
- Melt butter and add to flour mixture along with the milk. Stir.
- Place into well-greased ovenproof dish.
- In the meantime, combine the sauce ingredients and stir until melted.
- Pour the sauce mixture over the top of the pudding mixture using the back of a spoon for even distribution.
- Bake at 180C for approximately 30-40 minutes.

45. Cadbury Clinkers Rocky Road Recipe

Serving: 12 | Prep: 10mins | Cook: 0S | Ready in: 10mins

Ingredients

- 500g milk chocolate melts
- 20g coconut oil
- 300g Cadbury Clinkers cut in half
- 100g marshmallows cut in half
- 200g raspberry lollies cut in half

Direction

- Line the base and sides of a 16.5 x 26cm lamington pan with baking paper.
- Chop the Clinkers, marshmallows and raspberry lollies in half and set aside.
- Place the chocolate and coconut oil or copha into a heatproof, microwave-safe bowl.
- Heat, uncovered, on Medium, stirring every minute with a metal spoon for 4-5 minutes, or until the chocolate and coconut oil/copha has just melted.
- Remove from the microwave and stir until smooth.
- Stir through the Clinkers, marshmallows and raspberry lollies.
- Spread the mixture into the prepared lamington pan and place in the fridge for 2 hours, or until completely set.
- Use a sharp knife to cut into slices (if you are having trouble cutting the slice, run your knife under hot water first and then dry completely before cutting - the heat will help to cut the slice evenly).

46. Cafe Choc Chip Cookies Recipe

Serving: 0 | Prep: 15mins | Cook: 15mins | Ready in: 30mins

Ingredients

- 180 g butter softened
- 1/3 cup caster sugar
- 125 ml sweetened condensed milk
- 1 1/2 cups self-raising flour
- 250 g dark choc bits

Direction

- Preheat oven to 180C. Using an electric mixer, beat the butter and sugar together until light and creamy. Beat in condensed milk.
- Add the flour and mix on low speed until smooth. Stir in the choc bits until well combined.
- Roll about 2 teaspoonfuls of the mixture into balls and place on baking paper lined trays. Press each ball with a floured fork.
- Bake for 12 - 15 minutes or until lightly golden. Remove from oven and allow to cool on the trays. Store in airtight containers.

47. Caramel Hedgehog Slice Recipe

Serving: 10 | Prep: 30mins | Cook: 45mins | Ready in: 75mins

Ingredients

- 125 g butter
- 2/3 cup caster sugar
- 2 tbs golden syrup
- 395 g sweetened condensed milk
- 1 packet Arnott's Milk Arrowroot biscuits crushed
- Topping
- 200 g hazelnut milk chocolate
- 165 g copha

Direction

- Combine butter, sugar and golden syrup in a saucepan and melt. Add the sweetened condensed milk and bring to boil.
- Combine with crushed biscuits and press into a slice tin.

- Meanwhile to make the topping, melt the copha and chocolate together, being careful to not burn the mixture. Pour over slice. Refrigerate or freeze.

48. Cheat's Christmas Shortbread Recipe

Serving: 0 | Prep: 10mins | Cook: 45mins | Ready in: 55mins

Ingredients

- 125 g caster sugar
- 125 g cornflour
- 2 cups plain flour
- 250 g butter melted

Direction

- Mix dry ingredients together.
- Mix in butter until well combined.
- Press into an ungreased 28cm x 18cm lamington pan and bake at 170C for 30 minutes.
- Remove from oven, cut into 24 squares, sprinkle evenly with caster sugar and prick each piece with a fork. Return to oven for 15 minutes. Cool in tin.

49. Cheesecake Log

Serving: 10 | Prep: 15mins | Cook: 0S | Ready in: 15mins

Ingredients

- 1 lemon zested juiced
- 1/2 cup condensed milk
- 1/4 cup milk
- 250g butternut snap biscuits
- 3/4 cup cream
- 125g cream cheese

Direction

- Finely grate ½ teaspoon rind from the lemon. Squeeze to extract two tablespoons of juice.
- Soften cream cheese and beat with the lemon rind until creamy.
- Add condensed milk and lemon juice, and beat until smooth and combined. Chill for two hours until well thickened.
- Pour milk into a shallow bowl and remove cream cheese mix from fridge.
- Dip one side of biscuit into the milk, then spread with approximately one tablespoon of cream cheese mix and sandwich together with another milk-dipped biscuit.
- Stand sandwiched biscuits on a serving plate and continue adding dipped and spread biscuits until all mix and biscuits are used.
- Chill until firm.
- Beat cream and spread generously over biscuit log, then sprinkle lightly with cinnamon or nutmeg or grated chocolate.
- Refrigerate for minimum two hours, or until biscuits have softened.
- Cut into diagonal slices to serve.

50. Cherry Cake

Serving: 16 | Prep: 20mins | Cook: 50mins | Ready in: 70mins

Ingredients

- 200 g butter
- 180 g sugar
- 125 g ground almonds
- 125 g self-raising flour
- 4 egg
- 1 tsp ground cinnamon
- 3 tbs rum
- 100 g dark cooking chocolate roughly chopped
- 720 g morello canned cherries drained

Direction

- Preheat oven to 180C or 160C fan forced. Grease a 25cm round cake tin and line the base with baking paper.
- Beat butter and sugar with electric mixer until light and fluffy. Add eggs, one at a time, beating after each addition.
- Stir in almonds, chocolate, rum, sifted flour and cinnamon, then lightly fold in drained cherries.
- Pour the mixture into prepared pan. Bake for 50 minutes, or until cooked when tested with a skewer.
- Stand for 5 minutes before turning onto wire rack. Remove baking paper from bottom of cake and then turn right way up. Serve cake warm dusted with icing sugar or ice cream.

51. Cherry Ripe Balls Recipe

Serving: 0 | Prep: 20mins | Cook: 0S | Ready in: 20mins

Ingredients

- 250g Arnott's Marie biscuits
- 3 Cadbury Cherry Ripe chocolate bars
- 1 tbs cocoa
- 3/4 cup desiccated coconut
- 400g condensed milk
- 100g dark chocolate
- 1/2 cup desiccated coconut *to decorate *extra
- 1/2 cup red sugar crystals *to decorate
- 1/2 cup chocolate sprinkles *to decorate

Direction

- Blitz biscuits, Cherry Ripe bars and cocoa in a food processor to form a fine crumb. Transfer to a bowl and stir through the coconut.
- In a small saucepan over gentle heat, stir condensed milk and chocolate until chocolate has melted and mixture is smooth. Pour over the crumbs and mix well.
- Combine extra desiccated coconut and red sugar crystals in a small bowl. Place chocolate sprinkles in another. Using damp hands, form Cherry Ripe mixture into small balls. Roll in either coconut mix or chocolate sprinkles to coat well.

52. Cherry Ripe Trifle Recipe

Serving: 6 | Prep: 15mins | Cook: 95mins | Ready in: 110mins

Ingredients

- 18 lamingtons
- 170 g raspberry jelly
- 100 g Cottee's chocolate pudding mix
- 300 g thickened cream
- 2 tbs icing sugar
- 150 g Cherry Ripe chocolate bars

Direction

- Make jelly according to packet directions. Chill in freezer for 45-60 minutes or until the mixture is just beginning to set.
- Make chocolate pudding according to packet directions and refrigerate for 15-20 minutes.
- Layer lamington fingers on base of a glass dessert bowl.
- Pour one of the jelly mixtures over the top of the lamington fingers and refrigerate for approximately 30 minutes until fully set.
- Remove the other jelly from freezer and refrigerate until needed.
- Chop one Cherry Ripe bar into small bite size pieces and place over trifle.
- Place second jelly mixture over the chopped Cherry Ripe.
- Cover jelly with the chocolate pudding.
- Whip cream and icing sugar until firm and pour over chocolate pudding and then top with the remaining chopped Cherry Ripe bars.

53. Choc Chip Muffins Recipe

Serving: 0 | Prep: 15mins | Cook: 25mins | Ready in: 40mins

Ingredients

- 3 cups self-raising flour
- 3 tbs cocoa powder
- 1 1/2 cups brown sugar
- 200 g choc bits
- 1 1/2 cups milk
- 120 g butter melted
- 2 eggs beaten

Direction

- Sift flour and cocoa.
- Add sugar and choc chips, stir.
- Add milk, butter and eggs. Stir until just combined.
- Spoon into muffin tin ¾ full.
- Bake at 180C for 20-25 minutes.

54. Choc Salted Caramel Tart Recipe

Serving: 6 | Prep: 265mins | Cook: 20mins | Ready in: 285mins

Ingredients

- 1 3/4 cup plain flour
- 1/4 cup cocoa powder
- 1/2 cup pure icing sugar
- 125 g unsalted butter room temperature
- 1 egg yolks
- 1 tsp vanilla extract
- 600 g Woolwoths Gold salted caramel dessert sauce chilled
- 200 g dark chocolate chopped
- 1/2 cup cream
- 10 chocolate shards *to decorate

Direction

- Place flour, cocoa, icing sugar and butter in a food processor and process until combined. Add yolk and vanilla and process until the dough comes together. Turn out onto a lightly floured surface and press together. Flatten into a disc, wrap in baking paper and chill for 1 hour.
- Pre heat oven to 180°C. Line a 20cm springform pan with baking paper. Roll pastry out until 3mm thick. Place into pan, press over base and 5cmup side, leaving top ragged. Prick base with a fork. Transfer to freezer for 10 minutes. Bake for 20 minutes. Cool completely.
- Spread salted caramel into pastry shell and chill for 2-3 hours or until set.
- Meanwhile gently heat chocolate and cream in a saucepan over low heat, stirring, until melted and smooth. Stand for 10 minutes or until thickened slightly. Pour over caramel and chill for 1 hour or until filling has set. Remove tart from fridge and bring to room temperature. Decorate with chocolate shards. Serve.

55. Choc Banana Cookies

Serving: 0 | Prep: 15mins | Cook: 40mins | Ready in: 55mins

Ingredients

- 125 g butter
- 1/2 cup caster sugar
- 1/3 cup brown sugar firmly packed
- 1 egg
- 1 3/4 cup self-raising flour sifted
- 1/4 cup banana mashed
- 1/2 cup dark choc bits

Direction

- Lightly grease two oven trays.

- Beat butter and both sugars together in a small bowl with an electric mixer until mixture is light and fluffy.
- Add egg and beat until well combined.
- Stir in sifted flour, bananas and choc-bits.
- Drop level tablespoons of mixture, about 3 cm apart, on the prepared oven trays.
- Cook at 180C, for about 20 minutes, or until the cookies are lightly browned. Cool on trays.

56. Choc Top Freckle Cookies Recipe

Serving: 0 | Prep: 25mins | Cook: 15mins | Ready in: 40mins

Ingredients

- 125g butter, softened
- 1 tsp vanilla extract
- 3/4 cup firmly packed brown sugar
- 200g dark chocolate, melted
- 1 egg
- 1 cup plain flour
- 1/3 cup cocoa powder
- 1/2 tsp bicarbonate of soda
- 1 cup 100's and 1000's
- Choc-Top Coating
- 200g dark chocolate, chopped
- 2 tsp vegetable oil

Direction

- Using an electric mixer, beat butter, vanilla and sugar until pale and creamy. Beat in chocolate and egg until smooth.
- Sift flour, cocoa and bicarbonate of soda over the butter mixture. Stir to form a soft dough. Cover. Refrigerate for 15 to 20 minutes or until mixture firms slightly.
- Preheat oven to 180C/160C fan-forced. Line two baking trays with baking paper.
- Roll rounded tablespoons of mixture into balls. Place 5cm apart on prepared trays. Flatten slightly. Bake for 12 minutes. Cool on trays for 5 minutes. Transfer to a wire rack to cool completely.
- To make the choc-top coating. Place all ingredients in a large microwave-safe bowl. Microwave, uncovered, on Medium (50%), stirring every 30 seconds with a metal spoon, for 1 to 2 minutes or until melted and smooth.
- Place 100's and 1000's in a small bowl. Dip the top of each biscuit in choc-top coating, allowing excess to drain. Press into 100's and 1000's to coat. Return to wire rack. Stand cookies for 30 minutes or until set. Serve.

Nutrition Information

- Calories: 273.177 calories
- Total Carbohydrate: 2.6 grams carbohydrates
- Sugar: 36.6 grams sugar
- Cholesterol: 24 milligrams cholesterol
- Total Fat: 12.9 grams fat
- Saturated Fat: 7.4 grams saturated fat
- Sodium: 99 milligrams sodium

57. Chocolate Brownies Recipe

Serving: 12 | Prep: 15mins | Cook: 35mins | Ready in: 50mins

Ingredients

- 125g butter
- 1 1/2 cups caster sugar
- 1/2 cup cocoa powder
- 2 eggs
- 1 tsp vanilla essence
- 1/4 tsp salt
- 1 cup plain flour
- 1 tsp baking powder
- 1 cup white choc bits

Direction

- Melt the butter in a medium saucepan.
- Stir in sugar, cocoa, vanilla and salt.

- Remove from heat and allow to cool slightly.
- Quickly whisk in eggs.
- Fold through sifted flour and baking powder.
- Mix in choc bits.
- Spoon the mixture into a greased and lined 18cm x 28cm slab tin.
- Bake at 170C for 25-30 minutes.
- The mixture will seem soft, but will harden upon cooling.
- Allow to cool in the tin before removing and slicing.

58. Chocolate Cheesecake Recipe

Serving: 8 | Prep: 15mins | Cook: 180mins | Ready in: 195mins

Ingredients

- 125 g chocolate biscuits crushed
- 60 g butter melted
- 250 g cream cheese
- 1/2 cup sugar
- 1 tsp vanilla essence
- 2 eggs separated
- 1 cup cream
- 125 g dark chocolate
- 1 pinch salt

Direction

- Combine crushed biscuit crumbs and melted butter, mix well.
- Press mixture on to base of a greased 20 cm springform pan. Refrigerate until required.
- Beat cream cheese until smooth, add ¼ cup sugar and the vanilla, beat well.
- Add lightly beaten egg yolks and chocolate, which has been melted over hot water.
- Beat egg whites and salt until peaks form, gradually beat in remaining sugar. Fold through chocolate mixture.
- Fold through the whipped cream.
- Pour mixture onto crumb base. Refrigerate for 3 hours until set.
- To serve, decorate with extra whipped cream and grated chocolates and / or strawberries.

59. Chocolate Christmas Balls Recipe

Serving: 0 | Prep: 20mins | Cook: 130mins | Ready in: 150mins

Ingredients

- 2 x 250 g chocolate ripple biscuits
- 395 g condensed milk
- 2 x 55 g Cherry Ripe chocolate bar roughly chopped
- 2 x 55 g Peppermint Crisp chocolate bars roughly chopped
- 1/4 cup coconut

Direction

- Process biscuits into fine crumbs.
- Mix biscuits, condensed milk, and chocolate bars together.
- Roll into tablespoon-sized balls and roll in coconut.
- Refrigerate.

60. Chocolate Crackles Recipe

Serving: 0 | Prep: 15mins | Cook: 15mins | Ready in: 30mins

Ingredients

- 4 cups Rice Bubbles
- 1 cup icing sugar
- 1 cup desiccated coconut
- 5 tbs cocoa powder
- 250 g copha melted

Direction

- Mix all ingredients together, spoon mixture into patty cake papers and refrigerate until set.

61. Chocolate Fruit Mince Puddings With Custard And Strawberries Recipe

Serving: 0 | Prep: 30mins | Cook: 50mins | Ready in: 80mins

Ingredients

- 2 cups Woolworths Select mixed fruit
- 1 cup Woolworths Select raisins
- 0.6 cup apple juice
- 1/2 cup Woolworths Select golden syrup
- 1/2 cup brewed espresso coffee (liquid) cooled
- 60 g Woolworths Select butter melted
- 1 cup Home Brand brown sugar loosely packed
- 1 1/2 cups fresh breadcrumbs day-old
- 200 g Woolworths Select dark cooking chocolate chopped
- 1 cup Macro Organic plain flour
- 2 tbs Home Brand cocoa powder
- 3 tsp Woolworths Select ground mixed spice
- 1 tsp bicarbonate of soda
- 500 ml custard warmed *to serve
- 500 g fresh strawberries *to serve

Direction

- Grease eight holes of a 12 hole (200 mL capacity) loose-based Texas muffin pan. Preheat oven 150C fan forced.
- Combine dried fruit, raisins, apple juice and golden syrup in a saucepan. Bring to a simmer, continue to simmer for 5 minutes until fruit is plump. Transfer to a large bowl and cool to room temperature, about 20 minutes.
- Spoon mixture into a food processor. Pulse until finely chopped. Return to bowl.
- Add coffee, butter, sugar, breadcrumbs and chocolate to the fruit mixture. Mix well. Sift the flour, cocoa powder, mixed spice and bicarbonate of soda together over the mixture and stir to combine.
- Spoon evenly into 8 prepared muffin holes. Bake for 45 minutes or until a skewer inserted into centre of puddings comes out clean.
- Set aside for 10 minutes in pan before turning out onto a wire rack. Serve warm puddings with warm custard and strawberries.

62. Chocolate Hot Cross Bun Bread And Butter Pudding Recipe

Serving: 0 | Prep: 15mins | Cook: 45mins | Ready in: 60mins

Ingredients

- 300 ml full cream milk
- 300 ml thickened cream
- 10 hot cross buns
- 5 eggs
- 1/2 cup caster sugar
- 150 g butter spreadable
- 3/4 cup milk chocolate buttons
- 1 tbs raw sugar
- 1 tsp allspice
- 1 tsp ground cinnamon

Direction

- Line your cake tin with baking paper. The tin I've used is 20cm in diameter and not springform (springforms risk leaking when you pour in your thin custard). If you don't have such a cake tin, you can use a casserole dish.
- In a large jug, whisk together milk, thickened cream, eggs, allspice, cinnamon and caster sugar until eggs are well incorporated (if they're not completely whisked in, you may find small sections of plain old cooked egg white through your pudding).

- Spread butter on either side of each slice of hot cross bun and arrange them flat in the base of your cake tin/casserole dish.
- Once the base of your tin is covered, sprinkle 1/4 of your milk chocolate chips on top.
- Retrieve your bun tops, spread butter on the underside and arrange them as desired on top of your first layer.
- Sprinkle the rest of your chocolate chips on top, allowing them to fall in and fill the cracks left between the bun tops.
- Serve warm with cream and/or ice cream.
- Pour your milk and cream mixture into your cake tin, sprinkle the top of your pudding with raw sugar, and set aside in the fridge for an hour to allow the hot cross buns to soak up the custard.
- Preheat your oven to 180C.
- Once at temperature, place your pudding in the oven to bake for 45 minutes, or until the centre of your cake has set.
- Cut each hot cross bun horizontally in to three sections, set the tops aside.

63. Chocolate Mint Slice Christmas Balls Recipe

Serving: 0 | Prep: 20mins | Cook: 0S | Ready in: 20mins

Ingredients

- 200g Mint Slice biscuits
- 125g cream cheese, softened
- 150g milk chocolate
- 20 red mini M&Ms
- 10 spearmint leaf lollies

Direction

- Crush the Mint Slice biscuits in a food processor or Thermomix. Place crushed biscuits into a medium sized bowl.
- Add 125g of cream cheese and mix well until completely combined.
- Roll the mixture into heaped teaspoon-sized balls and place onto a baking paper lined tray in the fridge.
- Slice the spearmint leaves into tiny slithers (you'll get about 5 out of each leaf) and set aside.
- Melt the chocolate in a deep and narrow heatproof bowl or ramekin on Medium heat (50% power) in the microwave on 30 second bursts for 2 - 3 minutes, stirring each time.
- Dip the balls into the chocolate mixture with a fork and return to the baking tray, allowing any excess chocolate to drip off.
- Place one red M&M mini and two spearmint leaf slithers onto the top of each of the balls. Place back into the fridge to set.

64. Chocolate Orange No Bake Cheesecake

Serving: 8 | Prep: 360mins | Cook: 0S | Ready in: 360mins

Ingredients

- 14 digestive biscuits crushed
- 110 g butter melted
- 2 tsp cocoa powder
- Filling
- 85 g orange jelly
- 250 ml cream
- 160 g chocolate cream cheese
- 2 tsp cocoa powder

Direction

- Line a 20-22 cm springform tin with baking parchment.
- To make the base, stir the cocoa and biscuit crumbs into the melted butter.
- Spread evenly across tin and allow to set.
- Make jelly up to 250 mL and allow to partially set.
- Pour cream into liquidiser and whip to soft peak stage.

- Add chocolate cream cheese, jelly and cocoa to liquidiser. Whizz until blended.
- Pour mixture over the base and leave to set for at least 4 hours or, preferably, overnight.
- Decorate with sugared orange slices.

65. Chocolate Raspberry Trifle Cake

Serving: 0 | Prep: 60mins | Cook: 5mins | Ready in: 65mins

Ingredients

- 300 g frozen raspberries
- 1/2 cup caster sugar
- 1/4 cup water
- 500 g mini jam sponge roll
- 1/3 cup sherry
- 250 g mascarpone
- 1/2 cup cream
- 2 tbs icing sugar
- Topping
- 1/2 cup cream
- 200 g dark chocolate
- 100 g frozen raspberries *to decorate

Direction

- Line a 20 cm springform pan with baking paper.
- Tear 1 packet of jam rolls into bite size pieces and place on bottom of pan in an even layer.
- Sprinkle with sherry.
- Place raspberries, caster sugar and water into a saucepan over a low heat.
- Stir until sugar has dissolved, then bring to boil and remove from heat.
- In another bowl, mix mascarpone, cream and icing sugar.
- Gently pour half of the raspberry mixture evenly over jam rolls.
- Place half of the cream mixture over raspberry mixture.
- Add another layer using the remaining jam rolls with sherry, then top with raspberry and cream layers.
- Cover tightly with gladwrap and place a plate on top to weight down. Refrigerate overnight.
- Topping: Melt chocolate and cream over low heat, and stir to gently to combine.
- Remove cake from pan.
- Spread over cake and decorate with raspberries.
- Place back in fridge to set.

66. Chocolate Rum Balls Recipe

Serving: 0 | Prep: 15mins | Cook: 150mins | Ready in: 165mins

Ingredients

- 2 x 350 g chocolate cake mix
- 3 tbs strawberry jam
- 1 tbs rum
- 2 x 250 g milk chocolate chopped
- 300 g desiccated coconut

Direction

- Bake cake as per packet cooking instructions, allow to cool, then break up into large mixing bowl.
- Add rum and 3 heaped tablespoons of jam. Use hands to knead together until moist and well combined. Add more jam if necessary.
- Roll cake and jam mixture into 3 cm diameter balls.
- Melt chocolate in a heatproof bowl over saucepan of simmering water.
- Dip and roll chocolate balls in melted chocolate, allowing chocolate to drip off before rolling to coat in coconut.
- Place chocolate and coconut coated rum balls on a paper lined tray in the refrigerator to firm.

67. Chocolate Slice Recipe

Serving: 0 | Prep: 15mins | Cook: 25mins | Ready in: 40mins

Ingredients

- 1 cup self-raising flour
- 1 cup coconut
- 125 g butter melted
- 1/2 cup sugar
- 1 tbs cocoa powder optional
- Icing
- 3/4 cup icing sugar
- 1 tbs cocoa powder
- 50 g margarine
- 2 tbs hot water

Direction

- Mix together all base ingredients until well combined.
- Press into a slice tin.
- Bake for 10 minutes at 180C.
- Remove from oven and let cool.
- Make chocolate icing using desired quantities of ingredients and spread over base.

68. Chocolate Spiders Recipe

Serving: 10 | Prep: 15mins | Cook: 60mins | Ready in: 75mins

Ingredients

- 100 g fried noodles
- 2 tbs crunchy peanut butter
- 200 g milk cooking chocolate

Direction

- Microwave the chocolate and peanut butter until melted.
- Mix well to form a smooth paste.
- Add the noodles and coat well with the chocolate mixture.
- Spoon the mixture onto a tray lined with baking paper and refrigerate until set.

69. Chocolate And Salted Caramel Cookie Sandwiches Recipe

Serving: 0 | Prep: 10mins | Cook: 15mins | Ready in: 25mins

Ingredients

- 300 g chocolate shortcrust pastry
- 1 jar salted caramel spread
- 1 tbs icing sugar

Direction

- Preheat oven to 180C. Line a tray with baking paper.
- Cut the pastry sheet into shapes and place on the tray. They won't expand so you don't need to leave a lot of room between each cookie.
- Bake the cookies for 10-15 minutes then transfer to a wire rack to cool.
- When they have completely cooled, turn a cookie upside down and add half a teaspoon of salted caramel to the middle. Using another cookie, gently squeeze them together to create a sandwich.
- Refrigerate the sandwiches so the caramel sets and dust with icing sugar before serving.

70. Christmas Cake Balls Recipe

Serving: 0 | Prep: 15mins | Cook: 15mins | Ready in: 30mins

Ingredients

- 800 g dark fruit cake
- 250 g dark chocolate

- 125 g butter
- 2 tbs rum
- 1 orange zested *optional
- Icing
- 250 g dark chocolate
- 40 silver cachous

Direction

- Melt the butter and chocolate in a bowl over hot water.
- Crumble the fruit cake into a large bowl.
- Add the rum and mix it through.
- Stir in melted butter and chocolate mixture until it is combined and pour it into the cake mixture. Mix well until all is combined.
- Line baking trays with greaseproof paper. Roll a teaspoon of the mixture into a ball, place on trays.
- Continue until all the mixture is used up.
- Refrigerate for 1-2 hours to set.
- Make white glace icing or melt chocolate. Ice the balls, allowing the icing/chocolate to trickle down the sides.
- Put a small piece of glace cherry or a silver cachou on top of each one and return to the refrigerator to set.

71. Christmas Carrot Balls Recipe

Serving: 0 | Prep: 15mins | Cook: 20mins | Ready in: 35mins

Ingredients

- 250 g caster sugar
- 250 g carrot finely grated
- 50 g ground walnuts
- 1 tbs lemon juice
- 1 lemon, rind finely grated
- 1 packet hazelnuts
- 2 packets hazelnut meal

Direction

- In a saucepan place carrot, sugar and cook over a medium heat. Stir continuously until mixture comes together as a smooth paste.
- Remove from heat and allow to cool.
- Add ground walnuts, grated lemon rind and lemon juice. Mix together well to form a dough.
- Divide in to 25 and add a hazelnut to each portion. Form balls around hazelnut from each portion.
- Roll each ball in hazelnut meal to cover. Put into paper lined containers to store.

72. Christmas Choux Pastry Wreath With Cream Filling Recipe

Serving: 0 | Prep: 15mins | Cook: 20mins | Ready in: 35mins

Ingredients

- 250 ml water
- 90 g unsalted butter brought to room temperature
- 160 g continental flour
- 1 pinch salt
- 4 eggs room temperature
- Cream filling
- 500 ml milk
- 55 g caster sugar
- 80 g vanilla custard powder
- 250 g unsalted butter brought to room temperature
- Glaze icing
- 150 g icing sugar
- 2 tbs milk hot
- 1 tsp lemon juice

Direction

- Preheat a fan-force oven to 220C degrees. Prepare a baking tray with baking paper or lightly grease with butter.
- In a saucepan over medium heat, add water and 90g butter and bring to the boil. Add flour

and salt and stir to cook until dough forms and it no longer sticks to the sides. The dough must be nice and glossy. Leave to cool.
- While the dough cools make the filling. In saucepan heat half of the milk with caster sugar. Add the rest of the milk mixed and custard powder. Keep stirring and cook until custard has thickened. Leave to cool, but stir occasionally. When custard has completely cooled, add 250g butter and mix was an electric mixer until it forms a smooth cream.
- In a mixing bowl, add the dough and beat in one eggs at a time. Beat on high speed until all eggs are incorporated into dough.
- Fill a piping bag with large star nozzle with dough mixture. Pipe a small wreath shape (8cm in diameter) on to prepared tray. Bake for 25 minutes or until golden brown. Leave to cool, cut top off each wreath and spoon or pipe filling then replace top to sandwich two halves together.
- To make the glaze, mix together sugar, lemon juice and hot milk in a small bowl. Brush each wreath with the glaze. Keep wreaths in fridge until you are ready to serve.

73. Christmas Cookie Strips

Serving: 0 | Prep: 15mins | Cook: 15mins | Ready in: 30mins

Ingredients

- 300 g icing sugar
- 600 g unsalted butter room temperature
- 1 egg lightly beaten room temperature
- 900 g plain flour
- 375 g dark cooking chocolate
- 250 g walnuts ground
- 500 g apricot jam

Direction

- Preheat oven to 190C and grease and line baking sheets.

- Cream sugar and butter together in the bowl of an electric mixer. Slowly add egg and continue to mix.
- Turn off mixer and add flour and fold through manually until mixture forms a dough.
- Put the dough into a pipping bag with large nozzle and pipe long strips of mixture onto lightly greased baking sheet.
- Place in preheated oven and bake for 15 minutes or until lightly brown. Set aside to cool.
- Once cool spread jam over the base of one cookie and stick onto the base of another.
- Melt chocolate according to packet instructions. Dip biscuits into chocolate before covering with ground walnuts. Keep the cookies in an airtight container until ready to eat.

74. Christmas Cookies Recipe

Serving: 0 | Prep: 60mins | Cook: 10mins | Ready in: 70mins

Ingredients

- 175 g unsalted butter
- 300 g caster sugar
- 1 egg
- 1 egg yolk
- 1 tsp vanilla essence
- 1 pinch salt
- 300 g plain flour
- 1 lemon rind grated
- 1/2 cup plain flour *extra for dusting

Direction

- Pre-heat oven to 190C.
- Beat butter with an electric mixer. Gradually add the sugar and continue beating until light and fluffy.
- Using a wooden spoon, mix in whole egg and egg yolk. Add vanilla essence, lemon and salt. Stir to mix well.

- Sift flour into mix, stir to blend. Gather dough in a ball, cover with plastic wrap and chill in the fridge for 30 minutes.
- Lightly flour a clean surface with the extra flour and roll dough out until 1cm thick. Any thinner and they'll fall apart when you lift them. Also be sure to use enough flour on your surface or else the dough will stick and fall apart.
- Cut out shapes and place on baking trays.
- Bake for about 8-10 minutes, or until golden brown. Leave to cool for 5 minutes before transferring to a cooling rack.
- Decorate if desired.

75. Christmas Cookies With Walnut Filling Recipe

Serving: 0 | Prep: 15mins | Cook: 15mins | Ready in: 30mins

Ingredients

- 290 g plain flour
- 240 g unsalted butter room temperature
- 2 eggs lightly beaten room temperature
- 1 tbs cold water
- 100 g walnuts ground
- 100 g icing sugar
- 1 egg yolk room temperature
- 1 tsp vanilla sugar
- 1 cup icing sugar

Direction

- Preheat oven to 170C degrees. Lightly grease a baking tray.
- Sift flour into a bowl. Add butter, 1 egg and water and mix to make a dough.
- In another bowl, mix together 100g icing sugar, finely ground walnuts, 1 egg and yolk to make the filling.
- Transfer the dough to a lightly floured working surface. Dust with a little bit of flour and with a rolling pin roll out the cookie dough into a round shape 1cm thick. With a 10cm diameter round cookie cutter cut the dough into small disks.
- On each disk, place one heaped teaspoon of filling in the centre and gently press the edges together.
- Place cookies on a prepared baking tray and bake in a preheated oven for about 15 minutes, or until lightly brown.
- When still warm, dust cookies with icing sugar mixed with vanilla sugar.

76. Christmas Fruit Punch Recipe

Serving: 18 | Prep: 20mins | Cook: 0S | Ready in: 20mins

Ingredients

- 2 cups sugar
- 600 ml boiling water
- 6 sprigs mint crushed fresh
- 900 ml orange juice fresh
- 600 ml cold black tea
- 900 ml pineapple juice
- 300 ml lemon juice fresh
- 3 L dry ginger ale
- 3 L lemonade
- 1 cup fresh strawberries chopped fresh
- 1 tray ice cubes *to serve

Direction

- Dissolve sugar in boiling water and add crushed mint. Cool.
- Remove the crushed mint, then mix the sugar solution, cold tea and juices in a very large bowl.
- Decant into storage jugs and refrigerate until required.
- When ready to serve, mix with dry ginger ale and lemonade in roughly equal proportions, in a serving jug or glasses.
- Add ice and a few chopped strawberries and/or mint leaves if desired to garnish.

77. Christmas Funfetti Popcorn With Honey Butter Toffee Recipe

Serving: 0 | Prep: 10mins | Cook: 15mins | Ready in: 25mins

Ingredients

- 1/2 cup popcorn
- 2 tbs vegetable oil
- Toffee
- 1 cup sugar
- 1/4 cup water
- 1 tbs honey
- 50 g butter
- Toppings
- 100 g pretzels
- 200 g Mars peanut M&M's
- 1/2 tsp salt
- 1/2 cup hundreds and thousands

Direction

- Put sugar in a saucepan, add water and stir over a low heat until dissolved.
- Add butter and honey, and bring to the boil. Cook without stirring until it reaches 138C degrees, or until it turns a golden brown colour. You can test by dropping teaspoonfuls into a cold glass of water to see if toffee hardens.
- While toffee is cooking, make the popcorn. Place oil into a saucepan on high heat, drop a grain in and if it spins slowly, the oil is hot enough. Add popcorn, replace lid and agitate until popping sound slows down.
- Place baking paper on a large tray. Cover with popcorn. Break pretzels into pieces over popcorn.
- When toffee is ready, wait until the bubbles subside and then drizzle spoonfuls of toffee over the popcorn pretzel mix. Add as much toffee as desired then work quickly to sprinkle M&M's, salt and sprinkles over the top. Allow toffee to set.
- Break into pieces and put into cellophane bags, or into jars.

78. Christmas Honey Biscuits Recipe

Serving: 10 | Prep: 15mins | Cook: 15mins | Ready in: 30mins

Ingredients

- 225 g Capilano* Light & Smooth Honey
- 225 g sugar
- 225 g butter
- 1/2 cup water
- 570 g plain flour
- 1 tsp ground cloves heaped
- 1/2 tsp ground cinnamon
- 1 tsp bicarbonate of soda
- 1 tsp ginger

Direction

- Melt the honey, sugar, butter and water. Cool.
- Sift the flour, soda and spices into a mixing bowl.
- Add the melted mixture and stir thoroughly.
- Let stand overnight.
- The dough will harden, knead well after standing.
- Roll out dough onto a floured surface.
- Using Christmas shapes, cut out biscuits.
- Place on a greased tray and bake at 180C for 15 minutes until golden brown.
- Biscuits will be soft out of the oven, but will harden on cooling.

79. Christmas Jelly Slice Recipe

Serving: 8 | Prep: 10mins | Cook: 0S | Ready in: 10mins

Ingredients

- 1 packet sweet plain biscuits
- 175 g unsalted butter melted
- 400 g sweetened condensed milk
- 1 tbs gelatine powder
- 1 tsp gelatine powder
- 1 packet raspberry jelly

Direction

- Butter a slice tray 16cm x 26cm x 3cm. Dissolve jelly in 1 and a 1/2 cups of boiling water, then place in fridge for about 45 minutes until cool (not set).
- Place biscuits in a food processor and pulse into a fine crumb. Transfer to a bowl and mix in melted butter. Press mixture firmly into lined slice tray. Refrigerate for 30 minutes.
- Dissolve gelatine in 1/2 cup hot water. Place condensed milk in a bowl and combine with gelatine mixture. Pour this mixture over biscuit base and return to fridge to set for 30 minutes.
- Pour cold red jelly on top of slice. Return it to the fridge. Once set, use a warm knife to slice into squares.

80. Christmas Kourampiedes Recipe

Serving: 0 | Prep: 20mins | Cook: 25mins | Ready in: 45mins

Ingredients

- 500 g butter
- 1 cup sugar
- 2 cup toasted blanched flaked almonds
- 1 orange zested
- 1 kg plain flour sifted
- 3 cup icing sugar sifted *to decorate
- 3 drops vanilla essence *optional

Direction

- Preheat oven to 180C or 160C for fan forced. Grease 2 baking trays.
- With an electric mixer beat the butter until fluffy and adding the sugar gradually.
- Add the orange zest and flour until mixture is smooth and a little tight. Stir through the toasted almonds.
- Bake until golden brown for about 15-20 mins.
- After baking sift extra icing sugar over them.
- To shape the cookies, take a small piece of dough in your hands and press into shape of cookie cutter. Make sure there is enough to place the cookie cutter in the centre of the dough. You can shape whichever way you like at Christmas type I use Christmas Cookie Cutters shaping them as Trees, Bells, Gingerbread Man. Otherwise shape them into a round ball and with the one of your palms press down on them slightly.

81. Christmas Muffins Recipe

Serving: 0 | Prep: 15mins | Cook: 35mins | Ready in: 50mins

Ingredients

- 410 g fruit mince
- 2 cup self-raising flour
- 2 tsp ground cinnamon
- 1/2 cup brown sugar
- 1 egg
- 3/4 cup buttermilk
- 1/2 cup vegetable oil

Direction

- Mix together fruit mince, egg, buttermilk and oil in a large bowl.
- Add sifted dry ingredients and stir until just combined.
- Spoon mixture into prepared 12 hole muffin pan.
- Bake at 180C for 20-25 minutes.

82. Christmas Muffins Recipe

Serving: 0 | Prep: 0S | Cook: 20mins | Ready in: 20mins

Ingredients

- Muffins
- 3 1/2 cup fruit mince
- 150 g butter
- 1 tsp ground ginger
- 1 tsp bicarbonate of soda
- 250 ml water
- 2 egg
- 1 cup plain flour
- 1 cup self-raising flour

Direction

- Preheat oven to 180°C. Place muffin cases in muffin tray.
- Combine fruit mince, butter, ginger, bicarb and water in a saucepan and bring to the boil. Allow to cool.
- Stir in eggs and flour and mix until combined. Spoon into muffin cases and bake for 20 minutes.

83. Christmas Pudding Popsicles Recipe

Serving: 0 | Prep: 495mins | Cook: 5mins | Ready in: 500mins

Ingredients

- 900 g Pauls Double Thick Custard Rich Chocolate
- 80 g honey roasted mixed nuts finely chopped
- 100 g fruit mince
- 50 g dried cranberries chopped
- 2 tbs brandy *optional
- 200 g dark chocolate chopped
- 100 g white chocolate chopped
- 20 g desiccated coconut
- 1 silver cachous *to decorate

Direction

- Place the custard, nuts, fruit mince, cranberries and brandy or rum, if using, in a large bowl. Stir to combine.
- Divide custard mixture among twelve 80ml (1/3 cup) popsicle moulds. Insert a popsicle stick in the centre of each. Freeze overnight or until set (6-8 hours).
- Remove popsicles from freezer and quickly unmould, placing on a tray lined with baking paper. Return to the freezer.
- Place the chocolate in 2 separate microwave-safe bowls. Microwave each on Medium for 30-second intervals, stirring with a metal spoon until melted. Cool slightly.
- Using 2 piping bags, drizzle each popsicle with chocolate and sprinkle with coconut and/or cachous to decorate.

84. Christmas Sago Plum Pudding

Serving: 10 | Prep: 15mins | Cook: 520mins | Ready in: 535mins

Ingredients

- 2 tbs sago
- 1 cup milk
- 1 1/2 tbs butter
- 3/4 cup sugar
- 1 tsp bicarbonate of soda
- 1 cup fresh breadcrumbs
- 1 1/2 cup mixed fruit
- 1/4 cup brandy
- 1 pinch salt

Direction

- Wash sago well. Add milk and stand overnight.
- Cream butter and sugar.

- Dissolve the bicarbonate soda in the sago mixture and add to the creamed butter. Mix well.
- Fold in breadcrumbs, fruit, salt and brandy.
- Pour into a greased basin and steam for 2 1/2 hours.

85. Christmas Squares Recipe

Serving: 0 | Prep: 10mins | Cook: 60mins | Ready in: 70mins

Ingredients

- 250 g copha melted
- 3 cups Rice Bubbles
- 1 cup icing sugar sifted
- 1 cup milk powder
- 125 g glace cherries roughly chopped
- 1/4 cup sultanas

Direction

- Combine rice bubbles, coconut, sifted icing sugar, powdered milk, chopped cherries and sultanas in a bowl. Mix well.
- Add melted copha and mix well.
- Press mixture into a lightly greased pan lined with baking paper.
- Refrigerate until firm.
- When ready cut into desired squares or mini squares or whatever shape your heart fancies!

86. Christmas Trifle Recipe

Serving: 0 | Prep: 120mins | Cook: 0S | Ready in: 120mins

Ingredients

- 300 g Swiss jam roll
- 600 g vanilla custard
- 250 ml thickened cream
- 85 g red jelly
- 60 ml Baileys Irish cream liqueur
- 1/4 cup icing sugar mixture
- 1 tsp vanilla essence
- 2 cups mixed berries *to taste
- 85 g green jelly

Direction

- Make the jelly as directed on the box.
- Once set, use a knife to cut the jelly into 3 cm chunks.
- Place the thickened cream into a bowl and whip until very thick.
- Beat in icing sugar and vanilla essence.
- Cut the jam roll into slices 2 cm thick and layer into a large glass bowl.
- Cover with liqueur or alcohol of choice.
- Allow to soak for 10 minutes and cover with berries.
- Dollop berries with the cream and custard,
- Add the jelly on top and then repeat the process with the cream and custard.

87. Cinnamon Rolls Recipe

Serving: 10 | Prep: 25mins | Cook: 90mins | Ready in: 115mins

Ingredients

- 3 tsp dry yeast
- 1 cup milk warmed
- 1/2 cup sugar
- 1/2 cup butter melted
- 1 tsp salt
- 2 eggs
- 4 cups plain flour
- Filling
- 1 cup brown sugar
- 2 1/2 tbs cinnamon sugar
- 1/3 cup butter softened
- Icing
- 8 tbs butter softened
- 1 1/2 cups icing sugar

- 1/2 cup cream cheese
- 1/2 tsp vanilla essence

Direction

- Dough: Mix all ingredients until a smooth ball forms.
- Leave in a warm place until doubled in size.
- Punch and roll until approximately ½ cm thick.
- Filling: Beat butter until creamy, add brown sugar and cinnamon and mix until smooth. Spread over the dough.
- Roll up lengthwise. Cut into pieces.
- Place buns on a greased biscuit tray and cover with a towel for about an hour.
- Heat oven to 190C and bake for 10-15 minutes until brown around the edges.
- Icing: While buns are baking, beat the icing ingredients together and spread generously over each roll while still hot.

88. Classic Pavlova Recipe

Serving: 0 | Prep: 10mins | Cook: 90mins | Ready in: 100mins

Ingredients

- 5 egg whites
- 1 1/4 cups caster sugar
- 1 1/2 tsp vanilla essence
- 1 1/2 tsp white vinegar
- 1 1/2 tbs cornflour
- 1 pinch salt

Direction

- Preheat oven to 120C.
- Beat eggs whites until stiff.
- Add caster sugar slowly and then salt.
- Beat for a further 5 minutes until thick, stiff peaks form.
- Beat in vanilla and vinegar, then fold in cornflour.
- Spoon mixture onto a baking paper covered tray, shape into a 20 cm circle and pile high.
- Bake for about 1-1½ hours and let cool in the oven with door ajar.
- When cool cover top with whipped cream and toppings of choice.

89. Coconut Mango Cake Recipe

Serving: 8 | Prep: 20mins | Cook: 30mins | Ready in: 50mins

Ingredients

- 1/2 cup canned mango in syrup chopped
- 125 g butter chopped
- 1/2 tsp coconut essence
- 3/4 cup caster sugar
- 2 eggs
- 1 cup desiccated coconut
- 1 1/4 cups self-raising flour
- Icing
- 1 egg white
- 1 cup icing sugar
- 1 cup desiccated coconut
- 1/4 cup mango fresh *to decorate

Direction

- Cake: Grease a 20cm ring pan and line with baking paper.
- Drain mangoes over a small bowl and reserve 2 tablespoons of syrup.
- Beat the butter, essence and sugar in a small bowl with an electric mixer until combined.
- Add eggs one at a time, beating until just combined between additions.
- Transfer mixture to a large bowl and stir in mango, coconut and flour, and mix well.
- Pour mixture into a greased pan.
- Bake at 180C for about 30 minutes. Stand in the pan for 5 minutes before turning onto a wire rack to cool.
- Icing: Beat egg white in a small bowl with electric beater until frothy.

- Gradually beat in icing sugar, then stir in desiccated coconut and enough reserved syrup to make icing spreadable.
- Spread icing over cake and decorate with extra mango slices.

90. Condensed Milk Custard Cake Recipe

Serving: 8 | Prep: 20mins | Cook: 45mins | Ready in: 65mins

Ingredients

- 1 3/4 cups self-raising flour
- 395g can condensed milk
- 4 eggs
- 125g butter, melted
- Icing sugar, to dust
- Custard
- 1/3 cup custard powder
- 1/4 cup caster sugar
- 1 1/3 cups milk

Direction

- To make the custard, place the custard powder and sugar in a small saucepan. Add a splash of milk and stir until a smooth paste forms. Whisk in the remaining milk. Place over medium heat and cook, stirring, for 5 minutes or until the custard boils and thickens. Remove from heat.
- Transfer custard to a heatproof bowl. Place plastic wrap directly on the surface of the custard to prevent a skin forming. Set aside to cool. Place in the fridge until required.
- Preheat oven to 180C. Line the base and side of a round 20cm cake pan.
- Place the flour in a large bowl. Make a well in the centre. Add the condensed milk, eggs and melted butter. Use a whisk to mix until combined.
- Pour the batter into the prepared pan. Bake for 45 minutes or until a skewer inserted in the centre comes out clean. Set aside for 5 minutes before turning out onto a wire rack to cool completely.
- Use a serrated knife to slice the cake in half horizontally. Spread the custard over the cut side of the cake. Top with remaining cake half to sandwich the custard. Dust with icing sugar to serve.

91. Condensed Milk Slice

Serving: 0 | Prep: 30mins | Cook: 0S | Ready in: 30mins

Ingredients

- 225g milk coffee biscuits
- 375g condensed milk
- 2 cups coconut
- 1/2 cup lemon juice

Direction

- Place a layer of biscuits in a slice pan.
- Mix together condensed milk, coconut and lemon juice.
- Pour mixture on top of biscuits. Add another layer of biscuits on top.
- Refrigerate and slice before serving.

92. Cookie Monster Pancakes Recipe

Serving: 4 | Prep: 5mins | Cook: 5mins | Ready in: 10mins

Ingredients

- 3 cups plain flour
- 3 tbs baking powder
- 2 tbs sugar
- 1/2 tsp salt
- 2 eggs
- 1 tbs vanilla essence

- 4 tbs butter melted
- 1 cup choc chip cookies chopped
- 1 chocolate sauce
- 2 tbs whipped cream *optional
- 2 choc chip cookies *to decorate
- 1 knob butter *extra for frying
- 2 1/2 cups milk

Direction

- Mix the flour, baking powder, sugar and salt together in a big bowl.
- In a smaller bowl, mix together milk, eggs and vanilla
- Add the wet ingredients to the dry and mix gently until just combined. Add chopped cookies to the batter.
- Add the melted butter and mix until just incorporated.
- Melt a couple of teaspoons of butter in a non-stick frying pan over medium-high heat.
- Pour about a ¼ cup of pancake batter into the pan for each pancake.
- Cook until you see little bubbles forming in the batter then flip them and cook for 3-4 minutes.
- Serve with butter, more chunks of cookies and chocolate sauce or syrup and, if you're feeling wild, whipped cream.

93. Cookies And Cream Cheesecake

Serving: 20 | Prep: 60mins | Cook: 5mins | Ready in: 65mins

Ingredients

- Base
- 250 g chocolate ripple biscuits
- 150 g butter melted
- Filling
- 2 tsp gelatine powder
- 1/4 cup water
- 375 g cream cheese
- 300 ml thickened cream
- 1 tsp vanilla essence
- 1/2 cup caster sugar
- 180 g white chocolate melted
- 150 g Oreo biscuits roughly chopped
- 20 mini Oreo biscuits *to decorate

Direction

- Sprinkle the gelatine over the water in a small heat-proof jug, stand jug in small saucepan of simmering water, stir until the gelatine dissolves. Cool 5 minutes.
- Beat cream cheese, cream, vanilla and sugar with an electric beater until smooth.
- Melt chocolate over boiling water or in the microwave.
- Add melted chocolate, gelatine, and Oreos to mixture.
- Combine well.
- Spoon mixture over base of crushed biscuits combined with butter or a whole biscuit placed in the base of paper case.
- Refrigerate.
- Top with mini Oreo to decorate.

94. Cookies And Cream Cheesecake Recipe

Serving: 10 | Prep: 25mins | Cook: 0S | Ready in: 25mins

Ingredients

- 250g sweet plain biscuits crushed
- 150g butter melted
- 2 tsp gelatine powder
- 2 tbs boiling water
- 250 g cream cheese brought to room temperature chopped
- 1/2 cup caster sugar
- 300ml thickened cream
- 1 tsp vanilla extract
- 150g Oreo biscuits broken into pieces
- 5 chocolate wafers roughly chopped *to serve

Direction

- Lightly grease a 20cm x 30cm slice pan. Line base and sides with baking paper, allowing it to overhang on the long sides.
- In a bowl, combine crushed biscuit crumbs and butter, and mix well. Press firmly into the base of prepared tray. Chill for 20 minutes until firm.
- In a small jug, whisk gelatine briskly into hot water with a fork until dissolved. Cool slightly.
- In a bowl, using an electric mixer, beat cream cheese and sugar together until smooth and creamy. Beat in cream, vanilla and gelatine mixture.
- Fold through Oreo biscuits. Pour over base.
- Chill for 3 hours or overnight until firm.
- Top with chopped Oreo wafers.
- Cut into squares to serve.

95. Cranberry Cheesecake Dream Slice Recipe

Serving: 20 | Prep: 45mins | Cook: 220mins | Ready in: 265mins

Ingredients

- 250 g butter softened
- 1 orange grated zested
- 1 cup brown sugar firmly packed
- 2 cups plain flour
- 1 1/2 cups rolled oats
- 1/4 tsp salt
- 1/4 tsp ground cinnamon
- 375 g dark chocolate chips
- 1 cup dried cranberries
- 250 g cream cheese softened
- 400 g condensed milk
- 1/4 cup orange juice
- 1 tsp vanilla essence
- 1 egg
- 1 tbs plain flour

Direction

- Preheat oven to 180C and grease the bottom and sides of a 23 x 33mcm lamington pan and/or line with baking paper.
- In a small bowl mix the flour, oats, salt and cinnamon until blended.
- Toss chocolate chips and cranberries through flour mixture.
- Mix butter, brown sugar and orange zest with an electric mixer until creamy.
- Add flour mixture to bowl and mix on low speed until a crumbly dough is formed. Measure 2 cups of the crumbly dough and set aside.
- Tip the remaining dough into the prepared pan and press to form a thick bottom crust. Place in oven on centre rack and bake for 15 minutes.
- Mix cream cheese with electric mixer on low-medium speed until smooth.
- Slowly add condensed milk, egg, orange juice, vanilla, and remaining 1 tablespoon flour to blend.
- Remove pan from oven and pour cream cheese mixture over hot crust.
- Sprinkle remaining crumb dough evenly over the top, then return to the oven for about 30 minutes, until edges are brown and top looks firm and golden.
- Cool until safe to handle, then refrigerate until firm. To serve cut into squares.

96. Cranberry, Pistachio And White Chocolate Hedgehog Recipe

Serving: 0 | Prep: 10mins | Cook: 0S | Ready in: 10mins

Ingredients

- 1/3 cup roasted unsalted pistachios
- 1/2 cup dried cranberries
- 150 g sweet plain biscuits broken into pieces
- 180 g white chocolate coarsely chopped
- 60 g butter
- 3/4 cup sweetened condensed milk

Direction

- Grease a small rectangular slice pan and line with baking paper, letting the paper hang over the sides.
- Place the broken biscuits, pistachios and cranberries into a bowl and set aside.
- In a small saucepan, melt condensed milk and butter until smooth, then add the chocolate and stir until melted.
- Pour the chocolate mix into the bowl and mix well.
- Spread the mixture into the tray and place into the fridge for at least 3 hours (preferably overnight).
- Slice into 12 large pieces.

97. Cream Cheese Lattice Slice

Serving: 10 | Prep: 40mins | Cook: 75mins | Ready in: 115mins

Ingredients

- 2 x 200g Lattice biscuits
- 125g cream cheese
- 125g butter
- 1/2 cup caster sugar
- 1 tsp vanilla essence
- 2 tsp lemon juice
- 2 tsp gelatine powder
- 1/4 cup hot water cooled

Direction

- Dissolve gelatine in hot water and cool.
- Beat together cream cheese, butter and caster sugar until well combined and creamy.
- Add remaining ingredients and beat well.
- Place lattice biscuits in base of a slice tin, sugar side down.
- Refrigerate until firm.
- Spread cream cheese mixture evenly over biscuits and top with more biscuits, sugar side up.

98. Creamed Rice Recipe

Serving: 4 | Prep: 15mins | Cook: 45mins | Ready in: 60mins

Ingredients

- 1/2 cup rice
- 1/2 cup water
- 1L milk
- 1/4 cup sugar
- 1 tsp vanilla essence

Direction

- In a saucepan, bring rice and water to the boil.
- Gradually add milk and sugar, and simmer for 30 minutes.
- Stir occasionally to prevent rice catching on saucepan base.
- Add more milk if rice has thickened too much.
- Add vanilla and more sugar if needed.

99. Crustless No Bake Cheesecake Recipe

Serving: 4 | Prep: 95mins | Cook: 0S | Ready in: 95mins

Ingredients

- 400 g condensed milk
- 250 g cream
- 1/3 cup lemon juice
- 250 g cream cheese brought to room temperature

Direction

- Allow cream cheese to stand at room temperature for a couple of hours to soften.

- Combine all ingredients and mix on low speed with an electric mixer, beat well for approximately 2 minutes.
- Pour into a greased tin and refrigerate for 1½ hours.

100. Cupcakes Quick And Easy Recipe

Serving: 0 | Prep: 10mins | Cook: 35mins | Ready in: 45mins

Ingredients

- 125g unsalted butter
- 1 tsp vanilla essence
- 3/4 cup caster sugar
- 2 eggs
- 1/2 cup milk
- 1 1/2 cups self-raising flour

Direction

- Line 2 x 12 hole cup cake pan trays with paper cases.
- Combine all ingredients in medium bowl of electric mixer, beat on low speed until all ingredients are combined.
- Then beat on medium speed until mixture is smooth and has changed in colour.
- Divide into paper cases and bake at 180C for approximately 20 minutes.
- Turn onto a wire rack to cool.

101. Custard Cake Recipe

Serving: 10 | Prep: 15mins | Cook: 70mins | Ready in: 85mins

Ingredients

- 2 cups self-raising flour
- 250 g butter room temperature
- 2 tsp vanilla essence
- 2 cups caster sugar
- 4 eggs
- 3/4 cup custard powder
- 1 cup milk

Direction

- Preheat a fan-forced oven to 160C.
- Put all the ingredients in a large mixing bowl. Mix with electric mixer until just combined.
- Pour into lined 23cm deep square tin. Cook 1 hour.
- Check cake with skewer. Sometimes it takes another 5-10 minutes to cook in the middle.

102. Custard Tart Recipe

Serving: 6 | Prep: 20mins | Cook: 90mins | Ready in: 110mins

Ingredients

- 1 1/4 cup plain flour
- 1/4 cup self-raising flour
- 1/4 cup caster sugar
- 90g butter
- 1 egg
- 2 tsp water
- 1 tsp ground nutmeg
- Custard
- 3 egg lightly beaten
- 1 tsp vanilla essence
- 2 tbs caster sugar
- 2 cup milk

Direction

- Sift flours and sugar into a bowl. Rub in butter.
- Add egg and enough water to make a dough.
- Knead on a floured surface until smooth and refrigerate for 30 minutes.
- Roll dough out on a lightly floured surface, and line a 23cm pie plate, trimming the edges.

- Pinch a frill around the edge or decorate as desired.
- Bake blind at 190C for 10 minutes, remove rice or beans and bake for a further 10 minutes.
- Allow pastry to cool.
- Custard: Whisk eggs, vanilla essence and sugar in a bowl until combined.
- Heat milk until hot, then quickly whisk into the egg mixture.
- Pour the custard into the pastry case. Bake at 180C for 15 minutes.
- Sprinkle custard evenly with nutmeg, and bake for a further 15 minutes or until custard is just set. Allow to cool.
- Refrigerate until cold.

103. Czech Christmas Cookies

Serving: 0 | Prep: 15mins | Cook: 15mins | Ready in: 30mins

Ingredients

- 120 g unsalted butter room temperature
- 200 g plain flour
- 40 g caster sugar
- 2 egg yolks
- 100 g walnuts ground
- 100 g unsalted butter room temperature
- 3 tbs milk cold
- 12 tbs caster sugar
- 2 tbs water
- 80 g unsalted butter
- 1 packs hazelnuts

Direction

- Preheat oven to 160C and grease sheet molds.
- Sift flour in a bowl, add butter, sugar and yolk - combine until mixture forms a dough. Cover with cooking foil and leave for about 20 minutes in fridge.
- For filling mixture: In a separate bowl place ground walnuts, butter and cold milk and combine. Cover and leave in fridge just before use, take out 30 minutes prior to filling cookies.
- For chocolate topping: melt 80g butter in small saucepan over medium heat, add 12 teaspoons sugar, stir, add 2 tablespoons water and 2 tablespoon cocoa stir and cook until you get smooth sauce. Cover with lid and take it from stove.
- Now create a small basket or cup shape by taking a little bit of dough and with your thumb press gently into cookies shapes. Place them on oven tray and bake in preheated oven on 160C until lightly brown. Let them to cool, then gently slide out from the shapes. Allow to cool and fill the following day.
- Add a portion of filling to each of the cookie cups.
- Coat with chocolate and top with a hazelnut.

104. Dark Chocolate And Strawberry Galette Recipe

Serving: 6 | Prep: 50mins | Cook: 30mins | Ready in: 80mins

Ingredients

- 1 cup plain flour
- 250 g unsalted butter
- 150 ml cold water
- 1/2 cup unsweetened cocoa powder
- Galette filling
- 1 cup Pauls thick chocolate custard
- 1 cup fresh strawberries sliced
- 50 g dark chocolate *optional

Direction

- Galette: Sift plain flour and cocoa powder into a large bowl. Rub through the butter with your hands until most of the butter is through the flour. You still need to see streaks of butter.
- Make a well in the centre of the flour mixture and pour in half of the water, mixing until you

have a firm dough that isn't sticky - adding extra water if needed. Cover with plastic wrap and leave to rest for 20 minutes in the fridge.
- Turn out onto a lightly floured surface, knead gently and form into a smooth rectangle. Roll the dough in one direction only, until doubled in size. You should see a marbled effect from the butter in the cocoa.
- Fold the top third down to the centre, then the bottom third up and over that. Give the dough a quarter turn (to the left or right) and roll out again to double the length. Fold as before, cover with plastic wrap and chill for at least 20 minutes before rolling to use.
- Get the pastry out of the fridge, and roll out in a rectangle that is 1 cm thick.
- Filling: Pour the chocolate custard into the centre of the galette, and spread out - leaving about 3cms from the edge. Place the strawberries on top. Grate some dark chocolate over this before baking, if you so desire.
- Fold the edges over the filling leaving the centre exposed. Pinch together the dough in some parts to ensure it stays together whilst cooking.
- Bake for about 25-30 minutes, or until the custard has just set.

105. Dark Chocolate, Fig And Orange Parfait Recipe

Serving: 4 | Prep: 15mins | Cook: 0S | Ready in: 15mins

Ingredients

- 125 g cream cheese
- 1/4 cup brown sugar firmly packed
- 180 g dark chocolate cooled melted
- 1/2 cup whipped cream
- 1 cup fruit mince *see notes
- 120 g Sunbeam dry roasted hazelnuts roughly chopped
- 1 packet sponge finger biscuits *to serve

Direction

- Place cream cheese and brown sugar in a bowl, beat until smooth. Gradually beat in cooled melted chocolate.
- Gently fold in whipped cream.
- Using 4 parfait glasses add spoonfuls of chocolate mousse, spoonfuls of fruit mince, sprinkle with spoonfuls of hazelnuts, and layer with another spoonful of chocolate mousse, fruit mince and hazelnuts.
- Serve with sponge fingers to dip.

106. Delicious Spotty Dotty Cookies Recipe

Serving: 0 | Prep: 30mins | Cook: 25mins | Ready in: 55mins

Ingredients

- 100 g butter melted
- 1/2 cup caster sugar
- 1 tsp vanilla essence
- 1 egg lightly beaten
- 1 1/2 cups self-raising flour
- 1 cup Smarties

Direction

- Preheat oven to 180C.
- Line baking trays with baking paper.
- Combine butter, sugar, vanilla and egg in a bowl.
- Add flour and stir until combined.
- Cover and refrigerate for 15 minutes until firm.
- Roll teaspoons of mixture into small balls. Place on tray and press down slightly.
- Top with Smarties, sprinkles, or chocolate chips.
- Bake for 10-12 minutes until light golden.
- Stand on tray for 5 minutes then transfer to wire rack to cool.

107. Dessert Cob Loaf Recipe

Serving: 10 | Prep: 10mins | Cook: 30mins | Ready in: 40mins

Ingredients

- 1 cob loaf large
- 180g marshmallows
- 400g milk chocolate broken into squares
- 100g McVitie's Digestive Biscuits quartered

Direction

- Preheat oven to 200C. Line a tray with large sheet of aluminium foil topped with a smaller piece of baking paper.
- Using a sharp knife, carefully cut a circle into the top of the cob loaf to create a 'lid'. Remove, then pull bite-sized chunks of bread from inside the loaf, leaving the crust intact. Set the lid and bread chunks aside.
- Fill the empty cavity of the bread with layers of marshmallows, chocolate squares and pieces of biscuit. Top with the lid.
- Place on the lined tray and lift the foil to wrap the loaf. Bake for 20-30 minutes until the chocolate-marshmallow filling has melted and is gooey.
- Serve with chunks of bread for dipping.

108. Divine Vanilla Slice Recipe

Serving: 0 | Prep: 15mins | Cook: 0S | Ready in: 15mins

Ingredients

- 600 ml cream
- 100 g Cottee's instant vanilla pudding mix
- 200 g Lattice biscuits
- 2 tbs custard powder
- 1 tsp vanilla essence
- Icing
- 1 cup pure icing sugar sifted
- 1 tsp butter melted
- 1 tbs milk
- 1/2 tsp vanilla essence
- 1/2 cup desiccated coconut *to taste

Direction

- Filling: Place cream, instant pudding, custard powder and vanilla into the bowl of a food processor and process on medium speed until combined and thick, it must be thick and not fall from a spoon.
- Alternatively, place these ingredients into a bowl and use an electric hand mixer.
- Casing: With a wooden spoon, pile a good amount of cream mixture onto a biscuit.
- Place another biscuit on top and smooth down the sides, filling in the sides with more cream mixture if there are hollows. Continue for the remaining biscuits.
- Icing: Sift icing sugar into a bowl.
- Add butter, milk and essence and mix together with a fork until a firm consistency is reached. Add a very small amount of extra milk, if required.
- Spread icing onto each slice, then dip into the coconut while it is still wet.
- If possible, store for 2 days in an airtight container in the fridge to allow the biscuits to soften.

109. Double Choc Ripple Cake Log Recipe

Serving: 10 | Prep: 20mins | Cook: 0S | Ready in: 20mins

Ingredients

- 500ml thickened cream
- 1/4 cup cocoa powder
- 1/4 cup icing sugar
- 200g Choc Ripple biscuits
- 25g dark chocolate, to serve

- Fresh raspberries, to serve

Direction

- Whip cream until thick. Add cocoa and icing sugar and continue beating until fully combined.
- Spread a layer of chocolate cream along the middle of a long serving plate. Take one Choc Ripple biscuit and spread chocolate cream on the base. Stand the biscuit upright in the cream. Take a second biscuit, spread the base with cream and sandwich it with the first biscuit.
- Continue layering the biscuits with chocolate cream to form a long log.
- Use remaining cream to completely cover the log. Refrigerate overnight or at least 4 hours to set and to allow the biscuits to soften.
- Grate chocolate over the top and decorate with fresh raspberries.

110. Easiest Jam Drops Recipe

Serving: 0 | Prep: 5mins | Cook: 15mins | Ready in: 20mins

Ingredients

- 2 eggs
- 3/4 cup sugar
- 2 cups self-raising flour
- 125g unsalted butter
- 1/2 cup strawberry jam

Direction

- Cream butter and sugar. Add eggs one at a time and beat in.
- Add flour and mix into a stiff dough.
- Break dough into small pieces, press hole in centre with a cork, and fill with jam.
- Bake at 180C for about 15 minutes.

111. Easter Bunny Cookies

Serving: 0 | Prep: 210mins | Cook: 10mins | Ready in: 220mins

Ingredients

- 3 cups plain flour
- 1/2 tsp baking powder
- 1 cup butter softened
- 1 1/3 cup caster sugar
- 2 eggs
- 2 tsp vanilla extract
- 1 royal icing

Direction

- Preheat oven to 180C (160C fan-forced). Line two baking trays with baking paper and set aside. Sift flour and baking powder together.
- Using a mixer, beat butter until pale and creamy. With the mixer running, add sugar and then eggs one at a time. Add vanilla and then flour, mixing until the flour is just combined. Divide mixture into two discs and refrigerate for 20 mins. Roll out on a floured board to around 4mm thick. Cut bunny shapes out with the cookie cutter, taking care to dip the cutter into flour between each cut. Work as quickly as possible because this mixture needs to be firm to make clean cuts. Bake for 7- 10 minutes and remove from oven when still pale. Cool on a wire rack.
- Prepare a quantity of Royal icing and place into a Ziploc bag. Snip the tip with a very small opening and pipe around the very edge of each bunny cookie.
- Remove the remaining icing from the bag and stir in 1-2 tbsp of water. Place into a Ziploc bag and snip the end. Now fill inside the previous line that you have piped to fill in the blank area. Use a toothpick or skewer to help the mixture join together so you have no gaps. While the icing is still drying you can place on the decorations for the bunny nose and waistcoat buttons. Leave to dry for 2 hours or

overnight until the icing has hardened. Store in an airtight container.

112. Easy Apple Cake Recipe

Serving: 12 | Prep: 30mins | Cook: 60mins | Ready in: 90mins

Ingredients

- 150g butter melted
- 2 cups stewed apple
- 1 cup sugar
- 2 eggs
- 2 cups self-raising flour
- 2 tsp baking powder
- 2 tsp ground cinnamon
- 1/2 cup mixed nuts chopped optional

Direction

- Place all ingredients into a bowl. Stir until well combined.
- Add nuts if desired.
- Pour mixture into a springform tin and bake for 40-45 minutes at 140C.

113. Easy Banana Cake Recipe

Serving: 12 | Prep: 15mins | Cook: 45mins | Ready in: 60mins

Ingredients

- 125g unsalted butter
- 3/4 cup caster sugar
- 1 tsp vanilla essence
- 1 egg
- 2 bananas mashed ripe
- 1 1/2 cups self-raising flour
- 1/4 cup milk

Direction

- Melt the butter, sugar and vanilla in a medium-sized saucepan.
- Remove from the heat.
- Add mashed bananas and stir through until just combined.
- Add egg and mix well. Stir in the flour, then pour in the milk and fold in lightly.
- Bake at 170C for approximately 40 minutes.

114. Easy Banana Muffins Recipe

Serving: 0 | Prep: 15mins | Cook: 20mins | Ready in: 35mins

Ingredients

- 4 bananas ripe
- 1 cup sugar
- 2 tbs unsalted butter
- 1 egg beaten
- 2 cups self-raising flour
- 2 tbs milk
- 1 pinch salt

Direction

- Preheat oven to 180C. Grease a muffin tray.
- Beat eggs and bananas together, then add all other ingredients and mix well.
- Fill muffin tins ¾ full with mixture.
- Cook for approximately 20 minutes until risen and golden.

115. Easy Banana And Chocolate Bread And Butter Pudding Recipe

Serving: 4 | Prep: 20mins | Cook: 90mins | Ready in: 110mins

Ingredients

- 250 g brioche sliced
- 40 g butter room temperature
- 50 g dark chocolate melts
- 1 banana ripe sliced
- 3/4 cup thick vanilla custard
- 2 tbs milk
- 1/4 cup icing sugar *to decorate *optional

Direction

- Preheat oven to 160C or 140C fan-forced. Grease a large ovenproof baking dish [21cm x 15cm base with 3.5 cup capacity] with a little butter.
- Cut brioche slices in half. Spread slices with butter. Arrange slices in prepared dish.
- Arrange banana and chocolate between slices of brioche.
- Whisk custard and milk in a jug. Pour over brioche.
- Place baking dish in a larger roasting dish. Pour enough boiling water to come halfway up the sides of smaller baking dish. Bake for 1 hour or until set.
- Remove carefully pudding from bain-marie (roasting pan). Stand for at least 15 minutes before serving. Serve warm or at room temperature, sprinkled with icing sugar if you like.

116. Easy Bread And Butter Pudding Recipe

Serving: 4 | Prep: 15mins | Cook: 35mins | Ready in: 50mins

Ingredients

- 8 slices bread crusts removed
- 3 eggs
- 3 tbs caster sugar
- 300ml cream
- 1/4 cup apricot jam *to taste
- 1 tbs ground cinnamon *to taste
- 40g butter softened

Direction

- Preheat oven to 180C.
- Spread the bread with, butter, apricot jam and sprinkle with cinnamon.
- Cut the bread into triangles and arrange in a greased oven-proof dish.
- Whisk together the eggs, sugar and cream.
- Pour over the bread and bake for 25 minutes.

117. Easy Caramel Sauce Recipe

Serving: 10 | Prep: 5mins | Cook: 15mins | Ready in: 20mins

Ingredients

- 75 g butter
- 1/4 cup brown sugar
- 2 tbs milk

Direction

- Melt butter in a saucepan over low heat.
- Add brown sugar and mix until dissolved.
- Add milk and mix until smooth.

118. Easy Chocolate And Condensed Milk Truffles Recipe

Serving: 10 | Prep: 15mins | Cook: 50mins | Ready in: 65mins

Ingredients

- 250 g Arnott's Marie biscuits
- 1/3 cup cocoa
- 1 cup desiccated coconut
- 395 g sweetened condensed milk

Direction

- Process biscuits and blend well.
- Transfer mixture to a bowl.
- Add cocoa powder and one quarter of the coconut.
- Make a well in the centre.
- Add the condensed milk and mix together with a wooden spoon until evenly moistened.
- Chill for 30 minutes.
- Spread remaining coconut onto a plate.
- Roll level tablespoons of the mixture into balls. Roll in the coconut.
- Store in an airtight container in the refrigerator.

119. Easy Christmas Fruit Cake Recipe

Serving: 10 | Prep: 60mins | Cook: 180mins | Ready in: 240mins

Ingredients

- 250 g butter
- 1 kg mixed dried fruit
- 200 g brown sugar firmly packed
- 125 ml brandy
- 125 ml water
- 1/2 tsp bicarbonate of soda
- 2 tsp orange rind grated
- 1 tsp lemon rind grated
- 1 tbs treacle
- 5 eggs lightly beaten medium
- 250 g plain flour
- 50 g self-raising flour
- 2 tbs glace cherries optional *to decorate
- 2 tbs blanched almonds optional *to decorate

Direction

- Grease a deep 23 cm round cake tin, line base and sides with 3 layers of baking paper to 5 cm above edge of tin.
- In a large saucepan, place butter, fruit, sugar, brandy and water.
- Bring to boil, stirring, then simmer covered for 10 minutes.
- Stir in soda, cover and allow to cool.
- Stir rinds, treacle, eggs and flours into cooled mixture. Spread evenly into prepared tin.
- Decorate with the cherries and almonds.
- Bake at 140C for about 2¾ hours, checking after 2 hours.
- Cover hot cake tightly with foil, cool in tin.

120. Easy Cut Out Sugar Biscuits Recipe

Serving: 0 | Prep: 20mins | Cook: 15mins | Ready in: 35mins

Ingredients

- 250 g salted butter softened
- 1 cup white sugar
- 1 cup brown sugar
- 5 tbs vanilla essence
- 6 cups plain flour
- 3 eggs

Direction

- Beat together the sugar and butter until creamy.
- Add vanilla essence.
- Add eggs and mix until well combined.
- Add the plain flour a cup at time, until well mixed. The dough will be soft and slightly sticky.
- Divide it into two or three balls and cover with cling film, then place in the fridge for at least 1/2 hour.
- Prepare your trays with baking paper. Turn your oven on to 160C. Remove chilled dough from the fridge. Place a piece of baking paper onto your bench and the dough. Sprinkle some plain flour on top of the dough and roll out. Don't make it too thin!

- Cut out your shapes and bake for 12 minutes. If they are turning brown at the edges, take them out! Ice and enjoy!

121. Easy Festive Slice

Serving: 20 | Prep: 30mins | Cook: 260mins | Ready in: 290mins

Ingredients

- 400 g condensed milk
- 125 g butter melted
- 250 g mixed dried fruit
- 375 g biscuits crushed
- 1 cup coconut
- Topping
- 125 g cooking chocolate
- 2 tsp margarine

Direction

- Line a square cake tin with aluminium foil, and lightly grease.
- Combine all base ingredients and mix well. Pour mixture into tin and press down well using a spatula.
- Topping: Melt chocolate in microwave or over a bowl of simmering water. Stir in butter or margarine.
- Mix well and then spread over base. Place in refrigerator to chill.
- Cut into small squares to serve.

122. Easy Lemon Self Saucing Pudding Recipe

Serving: 4 | Prep: 15mins | Cook: 40mins | Ready in: 55mins

Ingredients

- 1 cup self-raising flour
- 1/2 cup caster sugar
- 1 tsp lemon rind grated
- 2 tbs butter melted
- 1/2 tsp vanilla extract
- 1/2 cup milk
- Sauce
- 1/3 cup caster sugar
- 1 tsp lemon rind grated
- 1 cup boiling water
- 1/2 cup lemon juice

Direction

- Preheat oven to 180C.
- Pudding batter: Sift the flour and pinch of salt together.
- Add sugar and grated lemon rind, mixing well. Stir in melted butter, vanilla and milk.
- Turn into a greased, ovenproof dish with deep sides.
- Sauce: Sprinkle mixture with the sugar and lemon rind.
- Combine boiling water and lemon juice, and carefully pour over the mixture in the dish.
- Bake for 30-40 minutes.
- Stand for 5-10 minutes before serving.

123. Easy Mango Fruit Cake Recipe

Serving: 10 | Prep: 10mins | Cook: 50mins | Ready in: 60mins

Ingredients

- 375g mixed fruit
- 425g canned mango in syrup
- 1/2 tsp bicarbonate of soda
- 1 cup self-raising flour
- 1 egg
- 1/2 cup walnuts chopped,

Direction

- Place fruit, mango and bicarbonate of soda into a saucepan.
- Boil for 5 minutes. Allow to cool.
- Add flour, egg and walnuts and mix well.
- Pour into a ring tin.
- Bake at 170C fan-forced for 40 - 45 minutes.

124. Easy No Bake Caramel Slice

Serving: 0 | Prep: 30mins | Cook: 5mins | Ready in: 35mins

Ingredients

- 200 g biscuits
- 400 g jersey caramels
- 1 tbs milk
- 1 cup milk chocolate chips
- 1 vegetable oil spray

Direction

- Spray loaf tin with vegetable oil.
- Line base with a single layer of biscuits.
- Heat Jersey caramels in a microwave proof bowl for 1½-2 minutes until completely melted. Stir.
- Add milk and combine until smooth. Pour caramel mix over biscuits and place in refrigerator for around 5-10 minutes or until firm.
- Melt choc chips in a small bowl in microwave for approximately 1½-2 minutes. Stir until melted and smooth.
- Spread melted chocolate over caramel and allow to cool completely before cutting.

125. Easy No Bake Caramel Slice Recipe

Serving: 0 | Prep: 30mins | Cook: 5mins | Ready in: 35mins

Ingredients

- 120g butter
- 1 tbs golden syrup
- 3 tbs brown sugar
- 3 tbs condensed milk
- 250g biscuits

Direction

- Crush the biscuits and set aside.
- Mix together butter, golden syrup, brown sugar and condensed milk.
- Microwave for 2 - 3 minutes at 30 second intervals until mixture is hot and bubbling.
- Add crushed biscuits. Press into slice pan to set.

126. Easy No Bake Cheesecake Recipe

Serving: 8 | Prep: 30mins | Cook: 210mins | Ready in: 240mins

Ingredients

- 2 cups Granita biscuits crushed
- 90 g butter
- 2 tsp hot water
- Filling
- 1 tbs gelatine powder
- 1/4 cup hot water
- 250 g cream cheese softened
- 1 tsp vanilla essence
- 1/2 lemon rind juiced
- 310 g canned mandarin
- 2 egg whites
- 1/2 cup caster sugar

Direction

- Base: Combine biscuit crumbs with hot water and butter.
- Press mixture into pie plate or spring form pan.
- Filling: Dissolve gelatine in hot water.
- Beat softened cream cheese until smooth.
- Gradually add sugar, gelatine, vanilla essence and lemon rind.
- Make lemon juice up to ½ cup with juice from the mandarins.
- Add liquid to cream cheese mixture and blend well.
- Beat egg whites until stiff and fold into cheese. Add mandarins.
- Pour into crumb-crust and chill until firm.
- Decorate as desired.

127. Easy No Bake Nut Slice

Serving: 10 | Prep: 15mins | Cook: 200mins | Ready in: 215mins

Ingredients

- 200 g condensed milk
- 3 tbs golden syrup
- 1/4 cup white sugar
- 160 g butter
- 170 g milk arrowroot biscuits
- 150 g pecans chopped
- 250 g dark chocolate melted

Direction

- Place the condensed milk, golden syrup, sugar and butter in a large saucepan and mix together over medium heat, or microwave, until boiling.
- Stir for 5-7 minutes until mixture thickens and turns golden brown.
- Remove from heat and add the biscuits and chopped nuts.
- Spoon mixture into a 30 cm x 20 cm greased and baking paper lined lamington tray.
- Allow to cool, then smooth the surface with the back of a spoon.
- Refrigerate until cold, then spread the melted chocolate over the slice and allow to set.
- Slice into small squares.

128. Easy No Bake Slice

Serving: 10 | Prep: 15mins | Cook: 75mins | Ready in: 90mins

Ingredients

- 1/2 cup shredded coconut
- 1/3 cup dried cranberries
- 1/3 cup sultanas
- 1 1/2 cup chocolate buttons
- 200 g sweet plain biscuits

Direction

- Crush biscuits into small and medium pieces.
- Combine the coconut, cranberries and sultanas with the biscuits.
- Melt the chocolate buttons in the microwave 1 minute at a time, stirring between until melted.
- Add chocolate to the dry ingredients.
- Spoon the mixture into a lined fridge-proof tray. Refrigerate for at least an hour to set.

129. Easy Orange Cake With Orange Icing Recipe

Serving: 10 | Prep: 20mins | Cook: 40mins | Ready in: 60mins

Ingredients

- Orange Cake
- 125g unsalted butter, softened

- 1/4 cup milk
- 1/4 cup orange juice
- 2 eggs
- 3/4 cup caster sugar
- 1 1/2 cups self-raising flour sifted
- 1 tbs orange zest, finely grated
- Orange icing
- 1/3 cup butter softened
- 1 1/2 cups icing sugar sifted
- 2 tbs orange juice *to taste
- 1/2 tsp orange zest, finely grated

Direction

- Combine all cake ingredients and beat thoroughly for 3 minutes.
- Pour mixture into a greased 20cm x 10cm loaf or 20cm ring tin.
- Bake in the centre of an 180C oven for 30-40 minutes.
- Turn onto a wire rack and allow to cool.
- Mix orange icing ingredients together in a bowl, then ice cake.

130. Easy Pavlova Recipe

Serving: 8 | Prep: 15mins | Cook: 80mins | Ready in: 95mins

Ingredients

- 6 egg whites
- 1 1/2 cup caster sugar
- 1/2 cup white sugar
- 2 tbs cornflour
- 2 tsp lemon juice
- 1 cup cream *to decorate
- 1 cup mixed berries *to decorate

Direction

- Line a baking tray with baking paper.
- Beat eggs whites until stiff peaks form.
- Gradually add the caster sugar to the egg whites and mix until mixture becomes thick and glossy.
- Mix white sugar and cornflour together in separate bowl.
- Fold sugar mixture and lemon juice into egg white mixture.
- Place mixture on baking tray and mould into a circle about a dinner plate size.
- Bake at 150C (fan forced) for 45 minutes to 1 hour. It will be ready when it is dry to touch. Allow to cool in the oven with the door ajar.
- Once cool, decorate with cream and topping of choice.

131. Easy Pikelets Recipe

Serving: 0 | Prep: 5mins | Cook: 15mins | Ready in: 20mins

Ingredients

- 1 cup self-raising flour
- 2 tbs caster sugar
- 1 egg lightly beaten
- 3/4 cup milk

Direction

- Combine flour and sugar in a medium bowl. Gradually whisk in egg and milk to make a thick, smooth batter.
- Drop dessertspoonfuls of mixture into a greased heavy-based pan. Cook until bubbles begin to appear on the surface of the pikelet. Turn and brown the other side.

132. Easy Mix Butter Cake Recipe

Serving: 10 | Prep: 10mins | Cook: 40mins | Ready in: 50mins

Ingredients

- 2 eggs
- 125g unsalted butter, softened
- 1 cup sugar
- 2 cups self-raising flour
- 2/3 cup milk
- 1 tsp vanilla essence

Direction

- Combine all ingredients in a small bowl of an electric mixer.
- Beat on low speed until blended, then beat on high speed for 3 minutes.
- Grease a 28cm x 18cm lamington tin, and line the base with greaseproof paper.
- Pour mixture into tin and bake in a moderate oven (180C) for 30-40 minutes.
- When cold, ice with icing of choice and sprinkle with coconut or coloured sprinkles.

133. Eggless Chocolate Cake Recipe

Serving: 6 | Prep: 15mins | Cook: 35mins | Ready in: 50mins

Ingredients

- 1 1/2 cups plain flour
- 1 cup sugar
- 4 tbs cocoa
- 1 tsp bicarbonate of soda
- 1/2 tsp salt
- 1 cup water
- 1/3 cup vegetable oil
- 2 tbs white vinegar
- 2 tsp vanilla extract

Direction

- Combine dry ingredients.
- Combine wet ingredients and stir into flour mixture.
- Pour mixture into a 20cm round tin and bake at 175-180C for 25-35 minutes (pan should be 1/3 to 1/2 full, to accommodate rising).
- Stand for 10 minutes before turning out. Cake will be delicate while still hot.
- Microwave: using a ring or Bundt microwaveable pan, lightly oil the pan.
- Cut a paper ring to line the bottom of the pan. Pour in batter and microwave on high 5-7 minutes on a rotating turntable.
- Stand for 2 minutes in the oven when done. Cool for 10 minutes.

134. Endive Tart Recipe

Serving: 1 | Prep: 10mins | Cook: 60mins | Ready in: 70mins

Ingredients

- 1 white endive
- 1 sheet puff pastry
- 25 g butter
- 10 g demerara sugar
- 1 dollop sour cream *to serve
- 1 splash olive oil
- 1 pinch salt *to taste

Direction

- Preheat oven to 160C.
- Season the endive with olive oil and salt, then wrap the endive in aluminum foil.
- Cook it in the oven for 30 minutes at 160C.
- Once cooked, let it rest for another 30 minutes inside the foil, then unwrap and cut it lengthwise into 4 wedges.
- In an individual aluminum tin (a tart tin or pie tin), coat the bottom of the tin with a thin layer of butter.
- Add 10 grams of demerara sugar to the buttered surface, spread evenly.
- Lay the endive in the tin to cover the whole surface (or as much as possible).

- Cover the endive with the puff pastry, poke some holes in the pastry with a fork.
- Cook the tart it in the oven for 30 minutes at 180C, checking every 10 minutes as the time may change depending on the oven.
- Once the pastry has puffed and is golden in colour, flip the tart upside down onto your serving plate.
- Serve immediately with a dollop of sour cream.

135. Fig And Craisin Fruit Cake

Serving: 10 | Prep: 45mins | Cook: 560mins | Ready in: 605mins

Ingredients

- 2 x 170g Craisins dried cranberries
- 350g dried figs, thinly sliced
- 1/2 cup brandy
- 250g butter, softened
- 1 1/2 cup brown sugar
- 4 eggs
- 1 1/2 cup plain flour
- 1/2 cup self-raising flour
- 2 tsp ground ginger
- 1 tsp ground cinnamon
- 1 1/2 cup pistachios
- 2 tbs golden syrup

Direction

- Combine the fruit and brandy in a large bowl and stand overnight.
- Grease and line a deep 23cm square cake pan with brown paper and 2 layers of baking paper.
- Beat butter and sugar with an electric mixer, until just combined. Add eggs, one at a time.
- Stir in fruit mixture and sifted flour and spices. Mix well. Spread mixture into prepared pan and press nuts into top.
- Cook at 150C for one hour.
- Cover cake loosely with foil and cook for 2 more hours.
- When cooked, remove from the oven and cover pan tightly with foil. Allow to cool completely. To serve brush with warmed golden syrup.

136. Flake Baked Bananas Recipe

Serving: 4 | Prep: 5mins | Cook: 30mins | Ready in: 35mins

Ingredients

- 4 bananas
- 4 x 30g Cadbury Flake Chocolates

Direction

- Leaving the skins on the bananas, cut a deep slit down the length of each banana and press a Flake into each.
- Wrap individually in foil.
- Bake in a pre-heated 180C oven for 20-25 minutes until the bananas are tender.
- Serve warm.

137. Flor's Leche Flan Recipe

Serving: 6 | Prep: 10mins | Cook: 55mins | Ready in: 65mins

Ingredients

- 1/2 cup brown sugar
- 1/4 cup water
- 7 eggs
- 2 egg yolks
- 3/4 cup caster sugar
- 750 ml evaporated milk
- 2 tsp vanilla essence

Direction

- Heat brown sugar and water in a small saucepan without stirring until it turn into a deep golden brown.
- Remove from heat and pour into an 8-cup ovenproof mould. Rotate mould to coat base and sides with caramel.
- In a large bowl beat the whole eggs and egg yolks until foamy.
- Gradually add the caster sugar, beating until thick and light.
- Heat milk and add very gradually, beating constantly.
- Stir in vanilla, then strain custard into caramel-lined mould.
- Place mould into a baking tin and pour boiling water around to come half way up mould.
- Bake at 150C for 45-55 minutes or until a knife inserted in centre of custard comes out clean.
- Remove from oven and cool. When cold, cover and chill in the refrigerator overnight.
- Run a knife around edge, invert a chilled serving plate over the mould, then grasping both together turn over so that the custard slips onto the serving plate.
- Serve chilled.

138. Flourless Peanut Butter And Choc Chip Cookies Recipe

Serving: 20 | Prep: 15mins | Cook: 25mins | Ready in: 40mins

Ingredients

- 1 cup crunchy peanut butter
- 1 cup brown sugar
- 1 cup milk chocolate chips
- 1 egg lightly beaten
- 1 tsp bicarbonate of soda
- 1/2 cup mixed nuts crushed optional

Direction

- Preheat oven to 200C.
- Lightly grease oven tray and line with baking paper.
- Place all ingredients in a mixing bowl and combine.
- Roll heaped spoonfuls of mixture into balls and place 3 cm apart on tray.
- Press each one down lightly.
- Bake for 8-10 minutes or until golden. Cool on tray.
- Store in airtight container.

139. Frozen Lemon Cream Pie Recipe

Serving: 8 | Prep: 30mins | Cook: 5mins | Ready in: 35mins

Ingredients

- 12 arrowroot biscuits
- 1/4 cup caster sugar
- 1/4 cup melted butter
- Filling
- 1 cup thickened cream
- 1/4 cup icing sugar, plus extra to dust
- 2 tsp vanilla extract
- 280g jar of lemon curd
- 250g cream cheese
- 1/2 cup condensed milk
- 1 lemon, zest only *to serve

Direction

- Preheat oven to 180C.
- Break biscuits into pieces, place in a food processor and process until fine crumbs. Add melted butter and sugar and process until well combined.
- Press the crumbs firmly into a 24cm round pie dish. Place on a baking tray and bake for 5 minutes until slight golden. Set aside to cool.
- To make the filling, whip the cream, icing sugar and vanilla until stiff peaks. Set aside.

- In a clean bowl, add lemon curd, cream cheese and condensed milk and beat until smooth. Gently fold in 3/4 cup of the whipped cream into the lemon curd mixture until combined.
- Pour the filling into the cooled pie shell. Top with remaining whipped cream and use the back of a spoon to spread it out. Freeze uncovered for at least 2 hours.
- Serve with a dust of extra icing sugar and lemon zest.

140. Frozen Mango Bars Recipe

Serving: 0 | Prep: 180mins | Cook: 10mins | Ready in: 190mins

Ingredients

- 1 1/4 cups sugar
- 1 1/4 cups water
- 3 425g can sliced mango drained
- 1 tbs lemon juice
- 300 ml thickened cream

Direction

- Combine the sugar and water in a saucepan. Stir over low heat until the sugar is dissolved.
- Bring to the boil and boil for about 5 minutes, or until syrup thickens slightly. Cool to room temperature.
- Blend or process mangoes, sugar syrup and lemon juice until smooth.
- Combine one cup of mango mixture with cream.
- Line a 20 cm x 30 cm lamington pan with foil.
- Pour mango cream mixture into pan. Freeze until firm.
- Pour remaining mango mixture over frozen mango cream in pan. Freeze for several hours, or until firm.
- Cut into slices when frozen and store in freezer.

141. Fruit Mince Cigars Recipe

Serving: 0 | Prep: 0S | Cook: 0S | Ready in:

Ingredients

- 1/2 packet filo pastry sheets
- 2 cups fruit mince *see notes
- 50 g butter melted

Direction

- Preheat oven to 180C.
- Use two sheets of filo pastry. Brush one sheet with melted butter and sprinkle with cinnamon sugar. Place next sheet on top and repeat.
- Place 1/2 cup of fruit mince along the short side of the sheets and roll up to form a cigar shape.
- Cut into desired lengths and bake at 180C until brown and crisp. Sprinkle with icing sugar before serving.

142. Fruit Mince Crumble Slice Recipe

Serving: 0 | Prep: 15mins | Cook: 35mins | Ready in: 50mins

Ingredients

- 2 cup fruit mince *see notes
- 250 g butter
- 1 cup brown sugar
- 1 egg
- 1 tsp vanilla extract
- 2 1/2 cup plain flour
- 2 cup rolled oats

Direction

- Preheat oven to 160C. Line a slice pan (18cmx28cm) with baking paper.
- Beat butter and sugar with an electric mixer until pale and creamy. Add in the vanilla and egg. Stir in flour and rolled oats until combined.
- Place half the mixture into the tin and press down firmly. Top with the fruit mince and crumble the remaining mixture over the top, pressing down gently. Bake for 35minutes.

143. Fruit Tart

Serving: 10 | Prep: 20mins | Cook: 20mins | Ready in: 40mins

Ingredients

- Shortcrust pastry
- 195 g plain flour
- 1 pinch salt
- 113 g unsalted butter softened
- 50 g caster sugar
- 1 egg lightly beaten
- Filling
- 500 g cream cheese
- 1 tsp vanilla extract
- 50 g caster sugar
- 3/4 cup thickened cream
- Apricot glaze
- 1/2 cup apricot jam
- 2 tbs water

Direction

- Preheat oven to 205C degrees and place rack in the centre of oven. Lightly grease a 20cm loose-based tart pan.
- To make the shortcrust pastry, beat butter using an electric mixer until softened. Add sugar and beat until light and fluffy. Add egg and beat until just incorporated. Add the flour and salt and mix until dough forms a ball. Remove from bowl. Flatten the pastry into a disc, cover with plastic wrap and place into the freezer for about 10-15 minutes to firm up.
- Roll out pastry to 1cm thickness. Place pastry into prepared pan, evenly pat the pastry onto the bottom and sides of the pan making sure it is not too thick. Prick the bottom and sides with a fork. Bake in oven for 5 mins.
- Reduce oven to 180C degrees and bake for another 15 mins or until golden brown. Remove from oven and place on wire rack to cool completely.
- To make the apricot glaze, heat apricot jam and water in a small saucepan over medium heat until the jam dissolves. Strain jam through a fine strainer or sieve to remove any lumps. This glaze can be used in tart shell and brushed over your fruit to make it shine and stay fresh. Spread a thin layer over the bottom and sides of your baked tart shell to prevent the shell going soggy.
- To make the cream filling, in a bowl of your electric mixer, beat cream cheese until smooth. Add vanilla, sugar and cream and then beat until fluffy. Place cream filling into tart shell and chill until firm and then cover with your choice of fruit.

144. German Snowballs Recipe

Serving: 15 | Prep: 15mins | Cook: 12mins | Ready in: 27mins

Ingredients

- 1 1/2 cup almond meal
- 1 1/4 cup wholemeal atta flour
- 170 g sunflower margarine
- 1/4 cup raw sugar
- 2 tbs vanilla essence
- 1 cup icing sugar
- 3 tbs vanilla sugar

Direction

- Preheat oven to 170C. Mix all ingredients except for the icing sugar into a bowl and kneed to a dough.
- Shape into little balls a 16g a piece and bake in preheated oven for 10-15 minutes.
- When ready and still warm, add into a bowl and immediately sprinkle over the icing sugar and vanilla sugar.
- Store in a metal box with lid.

145. Gingerbread Cookies Recipe

Serving: 0 | Prep: 60mins | Cook: 10mins | Ready in: 70mins

Ingredients

- 3 cups plain flour
- 120 g butter chopped
- 2 tsp bicarbonate of soda
- 1/2 tsp ground cloves
- 2 tsp ground ginger
- 1/3 cup brown sugar
- 1/2 cup golden syrup
- 1 egg
- 2 tsp ground cinnamon

Direction

- Preheat oven 160C.
- Combine ingredients in a large bowl.
- Knead until smooth.
- Roll between 2 sheets of baking paper until approximately 2.5 cm thick.
- Refrigerate until chilled.
- Place chilled dough on bench and cut out shapes.
- Place on baking paper-lined tray.
- Bake for 10 minutes until slightly golden.
- Ice when cool, if desired.

146. Gluten Free Rum Balls Recipe

Serving: 0 | Prep: 30mins | Cook: 0S | Ready in: 30mins

Ingredients

- 1/2 cup cocoa powder
- 1/2 cup white sugar
- 1 cup sultanas
- 2 1/2 cups gluten-free rice cracker crumbs
- 1/2 cup butter
- 1/2 cup milk
- 1/2 cup desiccated coconut *to decorate
- 1 tbs rum

Direction

- Place milk, sugar and butter into a saucepan over low heat, until butter and sugar have melted.
- Mix in dry ingredients and rum.
- Place in fridge for 30 minutes to set.
- Roll into walnut-sized balls and roll in coconut.

147. Golden Gaytime Frozen Cheesecake Recipe

Serving: 12 | Prep: 30mins | Cook: 5mins | Ready in: 35mins

Ingredients

- 200g butternut snap biscuits crushed
- 100g butter melted
- 2 Golden Gaytime ice creams
- Filling
- 500g cream cheese softened
- 3/4 cup brown sugar
- 1 tsp vanilla extract
- 300ml thickened cream
- Chocolate Sauce
- 1/3 cup thickened cream
- 100g dark chocolate chopped

Direction

- Lightly grease a 22cm round springform cake pan. Combine crushed biscuits and melted butter in a bowl. Stir to combine. Press over base of pan. Refrigerate for 30 minutes or until firm.
- Using electric beaters, beat cream cheese and sugar until smooth. Beat in vanilla and cream until light and fluffy. Spread mixture into pan and smooth the surface. Freeze overnight or until just firm.
- To make the chocolate sauce, combine cream and chocolate in a small saucepan over low heat. Stir for 2-3 minutes or until mixture is smooth. Cool for 30 minutes or until thickened slightly.
- Remove frozen cheesecake from pan and place on a serving plate. Drizzle cheesecake with chocolate sauce. Remove sticks from Golden Gaytimes and cut into chunks. Pile Gaytime chunks in the centre of the cheesecake. Serve immediately.

148. Gran's Christmas Fruit Balls Recipe

Serving: 4 | Prep: 10mins | Cook: 10mins | Ready in: 20mins

Ingredients

- 1 cup raisins
- 1 cup sultanas
- 1 cup dates
- 1 cup coconut
- 1 cup walnuts
- 400 g condensed milk

Direction

- Chop the fruit and nuts, and then add the coconut.
- Mix in condensed milk.
- Roll into 3 cm balls and roll in extra coconut.
- Bake at 150C until golden.

149. Guilt Free Choc Chip Peanut Butter Cookie For One Recipe

Serving: 1 | Prep: 5mins | Cook: 15mins | Ready in: 20mins

Ingredients

- 1/2 apple grated medium
- 1 tsp peanut butter
- 2 tbs self-raising flour
- 2 tbs plain flour
- 1/2 tsp honey
- 1 tsp chocolate chips
- 2 tsp honey *to serve
- 2 tsp peanut butter *to serve

Direction

- Preheat the oven to 180C fan forced.
- In a small bowl, place apple, peanut butter, honey and mix well.
- Add the flour and chocolate chips and mix to form a dough.
- Divide the dough and roll into two balls. Place on a lined baking tray and gently push down to flatten with a fork.
- Bake for 10-12 minutes, or until golden and cooked.
- Place peanut butter on one cookie and drizzle with honey and then sandwich the other cookie on top.

150. Healthier Chocolate Tart Recipe

Serving: 0 | Prep: 15mins | Cook: 45mins | Ready in: 60mins

Ingredients

- 14 medjool dates halved pitted
- 1 cup boiling water
- 1 cup water
- 1/2 cup coconut oil
- 3 cups shredded coconut
- 250 ml coconut cream
- 1/4 cup cocoa
- 1 tsp vanilla extract
- 1/4 tsp sea salt
- 2 tbs gelatine

Direction

- Preheat oven to 160C.
- Place dates in a small bowl and cover with 1 cup of boiling water. Cover bowl with foil and set aside for 30 minutes.
- Grease a 24cm flan tin with removable base and place on a dinner plate (dinner plate helps with moving to refrigerator).
- Meanwhile, spread shredded coconut onto a lined baking tray and brown in the oven (stirring every 5 minutes until golden). Set aside.
- Heat coconut oil in small saucepan over low heat until just melted.
- Combine coconut oil and shredded coconut in a medium-sized bowl. When the shredded coconut is fully coated with oil, line the base and sides of flan tin with the coconut mixture. Place the coconut base in the refrigerator for 30 minutes.
- When dates are ready, add to food processor with the water from the bowl and chop on high speed until a smooth thick liquid is formed. Add coconut cream, 1 cup of water, cocoa, vanilla and salt to the food processor and mix until well combined.
- Add the gelatine to the food processor and continue to mix for a further minute.
- When coconut base has been in the refrigerator for 30 minutes, pour chocolate mixture into base. Return to refrigerator and leave overnight to set.
- When ready to serve, remove from refrigerator and leave on counter top for 15 minutes before serving. Remove sides of tin and decorate with fruit of your choice.

151. Hidden Orange Pudding Recipe

Serving: 0 | Prep: 0S | Cook: 0S | Ready in:

Ingredients

- For The Crystallized Orange
- 1 orange
- 1 L water
- 1 kg white sugar
- 1/2 cinnamon stick
- 1 tbs marmalade
- 2 tbs Grand Marnier
- For The Pudding
- 500 g Sunbeam mixed fruit
- 1 carrot finely grated peeled
- 1 granny smith apple coarsely grated peeled
- 1/2 cup brandy
- 125 g butter
- 1/3 cup dark brown sugar
- 3 eggs
- 2 tbs treacle
- 3/4 cup plain flour
- 1 1/2 tsp mixed spice
- 1/2 cup Sunbeam almond meal

Direction

- To candy the orange, pierce orange several times with a skewer. Place into a stainless steel saucepan of boiling water, cover and gently boil for 30 minutes to soften.
- Remove from water, add the sugar, cinnamon and marmalade to saucepan and bring to the boil, stirring occasionally.
- Place orange back into sugar syrup, cover and cook over a medium heat for 45 minutes making sure to roll the orange around to cook evenly.

- Remove from the syrup (reserve syrup in saucepan) and dry overnight on a rack. Next day, add orange and liqueur to sugar syrup in saucepan and boil for 30 minutes. Remove and allow to dry overnight, the orange is now ready to use. Reserve the syrup in a clean sterilized jar and seal.
- Store in a cool pantry.
- To make the pudding, butter a 2 litre pudding basin and line the base with a double layer of baking paper.
- Place fruit, carrot, apple and brandy in a large mixing bowl and leave to soak for 20 minutes.
- Cream butter and brown sugar until light and fluffy. Gradually beat in eggs one at a time beating well after each addition, beat in treacle. Stir butter mixture into fruit mixing well.
- Sift plain flour and mixed spice onto fruit mixture, add almond meal and mix well.
- Half fill prepared pudding basin with the mixture. Place the candied orange in the centre of the bowl, gently add the remaining pudding mixture so it is buried inside. Cover with a disc of baking paper. Then take a large sheet of each baking paper and foil and fold in half then make a pleat. Place the sheet over the pudding basin and secure with string.
- Sit pudding on a wire trivet in a saucepan filled with simmering water to a depth of 6cm. Cover and stream for 6 hours. Making sure to replenish water with boiling water from kettle.
- Store the pudding for several weeks in the refrigerator. When required, steam again for 3 hours. Serve garnished with fine candied orange shreds and a generous drizzle of the reserved orange liquid syrup.

152. Honey Joys Recipe

Serving: 0 | Prep: 30mins | Cook: 25mins | Ready in: 55mins

Ingredients

- 90g butter
- 1/3 cup sugar
- 1 tbs Capilano* Light & Smooth Honey
- 4 cups Kellogg's Corn Flakes

Direction

- Preheat oven to 150C.
- Line 24-hole patty pan with paper cases.
- Melt butter, sugar and honey together in a saucepan until frothy.
- Add corn flakes and mix well.
- Working quickly, spoon mixture into patty cases.
- Bake for 10 minutes.
- Cool.

153. Impossible Pudding Recipe

Serving: 6 | Prep: 20mins | Cook: 40mins | Ready in: 60mins

Ingredients

- 4 egg
- 2 cups milk
- 125g butter cooled melted
- 1 cup desiccated coconut
- 1 cup caster sugar
- 1/2 cup plain flour
- 1 tsp vanilla essence

Direction

- Lightly beat eggs in a large bowl. Add milk, butter, sugar, coconut, flour and vanilla. Mix well.
- Pour into an 18 cm pudding bowl or casserole dish. Bake at 180C for 35-40 minutes or until custard is set and top is golden.

154. Individual Banoffee Pies Recipe

Serving: 0 | Prep: 10mins | Cook: 10mins | Ready in: 20mins

Ingredients

- 250 g butternut snap biscuits
- 380 g Top 'n' Fill Caramel
- 2 banana cut diagonally medium sliced
- 300 ml thickened cream
- 100 g instant vanilla pudding mix
- 1 tbs caster sugar
- 1 drop vanilla essence
- 30 g Flake chocolate bar crumbled

Direction

- Preheat oven to 180C (160C fan forced).
- Place biscuits over the top of each rounded bottom muffin pan.
- Bake for approximately 6 minutes until softened.
- Whilst still warm, gently push the centre of each biscuit into the muffin hole with the back of a spoon. Allow to cool before removing from tray.
- In a bowl, place the cream, pudding mix, caster sugar and vanilla essence. Beat with electric mixer until thick and firm peaks form. Set aside.
- Half fill each biscuit cup with caramel.
- Top with a banana slice, a tablespoon of cream mixture and then crumbled flake.

155. Individual Sticky Date Puddings Recipe

Serving: 0 | Prep: 30mins | Cook: 50mins | Ready in: 80mins

Ingredients

- 270 g pitted dates chopped
- 1 tsp bicarbonate of soda
- 1 tsp vanilla essence
- 60 g butter
- 185 g self-raising flour
- 125 g soft brown sugar
- 2 eggs
- Sauce
- 90 g butter
- 140 g soft brown sugar
- 2 tbs golden syrup
- 185 ml cream

Direction

- Preheat oven to 180C.
- Lightly grease or spray a 12 hole muffin pan.
- Place dates and 250 mL water in a small saucepan, bring to the boil, then remove from heat and stir in the bicarbonate of soda and vanilla.
- Add the butter and stir until dissolved.
- Sift flour into a large bowl, add the sugar and stir. Make a well in the centre, add the date mixture and eggs, and stir until just combined.
- Spoon the mixture into the prepared pan and bake for 15-20 minutes, or until a skewer comes out clean.
- Meanwhile, to make the sauce, place all ingredients in a saucepan and stir over low heat for 3-4 minutes. Bring to the boil, then reduce heat and simmer for 2 minutes.
- To serve, turn the puddings out onto the serving plates, pour the sauce over and serve with ice-cream or cream.

156. Jelly Cheesecake Recipe

Serving: 8 | Prep: 15mins | Cook: 0S | Ready in: 15mins

Ingredients

- 500 g cream cheese
- 80 g butter melted
- 2 x 85 g jelly crystals
- 400 ml water

- 125 g biscuits

Direction

- Dissolve the lemon jelly crystals in ½ cup boiling water. Whisk the jelly with cream cheese until smooth.
- Combine the crushed biscuits and butter. Press into the base of a pan.
- Pour the cream cheese filling over the biscuits, and then spread evenly to cover the biscuit base. Refrigerate.
- Prepare second packet of jelly according to the packet instructions. Allow to cool, then gently pour over the cream cheese mixture.
- Set in fridge for roughly 4 hours or until firm.

157. Lamington Cheesecake Recipe

Serving: 12 | Prep: 180mins | Cook: 10mins | Ready in: 190mins

Ingredients

- 18 lamingtons
- 250 g white chocolate
- 300 ml thickened cream
- 2 tsp gelatine powder
- 3 tsp water
- 125 g cream cheese
- 250 g mascarpone
- 1/2 cup caster sugar
- 1 tsp vanilla extract
- 250 g dark chocolate
- 1/2 cup thickened cream
- 1/2 cup desiccated coconut *to decorate

Direction

- Grease and line a 17 cm x 27 cm slice pan with baking paper.
- Lay lamington fingers side by side in pan.
- In a heatproof bowl, melt white chocolate and 150 mL of cream in microwave in short bursts, stirring regularly until chocolate is melted and cream is completely mixed into chocolate.
- Mix gelatine and water together. Heat in microwave for 20 seconds or until gelatine is dissolved. Stir into chocolate mixture.
- Beat cream cheese, mascarpone, sugar and vanilla until soft and creamy, then beat in chocolate mixture.
- In a separate bowl, beat remaining cream until soft peaks form. Fold through mixture.
- Pour over lamingtons and set in fridge overnight.
- Once set, melt dark chocolate and extra thickened cream together then refrigerate for 20 minutes to make ganache and spread over cheese cake. Sprinkle with coconut.
- Refrigerate until topping sets.

158. Lemon Baked Cheesecake Recipe

Serving: 10 | Prep: 20mins | Cook: 480mins | Ready in: 500mins

Ingredients

- 250 g sweet plain biscuits crumbed
- 125 g butter melted
- 3 eggs lightly beaten
- 1/2 cup caster sugar
- 3 x 250 g cream cheese softened
- 3 tsp lemon rind grated
- 1/4 cup lemon juice

Direction

- Lightly grease a 22 cm springform tin.
- Combine biscuit crumbs and butter in a bowl.
- Using a glass, press crumb mixture evenly over base and side of tin.
- Refrigerate biscuit crust for 1 hour.
- Beat eggs and sugar in a bowl with an electric mixer until pale and thick.
- Add cheese, rind and lemon juice. Beat until mixture is smooth and creamy.

- Pour mixture into prepared tin and bake in moderate oven for about 45 minutes.
- Cool in oven with door ajar, then refrigerate for several hours or overnight.
- Decorate with cream and strawberries if desired.

159. Lemon Coconut Cake Recipe

Serving: 12 | Prep: 15mins | Cook: 40mins | Ready in: 55mins

Ingredients

- 1 1/2 cups self-raising flour
- 1/2 cup desiccated coconut
- 1 tbs lemon rind grated
- 1 cup caster sugar
- 125 g butter melted
- 2 eggs
- 1 cup milk

Direction

- Preheat the oven to 180C. Grease a 20 cm deep round cake tin.
- Combine all ingredients into a bowl, mixing well with wooden spoon until batter is smooth.
- Pour the mixture into cake tin and bake 40 minutes.

160. Lemon Curd Cheesecake With Lemon Jelly Topping Recipe

Serving: 8 | Prep: 180mins | Cook: 0S | Ready in: 180mins

Ingredients

- 250 g plain biscuits
- 250 g butter melted
- Filling
- 85 g lemon jelly
- 1 cup boiling water
- 250 g cream cheese
- 1/2 cup lemon curd
- 1 tsp lemon essence
- 2 lemons juiced zested
- Jelly topping
- 170 g lemon jelly
- 1 tbs gelatine powder
- 2/3 cup boiling water

Direction

- Mix 1 packet of jelly with 1 cup boiling water and allow to partially set in fridge. This will be used in the filling.
- Grease a 23 cm round springform cake tin.
- Process the biscuits to make fine crumbs.
- Combine melted butter with biscuit crumbs.
- Press the biscuit mix into the tin, covering base and sides to approximately ⅓ of the way up.
- Allow to set in fridge.
- For the jelly topping, use a separate 23 cm round sponge tin. Run water inside the tin to wet it, drain and shake off the water, don't wipe dry.
- Dissolve 2 packets of jelly and gelatine in ⅔ cup boiling water.
- Pour into the wet sponge tin, allow to set in fridge for approximately 45 minutes.
- For the filling, soften cream cheese in the microwave for approximately 2 minutes.
- Using an electric mixer, beat cream cheese, lemon curd, lemon essence, lemon juice and zest and partially set jelly mix.
- Spread filling over set base.
- Once jelly topping is set, place cake tin with jelly in some hot water then use a sharp knife to loosen jelly from edges of pan. The jelly should easily slide out of cake tin onto the top of the filling.
- Place in fridge overnight to set.
- Use a knife to loosen edges of cheesecake and open the springform tin.

161. Lemon Meringue Cheesecake Recipe

Serving: 10 | Prep: 20mins | Cook: 180mins | Ready in: 200mins

Ingredients

- 250 g sweet plain biscuits crushed
- 125 g butter melted
- Filling
- 250 g cream cheese
- 440 g condensed milk
- 2 egg yolks
- 2 tsp lemon rind grated
- 1/4 cup lemon juice
- Meringue
- 3 egg whites
- 1/2 cup caster sugar

Direction

- Base: Combine biscuit crumbs and butter and press firmly into base of a springform pan. Refrigerate until firm.
- Filling: Beat cheese until smooth, add condensed milk, lemon rind, lemon juice, and egg yolks and beat until smooth.
- Pour over base and refrigerate for approximately 2 hours or until firm to touch.
- Meringue: Whip egg whites until stiff peaks form. Gradually add sugar and beat until dissolved.
- Spread evenly over filling.
- Preheat the grill to high heat and cook for 4 - 5 minutes, checking regularly or until meringue browns.
- Allow to cool, then refrigerate until required.

162. Lemon Meringue Pie Recipe

Serving: 8 | Prep: 15mins | Cook: 45mins | Ready in: 60mins

Ingredients

- 180 g plain biscuits crushed
- 90 g butter melted
- 400 g NESTLÉ Sweetened Condensed Milk
- 1/2 cup fresh lemon juice
- 3 eggs separated
- 1/2 cup caster sugar

Direction

- Combine crushed biscuits and melted butter.
- Press into a 23 cm pie plate and refrigerate.
- Blend condensed milk and lemon juice. Add lightly beaten egg yolks and combine well.
- Pour evenly into the chilled crumb crust.
- Beat egg whites until stiff, then gradually beat in caster sugar. Spoon meringue on top of the filling.
- Bake in a preheated oven at 160C for 10-15 minutes, until meringue is golden.
- Let pie cool before serving.

163. Lemon Slice Recipe

Serving: 10 | Prep: 15mins | Cook: 25mins | Ready in: 40mins

Ingredients

- 250 g sweet plain biscuits
- 125 g butter melted
- 3/4 cup coconut
- 1/2 can NESTLE Sweetened Condensed Milk
- 1 lemon zested
- Icing
- 2 cups icing sugar
- 1 1/2 tbs butter melted
- 1/2 cup lemon juice *to taste

Direction

- Crush biscuits and mix in coconut.
- Add finely grated lemon rind and mix.
- Combine melted butter and condensed milk and add to dry mixture. Stir well.
- Press into a lined slice tin and set in fridge.
- Icing: Mix all icing ingredients (with lemon juice to taste) and ice when cooled.

164. Lemon Yoghurt Cake Recipe

Serving: 12 | Prep: 10mins | Cook: 45mins | Ready in: 55mins

Ingredients

- 1 3/4 cups sugar
- 2 eggs
- 1/2 tsp salt
- 3 tsp lemon juice
- 2 lemons grated
- 3/4 cup oil
- 1 cup natural yoghurt
- 2 cups self-raising flour

Direction

- In a bowl, mix rind, oil, eggs and sugar with a fork.
- Add remaining ingredients and combine well.
- Pour into greased ring tin and bake at 180C for 30 minutes.
- Leave to cool then turn out and dust with icing sugar.

165. Lemonade Scones Recipe

Serving: 0 | Prep: 5mins | Cook: 15mins | Ready in: 20mins

Ingredients

- 1 cup lemonade
- 1 cup cream
- 3 cups self-raising flour
- 1 egg

Direction

- Preheat oven to 220C.
- Add lemonade and cream to flour, mix to form a soft dough, then place on a floured surface.
- Knead dough to a 2cm thickness and cut with a floured cutter.
- Place close together on a tray, brush with beaten egg and bake for 10-15 minutes.

166. Limoncello Christmas Cake Recipe

Serving: 12 | Prep: 30mins | Cook: 2mins | Ready in: 32mins

Ingredients

- 225g butter
- 100g raw sugar
- 125g brown sugar
- 1 tbs molasses
- 4 eggs
- 340g plain flour
- 1 tsp cinnamon
- 1 tsp nutmeg
- 1kg dried mixed fruit
- 100g almonds, chopped
- 1/2 lemon, rind only
- 4 tbs limoncello

Direction

- Pour the limoncello over the dried fruit and chopped almonds and allow it to soak overnight.
- Grease and line a 23cm round tin with baking paper.
- Melt the butter in a small saucepan and then add the sugars, molasses and eggs. Add the

spices, flour and the butter mixture to the dried fruit in batches, and stir with a large wooden spoon until stiff and thick. If you think the mixture is too heavy, add a tbs or two of milk.

- Spoon into the cake tin and bake at 150C fan-forced for one hour. The cake should start to be a bit brown on top. Reduce the heat to 140C fan-forced and bake a further hour and a half.
- When cooked, remove from the oven and allow to cool.

167. Limoncello Tiramisu Recipe

Serving: 12 | Prep: 30mins | Cook: 0S | Ready in: 30mins

Ingredients

- 4 egg whites
- 24 Savoiardi sponge finger biscuits
- 1 punnet fresh strawberries
- Lemon syrup
- 1 1/2 cups water
- 1/4 cup sugar
- 3/4 cup lemon juice
- 1/2 cup limoncello
- Lemon mascarpone cream
- 500 g mascarpone
- 4 egg yolks
- 4 tbs caster sugar
- 1 tsp vanilla extract
- 2 lemons zested

Direction

- Combine lemon syrup ingredients in a shallow dish.
- Beat egg whites until soft peaks form.
- Blend together lemon mascarpone cream ingredients. Gently fold egg white into the cheese mixture.
- Dip biscuits into syrup mix to coat and lay in dish.
- Cover with half the mascarpone mixture and slices of fresh strawberries.
- Repeat layers and finish by topping with fruit slices.
- Leave in fridge for at least four hours or overnight.

168. Little Dutch Pancakes Recipe

Serving: 0 | Prep: 10mins | Cook: 20mins | Ready in: 30mins

Ingredients

- 2 cups self-raising flour sifted
- 2 tbs caster sugar
- 1 pinch salt
- 1 cup milk
- 1/2 cup water
- 3 eggs
- 1 splash maple syrup *to serve
- 1 pinch icing sugar *to serve
- 1 scoop vanilla ice cream *to serve

Direction

- Combine flour, sugar and salt into a large bowl.
- Add milk and water, and mix with an electric mixer until smooth, scraping sides if necessary.
- Add eggs and mix until combined and smooth.
- Heat poffertje pan and lightly grease indentations.
- Add the mixture until holes are full.
- Cook for a few minutes, then turn over.
- Poffertjes are cooked when they are golden brown and puffy.
- Remove from pan and drizzle with maple syrup, icing sugar and ice cream.
- Serve immediately.

169. Macadamia Christmas Cake Recipe

Serving: 0 | Prep: 0S | Cook: 0S | Ready in:

Ingredients

- Christmas cake
- 375 g Sunbeam sultanas
- 375 g Sunbeam mixed fruit
- 1/2 cup rum
- 250 g butter
- 1 cup brown sugar firmly packed
- 4 eggs
- 100 g dark chocolate melted
- 1 cup plain flour
- 2 tsp ground ginger
- 2 tsp ground cinnamon
- 2 cups Sunbeam macadamias halved

Direction

- Combine sultanas, mixed fruit and rum in a large bowl. Cover and allow to stand overnight.
- Preheat oven to 140°C. Line the base and sides of a 20cm deep square cake tin with a double layer of baking paper.
- Beat butter and brown sugar until light and creamy. Add eggs, one at a time, beating well after each addition. Add melted chocolate and beat until combined. Stir butter mixture into soaked fruit.
- Blend 1 cup of Macadamia nuts in a food processor until smooth, to make a meal.
- Sift plain flour, ginger and cinnamon onto fruit mixture, add macadamia meal and nuts and stir until combined.
- Pour into tin and level the top. Bake for 1½ - 1¾ hours or until a skewer inserted in the centre of cake comes out clean.

170. Macadamia And Fruit Mince Truffles Recipe

Serving: 0 | Prep: 90mins | Cook: 20mins | Ready in: 110mins

Ingredients

- 55 g Sunbeam macadamia nuts halved toasted
- 1/2 cup caster sugar
- 180 g dark chocolate chopped
- 1/3 cup thickened cream
- 1/2 cup fruit mince *see notes
- 360 g dark chocolate chopped

Direction

- Place macadamias on a baking paper-lined baking tray. Place sugar and 1/2 cup water in a small saucepan over medium-high heat. Cook, stirring, for 3 to 5 minutes or until sugar is dissolved. Bring to the boil. Reduce heat to medium. Boil, without stirring, for 5 to 8 minutes or until mixture turns dark golden. Pour over macadamias. Set aside for 30 minutes or until hard.
- Meanwhile, place chocolate and cream in a microwave-safe bowl. Microwave on HIGH (100%), stirring with a metal spoon every 30 seconds, for 1 to 2 minutes or until melted and combined. Set aside for 30 minutes or until mixture cools and thickens.
- Break up macadamia toffee. Transfer to the bowl of a small food processor. Process until chopped (do not allow mixture to become too fine or it will lose its crunch). Add fruit mince and half the macadamia mixture to the chocolate mixture. Stir to combine. Refrigerate for 10 minutes or until mixture is thick enough to shape into balls.
- Using 2 level teaspoons of chocolate mixture at a time roll into balls. Place on baking paper-lined tray. Refrigerate for 10 minutes.
- Meanwhile, place extra chocolate in a microwave-safe bowl. Microwave on HIGH (100%), stirring with a metal spoon every 30 seconds, for 1 to 2 minutes or until melted and smooth. Set aside for 10 minutes to cool.

- Dip 1 truffle into melted chocolate to coat. Using a fork, lift truffle out, allowing excess chocolate to drain. Return to tray. Sprinkle with a little remaining macadamia mixture. Repeat with remaining truffles. Refrigerate for 10 minutes or until set. Serve.

171. Magic Cake Recipe

Serving: 8 | Prep: 15mins | Cook: 70mins | Ready in: 85mins

Ingredients

- 4 eggs room temperature separated
- 1 tsp vanilla extract
- 150 g sugar
- 125 g butter melted
- 115 g plain flour
- 500 ml milk warmed
- 1/2 cup icing sugar *to decorate

Direction

- Preheat oven to 160C. Grease a 20cm x 20cm baking dish.
- Separate eggs and add egg whites into a mixing bowl and mix until egg whites are stiff. Set aside.
- Beat egg yolks with sugar until light. Add butter and vanilla extract and continue beating for another minute or two. Add the flour and mix until well combined.
- Slowly start adding the lukewarm milk and beat until all ingredients are mixed together. Add the egg whites a third at a time, gently fold in using a spatula. Repeat until all egg whites are folded in.
- Pour batter into baking dish and bake for 50-70 minutes, or until the top is golden. The cake will be wobbly in middle due to custard.
- Sprinkle icing sugar on cake when cooled.

172. Magic Peanut Butter Biscuits Recipe

Serving: 10 | Prep: 30mins | Cook: 20mins | Ready in: 50mins

Ingredients

- 200 g peanut butter
- 250 g Splenda sugar substitute
- 1 egg
- 1 vanilla extract

Direction

- Preheat oven to 180C.
- In a bowl, combine all ingredients.
- Stir with a spoon until just combined.
- Roll into walnut-sized balls and place on lined tray.
- Use a fork dipped into Splenda and press to make a cross-hatch pattern into tops of dough.
- Bake for 12 minutes.
- Cool for several minutes before removing from tray.

173. Malteser Layer Cake Recipe

Serving: 12 | Prep: 20mins | Cook: 0S | Ready in: 20mins

Ingredients

- 2 x 600g chocolate mud cakes
- 400g tub chocolate frosting
- 600g Maltesers chocolates

Direction

- Place one mud cake on a serving platter and top with some of the chocolate frosting. Place second cake icing side down on top of the chocolate frosting, stacking the cakes. Spread remaining frosting over the entire top and sides of the two cakes.

- Beginning in the centre and working in a circle, arrange Maltesers over the top and sides of the cake, pressing into the icing.

174. Malteser And Banana Cake Recipe

Serving: 8 | Prep: 15mins | Cook: 40mins | Ready in: 55mins

Ingredients

- 125 g butter
- 1/2 cup caster sugar
- 2 egg
- 2 tbs milk
- 1/2 tsp bicarbonate of soda
- 1 1/2 cup self-raising flour
- 2 1/2 banana mashed ripe
- 2 tbs vanilla sugar
- 165 g Maltesers
- 1 tbs icing sugar *to decorate

Direction

- Preheat oven 180C.
- Cream butter and sugar until light and fluffy with electric mixer.
- Gradually add eggs on a low speed. Blend bicarbonate of soda with warm milk.
- Fold through butter mixture with dry ingredients.
- Stir through mashed bananas, vanilla sugar and Maltesers.
- Pour into a greased ring tin lined with baking paper.
- Bake 30-40 minutes or until skewer comes out clean.
- Let sit in tin for 5 minutes then turn onto wire cake rack to cool.
- Dust with icing sugar when cool.

175. Mango Brulee With Passionfruit Cream Recipe

Serving: 8 | Prep: 0S | Cook: 4mins | Ready in: 4mins

Ingredients

- 4 Calypso mangoes
- 0.6 cup white sugar
- Passionfruit Cream
- 300 ml thickened cream
- 1/4 cup sour cream
- 1 tsp vanilla bean paste
- 2 passionfruit pulp removed

Direction

- To make passionfruit cream: whip the cream, sour cream and vanilla together until thick. Fold through the passionfruit. Cover and refrigerate until ready to serve.
- Cut the cheeks from the mangoes. Score the mango cheeks. Spoon the sugar onto a plate.
- Heat a large, non-stick frying pan over high heat. Dip 2-3 mango cheeks (see notes), cut-side down, into sugar. Place a sheet of baking paper into the hot pan, then add mangoes, cut-side down. Cook for 3-4 minutes, or until sugar has caramelised. Using tongs, lift mango cheeks onto a tray, cut side up. Discard the paper. Repeat with remaining mangoes and sugar.
- Serve mangoes with passionfruit cream.

176. Mango Cake With Curd Recipe

Serving: 12 | Prep: 15mins | Cook: 60mins | Ready in: 75mins

Ingredients

- 6 eggs separated
- 250 g unsalted butter brought to room temperature

- 8 tbs continental flour
- 15 g baking powder
- 8 g vanilla sugar
- 1 kg milk curd (see notes)
- 825 g canned mango in syrup
- 250 g icing sugar

Direction

- Preheat fan forced oven to 170C degrees. Grease a 26cm round deep pan with extra butter and dust bottom and sides with extra flour.
- In a bowl, mix butter and sugar with electric mixer until fluffy. Add egg yolks one at the time. Add flour, curd or ricotta cheese, baking powder, vanilla sugar and mix all well.
- In another bowl, mix egg whites with electric mixer until soft peaks form, then very gently fold into yolk mixture.
- Pour batter into prepared pan. Top with strained sliced mangoes. Press the fruit gently into batter with fork. Bake for about 1 hour, or when skewer comes out clean. Leave to cool, then sprinkle with icing sugar.

177. Mango Cheesecake Slice Recipe

Serving: 8 | Prep: 20mins | Cook: 45mins | Ready in: 65mins

Ingredients

- 4 Calypso mangoes
- 400 g Lattice biscuits
- 375 g cream cheese softened
- 1/2 cup caster sugar
- 395 g sweetened condensed milk
- 2 egg yolks
- 250 g sour cream
- 1 tsp vanilla bean paste
- 250 g mascarpone

Direction

- Preheat oven to 160C fan-forced. Grease and line a 22cm (base) square cake pan with baking paper, allowing a 3cm overhang on all sides.
- Arrange 16 biscuits, glazed side down, over the base of the cake pan, cutting to fit, so the base is covered.
- Peel and cut the fruit from 1 mango. Process the mango until smooth (you should have ¾ cup of puree). Pour the puree into a jug, wash and dry the food processor.
- Combine the cream cheese and sugar in the processor. Process until smooth. Add the sweetened condensed milk, egg yolks and sour cream, pulse until just combined. Add 3/4 cup mango puree, pulse to combine. Pour over the base. Arrange more biscuits, glazed side up, over the top.
- Bake for 40-45 minutes until set. Set aside to cool. Refrigerate for 4 hours, or overnight if time permits.
- Lift the slice onto a board or serving platter. Fold the vanilla through the mascarpone. Gently whisk with a balloon whisk to thicken if necessary. Spread over the biscuits. Cut the cheeks from the remaining mangoes. Using a large spoon remove the mango fruit from the cheeks and thinly slice. Arrange over the mascarpone. Cut into squares to serve.

178. Mango Cheesecake Recipe

Serving: 12 | Prep: 25mins | Cook: 390mins | Ready in: 415mins

Ingredients

- 1/4 cup cold water
- 1 tbs gelatine powder
- 125 g biscuits
- 75 g butter melted
- 500 g cream cheese softened
- 2/3 cup caster sugar
- 500 g mango diced

- 300 ml thickened cream
- 1 mango sliced *to serve

Direction

- Grease a 22cm-round (base) springform cake pan. Line side with baking paper, extending paper 1cm above edge of pan.
- Place water in a small heatproof jug. Sprinkle over gelatine. Microwave on HIGH (100%) for 20 to 30 seconds or until gelatine is dissolved, stirring halfway through cooking. Set aside to cool.
- Meanwhile, process biscuits until fine crumbs. Add butter. Process until combined. Press biscuit mixture over base of prepared pan. Refrigerate while preparing filling.
- Wipe processor clean. Process cream cheese, sugar and half the diced mango until smooth and combined. Add cream. Process for 30 seconds or until combined. With motor running, gradually add cooled gelatine mixture, processing until combined. Transfer to a bowl. Fold in remaining diced mango. Pour over prepared base in pan. Refrigerate overnight or until set.
- Serve chilled cheesecake topped with sliced mango.

179. Mango Fruit Cake Recipe

Serving: 8 | Prep: 15mins | Cook: 60mins | Ready in: 75mins

Ingredients

- 425 g canned mango in syrup
- 500 g mixed dried fruit
- 1/2 cup water
- 1 1/2 tsp bicarbonate of soda
- 1 1/2 cup self-raising flour
- 2 egg lightly beaten

Direction

- Grease a 15 cm x 25 cm loaf pan and line base and sides with baking paper.
- Combine the undrained mango slices, mixed dried fruit and water in a large pan.
- Bring to boil and simmer, uncovered, for 1 minute. Allow to cool.
- Stir in eggs and combined sifted bicarbonate of soda and flour.
- Mix well and pour mixture into prepared pan.
- Cook in a moderately slow oven, about 160C for 1 hour or until cooked.
- Cool cake in pan.

180. Mango Granita Recipe

Serving: 4 | Prep: 10mins | Cook: 0S | Ready in: 10mins

Ingredients

- 3 mangoes chopped
- 1 lime juiced
- 1 cup water
- 1 tbs caster sugar

Direction

- Blend three chopped mangoes in a food processor, or blender with the juice of one lime, 1 cup water and 1 tablespoon of caster sugar.
- Strain, then pour into a metal tray and freeze for 3-4 hours.
- Remove from freezer and blend mixture again to a smooth slushy consistency. Serve immediately.

181. Mango Ice Cream

Serving: 8 | Prep: 15mins | Cook: 0S | Ready in: 15mins

Ingredients

- 2 1/2 cups mango pulp

- 3 tablespoons sugar
- 400 g condensed milk
- 2 cups full cream milk
- 3 teaspoons lemon juice
- 1/2 teaspoon cornflour
- 1/2 teaspoon mango essence (optional)

Direction

- Blend mango pulp with sugar thoroughly.
- Combine condensed milk, milk, lemon juice, mango essence and blend well. Pour into an ice-cream mould and freeze for 2 hours.
- Remove from freezer and blend again adding cornflour.
- Freeze for another 2 hours. Remove and blend well.

182. Mango Ice Cream Recipe

Serving: 0 | Prep: 120mins | Cook: 5mins | Ready in: 125mins

Ingredients

- 375 ml thickened cream
- 375 ml full cream milk
- 750 ml mango puree
- 300 g milk powder
- 100 g sugar
- 1 tsp ground cardamom

Direction

- Combine cream and milk in saucepan, and bring to a simmer.
- Stir in milk powder and ground cardamom then allow to cool.
- Stir in mango puree and combine well.
- Freeze in dariole moulds.
- Cover once frozen.
- Allow to thaw slightly and sprinkle with blanched, chopped pistachios before serving.

183. Mango Log Recipe

Serving: 8 | Prep: 30mins | Cook: 0S | Ready in: 30mins

Ingredients

- 1 cooking oil spray
- Meringue
- 4 egg whites room temperature
- 1 cup caster sugar
- 1 tsp vanilla essence
- Mango puree
- 3 mangoes
- 1/3 cup caster sugar
- To serve
- 3 passionfruit
- 8 sprigs mint
- 8 scoops vanilla ice cream

Direction

- Preheat oven to 120C. Using an electric mixer, beat egg whites on high until soft peaks form.
- Reduce mixer speed to medium. Add sugar, 1 tablespoon at a time, beating constantly until well combined.
- Line a lamington tray with baking paper and spray with cooking oil.
- Spread meringue into a 1cm layer in the tray.
- Place in the oven until meringue starts to get colour.
- Mango puree: Dice the mangoes roughly and add to a blender, mix until it is a thick consistency and add the caster sugar.
- Spread the mango over the meringue, get one side of the baking paper and start rolling into a log. Do this gently and while the meringue is still warm and you will have a perfect log. Wrap the log with cling wrap and place in the freezer.
- To serve: Slice the frozen log into 1-2 cm slices. Add a ball of ice cream on the side, spread the passionfruit pulp around it in a ring and add the sprig of mint to finish off.

184. Mango Mousse

Serving: 8 | Prep: 15mins | Cook: 20mins | Ready in: 35mins

Ingredients

- 1 tbs gelatine powder
- 1/2 cup hot water
- 400 g canned mango in syrup crushed
- 1/2 cup orange juice
- 2 tbs rum
- 2 egg whites
- 2 tbs caster sugar
- 140 ml whipped cream

Direction

- Soak gelatin in hot water for 5 minutes.
- Combine mango pulp, orange juice and rum.
- Mix in gelatin and chill until thickened slightly.
- Beat egg whites until peaks form, add sugar gradually and beat until thick and glossy.
- In a chilled bowl whip the cream.
- Fold cream and egg whites into mango mixture and pour into a bowl and chill.
- Serve with whipped cream

185. Mango Mousse Recipe

Serving: 4 | Prep: 15mins | Cook: 5mins | Ready in: 20mins

Ingredients

- 3 Honey Gold mango cut into slices peeled
- 1 tbs lemon juice
- 1 tbs white sugar
- 1 cup cream
- 3 tsp gelatine powder dissolved large
- 1 passionfruit pulp optional

Direction

- Place all ingredients in blender and blend until mixture is smooth.
- Fold in passionfruit pulp.
- Place in large bowl or small individual bowls and refrigerate until set.
- Serve topped with whipped cream or pureed mango.

186. Mango Popsicles Recipe

Serving: 0 | Prep: 25mins | Cook: 0S | Ready in: 25mins

Ingredients

- Mango ice cream
- 2 mangoes
- 400 g double cream
- 3 cups fresh milk
- 1/2 cup caster sugar
- Vanilla ice cream
- 2 cups heavy cream
- 1 cup whole milk
- 1/2 cup sugar
- 1 vanilla bean pod split in half lengthwise
- 3/4 tsp vanilla extract

Direction

- Mango ice cream: Remove the mango flesh from the fruit, and place into a blender with the remaining ingredients.
- Puree until smooth (about a minute) and then chill in the freezer in a large plastic container with a lid.
- After 1 hour, remove from the freezer and stir, and then return to the freezer for another 4 hours or until set.
- Vanilla ice cream: Pour 1 cup of cream into a medium saucepan, then add the sugar. Scrape the seeds from the vanilla bean pod into the saucepan, and add the pod to the pot. Warm over medium heat, stirring, until the sugar is dissolved.

- Remove from the heat; add the remaining 1 cup cream, milk and the vanilla extract. Chill the mixture thoroughly in the refrigerator.
- Once mixture is chilled and ready to churn, remove the vanilla bean and then freeze the mixture in your ice cream maker according to the manufacturer's instructions.
- Assembly: To make the popsicles, use a teaspoon to make the bottom layer of mango. Return to the freezer to set slightly (for 1 hour), then spoon in a layer of vanilla. Allow the vanilla layer to set before filling up the rest with more mango. Insert a paddle pop stick into the center of the ice cream, then freeze overnight for best results.
- Dip the popsicles in warm water to remove them from the molds and serve.

187. Mango Rosé Jelly Jars Recipe

Serving: 6 | Prep: 15mins | Cook: 5mins | Ready in: 20mins

Ingredients

- 6 Calypso mangoes
- 3 cups rosé room temperature
- 3/4 cup caster sugar
- 1 tbs gelatine powder
- 300 ml thickened cream
- 2 tbs icing sugar
- 1 packet shortbread *to serve

Direction

- Combine 1 cup (250ml) rosé, sugar and gelatine in a medium saucepan. Gently whisk over medium heat for 3-4 minutes until mixture just comes to the boil. Cool for 10 minutes. Stir in remaining rosé. Strain into a jug. Set aside to cool for 1 hour.
- Cut the cheeks from the mangoes. Using a large spoon remove the mango fruit from the cheeks. Chop the mango and spoon into the base of jars or glasses. Cut the remaining fruit from the mangoes, discarding the skin. Process the mango until smooth (you should have about ½ cup puree). Cover and refrigerate until ready to serve.
- Pour the cooled rosé mixture over the mango. Cover and refrigerate 4 hours until set.
- Whip the cream and icing sugar together to firm peaks. Swirl through the mango puree then spoon over the jelly. Serve with shortbread or meringues.

188. Mango Slice

Serving: 8 | Prep: 15mins | Cook: 0S | Ready in: 15mins

Ingredients

- 200 g Lattice biscuits
- 420 g canned mango in syrup drained mashed
- 300 ml cream
- 100 ml instant pudding mix
- 2 tsp lemon rind

Direction

- Place 9 lattice biscuits in a suitable slice pan.
- In a bowl, add cream and mango puree and mix until combined.
- Add vanilla pudding mix and mix well. Mixture will now thicken.
- Add lemon rind and combine.
- Spread the mixture over the lattice biscuits. Place a further 9 biscuits on top.
- Refrigerate overnight or until firm.
- Once firm, cut slices to make individual portions, using biscuits as a guide.

189. Mango Tart

Serving: 8 | Prep: 45mins | Cook: 45mins | Ready in: 90mins

Ingredients

- 2 cup self-raising flour
- 1 pinch salt
- 1/2 cup butter
- 1 egg yolks
- 1/4 cup sugar
- 1 cup milk
- Filling
- 395 g condensed milk
- 1 lemon
- 4 egg yolks
- 1/2 cup sugar
- 1 mango ripe thinly sliced
- 2 egg

Direction

- Place flour in a bowl with the salt and sugar.
- Rub in the butter and egg yolk and enough milk to form a dry dough.
- Roll out to required size and line a tart plate with pastry.
- Bake at 180C for approximately 10 minutes or until golden brown.
- Filling: Place condensed milk, lemon juice and egg yolks into a blender and blend.
- Fill tart case with condensed milk mixture and place mango on top.
- Beat egg whites until stiff, gradually add sugar until stiff peaks form.
- Place on top of the tart filling and return to the oven until just browned.
- Chill and serve.

190. Mango And Coconut Muffins Recipe

Serving: 0 | Prep: 10mins | Cook: 25mins | Ready in: 35mins

Ingredients

- 1 cup wholemeal plain flour
- 1 cup wholemeal self-raising flour
- 1/2 cup coconut sugar
- 2 eggs
- 1/2 cup light milk
- 1/2 cup low-fat mango fruit yoghurt
- 1/4 cup coconut oil
- 2 tsp coconut essence
- 1 mango thinly sliced
- 1 mango cubed
- 1 tbs desiccated coconut

Direction

- Preheat oven to 190C or 170C fan-force. Lightly spray a 12 hole muffin pan with oil.
- Combine flours and sugar in a large bowl.
- Whisk eggs, milk, yoghurt, coconut oil and essence in a large bowl until combined.
- Stir egg mixture into flour mixture until just combined - be careful not to over-mix. Stir through chopped mango.
- Divide batter between muffin holes. Top with sliced mango and sprinkle with desiccated coconut.
- Bake for 22 minutes or until golden and a skewer inserted in centre comes out clean. Cool in muffin pan for 5 minutes. Transfer to a wire rack to cool or enjoy warm.

191. Mango And Coconut Parfait Recipe

Serving: 4 | Prep: 5mins | Cook: 15mins | Ready in: 20mins

Ingredients

- 4 gelatine leaf
- 150 g caster sugar
- 150 ml cream
- 200 ml coconut milk
- 100 ml milk
- 2 mango
- 1 cup roasted macadamias
- 200 g Persian fairy floss

Direction

- Make the Coconut Parfait first: Soak 2 gelatine leaves in a bowl of cold water for 4-5 minutes. In a small saucepan, combine 75g of caster sugar, 75ml of cream and coconut milk. Stir over a low heat until mixture comes to the boil. Remove from heat. Squeeze gelatine leaves to remove as much water as possible and then add it to the coconut mixture, whisking until it is dissolved. Pour this mixture equally into four glasses. Place in fridge and allow to set for a couple of hours or overnight.
- To make the Mango Parfait: Peel 1 mango and cut flesh away. Place into a blender and blend until smooth. Soak 2 gelatine leaves in a bowl of cold water for 4-5 minutes. In a small saucepan, combine 75g of caster sugar, 75ml of cream and milk. Stir over a low heat until mixture comes to the boil. Remove from heat. Squeeze gelatine leaves to remove as much water as possible and then add it to the milk mixture, whisking until it is dissolved. Pour this mixture into the blender with the mango and blend until combined. Pour this mixture equally over the set coconut parfait. Place in fridge and allow to set for a couple of hours or overnight.
- I serve my parfaits with extra diced mango and roasted macadamias and for something extra special some Persian Fairy Floss on top.

192. Mango And Raspberry Tiramisu Recipe

Serving: 12 | Prep: 40mins | Cook: 0S | Ready in: 40mins

Ingredients

- 3 mangoes
- 1 tbs caster sugar
- 2 eggs
- 1/4 cup caster sugar *extra
- 500 g mascarpone
- 1 orange zested
- 600 ml thickened cream
- 500 g Savoiardi sponge finger biscuits
- 2 cups orange juice
- 60 ml Cointreau
- 1 cup frozen raspberries
- 1 punnet fresh raspberries *to decorate
- 2 passionfruit *to decorate

Direction

- Scoop the flesh out of two mangoes into a food processor. Add the 1tbs caster sugar and blitz to make a puree. Set aside.
- Using handheld beaters or a stand mixer, whip cream until very thick and firm. In a separate bowl, whisk together eggs and 1/4 cup caster sugar for a few minutes until pale and frothy. Add mascarpone and orange zest and whip until well combined. Fold through the whipped cream. Refrigerate until ready to assemble.
- Combine orange juice and Cointreau in a shallow dish. Dip Savoiardi biscuits in one at a time to soften, then place in a single layer in the base of a rectangular baking dish. Spread over half of the mascarpone mix. Drizzle half of the mango puree then dot with the frozen raspberries. Place a second layer of soaked Savoiardi biscuits then top with the remaining mascarpone.
- Once complete, cover with cling film and refrigerate for several hours, but overnight is best. Reserve remaining mango puree.
- When you are ready to serve, decorate the tiramisu with sliced mango, fresh raspberries and passionfruit pulp. Drizzle over reserved mango puree.

193. Mango And Salted Caramel Ice Cream Cake Recipe

Serving: 8 | Prep: 20mins | Cook: 15mins | Ready in: 35mins

Ingredients

- 5 Calypso mangoes
- 1 1/4 cups self-raising flour
- 80 g butter chilled chopped
- 1/2 cup brown sugar
- 1 cup honey roasted macadamias roughly chopped
- 3 L vanilla ice cream
- Quick salted caramel
- 1/2 cup thickened cream
- 2 packets Werther's Original Chewy Toffees unwrapped
- 2 tsp sea salt flakes crushed

Direction

- Preheat oven to 180C fan-forced. Combine the flour and butter in a food processor. Process until the mixture resembles fine breadcrumbs. Add sugar and ½ cup of the macadamia nuts, process until crumble forms clumps. Spread out on a baking tray and bake for 15 minutes or until golden. Cool.
- Quick salted caramel: Pour the cream into a small saucepan, add the caramels. Stir over medium-high heat for 3-4 minutes until cream comes to the boil. Remove from the heat and stir until caramels have melted and sauce is smooth. Stir in the salt. Set aside to cool.
- Line the base and sides of a 4cm deep, 20cm x 30cm (base) baking dish with baking paper, allowing a 2cm overhang at both long sides. Scatter the crumble over the base of the pan to cover.
- Peel 3 of the mangoes. Chop the fruit. Swirl chopped mango, remaining macadamia nuts and ¾ cup salted caramel through the ice cream. Spoon over the crumble base. Smooth the surface. Cover and freeze overnight.
- Peel and chop the remaining 2 mangoes, spoon over the ice cream. Cut into pieces and serve drizzled with remaining salted caramel.

194. Mars Bar Slice Recipe

Serving: 0 | Prep: 10mins | Cook: 20mins | Ready in: 30mins

Ingredients

- 3 x 65 g Mars Bars chopped
- 90g unsalted butter, chopped
- 3 cups Kellogg's Rice Bubbles
- 200 g milk chocolate

Direction

- Grease a slice tray.
- Combine Mars Bars and butter in a saucepan. Stir constantly over low heat, without boiling, until the mixture is smooth.
- Stir in Rice Bubbles and press mixture evenly into greased tray.
- Melt the chocolate in the microwave on a low setting, stirring every 20-30 seconds.
- Spread the chocolate evenly over the slice mixture and refrigerate until topping is set.

195. Mars Bar Slice With A Twist Recipe

Serving: 0 | Prep: 15mins | Cook: 5mins | Ready in: 20mins

Ingredients

- 3 tbs butter chopped
- 259 g Mars Bar chopped
- 1 cup Kellogg's Rice Bubbles
- 1 cup apricots diced
- 1 cup Komplete muesli
- 150 g milk chocolate chopped

Direction

- Line a baking tray with foil or baking paper.
- Place Rice Bubbles, apricots and muesli in a large mixing bowl.

- Melt the butter and chopped Mars Bar together.
- Add melted butter and Mars Bars to Rice Bubble mixture and combine well.
- Place mixture in the lined tray.
- Melt the chopped chocolate in the microwave.
- Pour chocolate over Rice Bubble mixture and place in the fridge until set.

196. Marshmallow Easter Bunnies

Serving: 15 | Prep: 15mins | Cook: 0S | Ready in: 15mins

Ingredients

- 2 tsp gelatine powder
- 60 ml hot water
- 60 ml cold water
- 125 g sugar

Direction

- Put sugar and cold water into a bowl and beat on high speed for 2-3 minutes.
- Dissolve gelatine in hot water and, while still hot, add to the sugar mixture and beat until thick and white.
- Pour into sprayed rabbit moulds. Refrigerate until set.
- Toss in coconut.
- Add eyes and whiskers using red food colouring, if desired.

197. Marshmallow And Weet Bix Slice Recipe

Serving: 0 | Prep: 20mins | Cook: 20mins | Ready in: 40mins

Ingredients

- 4 Weet-Bix crushed
- 1 cup coconut
- 1 cup brown sugar
- 1 cup self-raising flour
- 125 g unsalted butter, melted
- 2 cup white sugar
- 1 1/4 cup water
- 1 tbs gelatine powder

Direction

- Combine Weet-Bix, coconut, brown sugar and flour, then pour melted butter over ingredients.
- Press into a lamington pan and bake at 180C for 15 minutes.
- Marshmallow topping: Place white sugar and ¾ cup water in a saucepan. Boil for 3-4 minutes, then remove from stove top.
- Soak gelatine in ½ cup water and add to sugar and water. Cool slightly, then beat until thick and pour over biscuit base.

198. Melt And Mix Christmas Cake Recipe

Serving: 0 | Prep: 0S | Cook: 0S | Ready in:

Ingredients

- Cake
- 500 g Sunbeam Gourmet Selection mixed fruit
- 1/2 cup Sunbeam slivered almonds
- 2 cup plain flour
- 1/2 tsp bicarbonate of soda
- 1 cup brown sugar firmly packed
- 1 tsp nutmeg
- 2 tsp ground cinnamon
- 250 g butter melted
- 3 egg lightly beaten
- 1/4 cup brandy

Direction

- Preheat oven 150°C. Double line a 20cm round tin with baking paper.
- Combine all ingredients together and stir until combined. Spoon into prepared tin and bake for 1 hour or until skewer inserted comes out clean.

199. Merry Mango Trifle Recipe

Serving: 8 | Prep: 20mins | Cook: 0S | Ready in: 20mins

Ingredients

- 800 g fruit cake sliced
- 1/4 cup sherry
- 500 g brandy custard
- 300 ml double cream whipped
- 4 mangoes fresh peeled sliced
- 120 g fresh raspberries *to serve

Direction

- Cover base of 2L dish with cake slices and sprinkle with sherry.
- Whip cream to soft peaks. Mix together custard and cream in a bowl. Pour half over cake and spread.
- Top with half the mango and repeat layer.
- Top with remaining custard and cream mixture and refrigerate for 3 hours or overnight.
- Top with raspberries to serve.

200. Mini Christmas Pudding Recipe

Serving: 0 | Prep: 25mins | Cook: 15mins | Ready in: 40mins

Ingredients

- 500 g mixed dried fruit
- 80 ml orange juice
- 125 g butter
- 2 tsp mixed spice
- 1 granny smith apple grated
- 2 eggs lightly beaten
- 3/4 cup wholemeal plain flour
- 1/2 tsp bicarbonate of soda
- 50 g fresh mint leaves only
- 50 g glace cherries
- 50 g walnuts *optional
- 50 g slivered almonds *optional

Direction

- In a saucepan add dried fruit, juice, butter and all spice and boil for a few minutes to soften fruit and spread the brown colour through. Add the grated apple. Allow to cool.
- While waiting for the fruit mixture to cool, grease 6 microwave-proof teacups and place chopped cherries and mint leaves (or halved walnut or sprinkle slivered almonds whichever desired) in the base of each cup.
- When the fruit mixture is cool enough, add the beaten eggs before stirring through the flour and soda. Divide the mixture evenly between the teacups and smooth tops.
- Arrange the 6 cups evenly on microwave turntable. Cook on Medium (50%) for 8 minutes, rotate cups and cook further 7 minutes on Medium until the centre is almost set.
- Rest the puddings in cups for 5 minutes before turning out.

201. Mini Christmas Puddings

Serving: 0 | Prep: 15mins | Cook: 25mins | Ready in: 40mins

Ingredients

- 700 g Christmas pudding
- 250 g milk chocolate melted

- 1/4 cup brandy
- 1/2 cup white choc bits
- 1 packet snake lollies

Direction

- Crumble the pudding and mix in the melted chocolate and brandy.
- Roll the mixture into almond sized balls.
- Melt a small amount of the white chocolate bits and drizzle over the mini puddings.
- Cut up the snakes into small pieces to garnish the top of the pudding (should look like holly leaves and red berries).
- Repeat the process until all the mini puddings have been decorated.

202. Mini Christmas Tree Cupcakes

Serving: 18 | Prep: 30mins | Cook: 50mins | Ready in: 80mins

Ingredients

- 225 g unsalted butter softened
- 225 g caster sugar
- 225 g self-raising flour
- 4 egg
- 1 tsp vanilla essence
- Icing
- 175 g fondant icing
- 175 g fondant icing
- 2 tbs raspberry jam

Direction

- Preheat oven to 175C.
- Place 18 mini paper baking cases in muffin tins.
- Dust two baking sheets with icing sugar.
- Combine all the cupcake ingredients into a large bowl and beat with an electric whisk until smooth and pale, approximately 2-3 minutes.
- Spoon the batter into the cases.
- Bake for 20 minutes. Cool in tray for 5 minutes before placing on a wire rack to cool.
- Icing: Roll the white fondant to 3 mm thick.
- Cut 18 circles using a 6 cm biscuit cutter and set them on one of the baking sheets.
- Roll the green fondant to 3 mm thick.
- Using a small Christmas tree biscuit cutter, cut shapes out of the icing and place them on the other baking sheet to firm a little.
- Brush each cupcake with a little raspberry jam, then place a white fondant disk on top.
- Top with a Christmas tree and decorate with the coloured balls.

203. Mini Mango Cakes

Serving: 4 | Prep: 15mins | Cook: 25mins | Ready in: 40mins

Ingredients

- 425 g canned mango in syrup sliced
- 90 g unsalted butter
- 3/4 cup caster sugar
- 2 egg lightly beaten
- 1/2 cup self-raising flour
- 2 tbs ground almonds
- 2 tbs coconut milk
- 2 tbs lime juice

Direction

- Preheat oven to 200C. Lightly grease a 4 x 1-cup muffin pan and line with mango slices.
- Beat butter and ½ cup of the sugar in a bowl until light and creamy. Gradually beat in eggs, beating well after each addition.
- Fold in flour, add almonds and coconut milk and spoon into muffin pan.
- Bake for 25 min or until a skewer inserted comes out clean.
- Syrup: Place lime juice, remaining sugar and ½ cup of water in a small saucepan and stir over

low heat until sugar dissolves, increase heat and simmer for 10 minutes.
- Pierce each cake with a skewer several times, then drizzle syrup over the top and allow to stand for 5 minutes to soak up liquid.

204. Mixed Berries Dessert Recipe

Serving: 2 | Prep: 5mins | Cook: 0S | Ready in: 5mins

Ingredients

- 300 g sour cream
- 100 g plain biscuits
- 2 tbs vanilla sugar
- 1 mango peeled sliced
- 225 g canned pineapple
- 2 tbs fresh blueberries
- 1/2 cup water
- 1 tsp cornflour
- 1 tsp caster sugar

Direction

- In a saucepan over medium heat, add blueberries, water and sugar and boil for 1 minute. Strain and reserve berries. Pour liquid back into saucepan. Add cornflour mixed with some water and bring to the boil to make thicken the sauce. Allow to cool.
- In a bowl, mix sour cream and vanillin sugar. Break biscuits into pieces and arrange in serving glasses. Layer sour cream, biscuits, fruit and sauce. Serve cold

205. Mixed Berry Trifle Recipe

Serving: 10 | Prep: 25mins | Cook: 0S | Ready in: 25mins

Ingredients

- 1 cup port
- 1 packet Unibic Savoiardi sponge finger biscuits
- 170 g raspberry jelly
- 1 punnet fresh strawberries
- 1 punnet fresh raspberries
- 1 punnet fresh blueberries
- 375 L cream
- 1 L custard
- 2 tbs brandy optional

Direction

- Before making the trifle, make the jelly according to the packet and allow to set firmly in the fridge.
- Soak the sponge fingers in port.
- Layer half the fingers in the bottom of a large glass bowl.
- Roughly cube half the jelly and pour over fingers.
- Cover the jelly with half the berries.
- Beat the cream until very thick and stir in custard and brandy.
- Pour half the cream mixture over the berries.
- Repeat the layers again - fingers, jelly, berries and cream mixture.
- Refrigerate until ready to serve.
- Top with grated chocolate if desired.

206. Mixed Fruit Pie Pops Recipe

Serving: 0 | Prep: 0S | Cook: 0S | Ready in:

Ingredients

- Pie pops
- 2 cup plain flour
- 1 tbs sugar
- 200 g unsalted butter
- 3 tbs water iced
- 3/4 cup fruit mince *see notes
- 2 tbs golden syrup
- 3 tbs water *extra

- 1 tsp mixed spice

Direction

- Place flour, sugar, butter and iced water into a food processor. Process until it starts to come together. Turn out onto a floured surface and form into two balls, wrap in cling film and refrigerate.
- Place fruit mince, golden syrup, mixed spice and extra water into a saucepan and simmer for 3 minutes while stirring. Cool completely.
- Preheat oven to 180°C. Roll out one pastry ball between two sheets of baking paper to 3mm thick, cut out Christmas shapes and place on a tray lined with baking paper.
- Press a lollipop stick into the centre of each shape. Place a teaspoonful of fruit mixture onto each cut out. Roll out remaining pastry and cut into shapes. Place a matching shape on top of fruit mixture pressing the edges together gently. Bake for 10mins.

207. Moist Orange Poppy Seed Cake Recipe

Serving: 12 | Prep: 15mins | Cook: 60mins | Ready in: 75mins

Ingredients

- 1 orange roughly chopped
- 185 g butter melted
- 3 eggs
- 1 cup caster sugar
- 1 1/2 cups self-raising flour
- 2 tbs poppy seeds

Direction

- Preheat oven to 170C.
- Grease and line an 18 cm cake pan or a loaf tin.
- Puree whole orange, peel on, in food processor
- Add melted butter, eggs, sugar and mix well.
- Add flour and poppy seeds and mix until well combined.
- Bake for approximately 45 minutes or until cooked when tested.

208. Monica's Lemon Cake Recipe

Serving: 12 | Prep: 15mins | Cook: 65mins | Ready in: 80mins

Ingredients

- 125 g butter
- 185 g sugar
- 185 g self-raising flour
- 4 tbs milk
- 2 eggs large
- 2 lemons zested
- Syrup
- 6 tbs fresh lemon juice
- 6 tbs icing sugar heaped

Direction

- Preheat oven to 160C.
- Grease and line a loaf tin with baking paper.
- Cream butter and sugar, beat in eggs.
- Add flour, lemon rind and milk and mix well.
- Pour into tin and smooth top.
- Bake for 30-40 minutes.
- Syrup: Mix lemon juice and sugar.
- After removing cake from oven, prick the top with a metal skewer.
- Pour over the lemon juice while cake is still hot.
- Leave until cold before removing from tin.

209. Mum's Wine Trifle

Serving: 0 | Prep: 360mins | Cook: 0S | Ready in: 360mins

Ingredients

- 1 round double unfilled sponge s cake sliced
- 85 g raspberry jelly
- 85 g lemon jelly
- 1/2 cup sweet sherry
- 2 cup thick custard
- 1 cup whipped cream *to decorate
- 1 cup fresh strawberries *to decorate

Direction

- Make up the jellies separately according to the directions on the packet and allow to cool.
- Line the base of a glass serving dish with cake slices and sprinkle with 2 tablespoons sherry.
- Layer with jelly, custard, fruit, cream and cake, sprinkling each layer of cake with 2 tablespoons of sherry. Make a final layer of custard, then decorate with cream and fruit.
- Allow to set in the fridge overnight.

210. Neenish Tart Slice Recipe

Serving: 20 | Prep: 75mins | Cook: 25mins | Ready in: 100mins

Ingredients

- 100 g unsalted butter brought to room temperature chopped
- 100 g caster sugar
- 1 egg
- 100 g plain flour
- 50 g self-raising flour
- 160 g raspberry jam
- Mock cream
- 140 g caster sugar
- 2 tbs milk
- 1/2 tsp gelatine powder
- 185 g unsalted butter brought to room temperature melted
- 2 tsp vanilla extract
- Glace icing
- 450 g pure icing sugar
- 25 g unsalted butter melted
- 1 tsp vanilla extract
- 80 ml milk
- 1 splash pink food colouring
- 3 tsp cocoa powder

Direction

- Preheat the oven to 180C/160C fan-forced. Line the base of a 19 x 29cm slice pan with baking paper, allowing the paper to overhang 3cm on each long side.
- Base: Use electric beaters to beat the butter, sugar and egg in a bowl until pale and creamy. Fold in the sifted flours until combined. Spread the mixture into the base of the prepared pan, smoothing the top. Bake for 20-25 minutes or until golden. Set aside to cool.
- Mock cream: Meanwhile, for the mock cream, stir the sugar, milk and 80ml water in a small saucepan over low heat, without boiling, until the sugar dissolves. Sprinkle the gelatine over the sugar mixture and stir until the gelatine dissolves. Set aside to cool to room temperature. Mixture will thicken slightly.
- Use electric beaters to beat the butter and vanilla in a bowl until very pale. With the motor running, gradually beat in the cooled milk mixture, beating until pale and creamy.
- Spread the cooled pastry base with jam. Top with the mock cream, smoothing the surface. Place in the fridge until required.
- Glace icing: For the glace icing, sift the icing sugar into a bowl. Stir in the butter, vanilla and slowly add the milk to make a thick icing (you may not need it all). Divide the icing evenly between two bowls. Tint the icing in one bowl with pink colouring. Sift the cocoa into the other bowl of icing until combined (you may need to add a little more milk, if necessary) until the icing is a spreadable consistency.
- Use a ruler to divide the slice in half, lengthways, and run a knife down the middle to lightly mark. Mark another two lines down the middle of each half (you will have 4 even

strips running lengthways across the slice). Spoon each batch of icing into a snap lock bag. Snip off one corner. Use the pink icing to mark out the edges of the two outside strips and then fill with icing. Repeat with chocolate icing to mark out and fill the remaining middle strips (see note). Set aside for 15 minutes or until set. Use a hot knife to cut the slice down the middle and then into slice into thin fingers, with a pink and brown iced half on each finger.

- Bake at 170C - 180C for 10 - 15 minutes.
- Cool pastry cases on a cake rack.
- To make the filling, dissolve gelatine in boiling water and cool.
- Cream butter and sugar, beat in the cooled dissolved gelatine. Add cream of tartar and the rum essence.
- Fill pastry cases with filling.
- When set, spread completely with white icing, allow to set then spread chocolate icing over half for effect.

211. Neenish Tarts

Serving: 0 | Prep: 60mins | Cook: 15mins | Ready in: 75mins

Ingredients

- Pastry
- 125g butter
- 125g white sugar
- 1 egg, beaten
- 250g plain flour
- 1 tsp baking powder
- 1 tsp cocoa *optional
- Filling
- 125g butter
- 2 tbs sugar
- 2 tsp gelatine powder
- 3 tbs boiling water
- 1 pinch cream of tartar
- 1/2 tsp rum essence
- 1 tbs icing sugar
- 1 tbs cocoa

Direction

- To make the pastry, mix butter and sugar until creamy using an electric beater.
- Combine egg. Sift in flour, baking powder and cocoa.
- Knead mixture on a lightly floured board. Roll out pastry and cut rounds to fit patty tins. Line base and sides of tins with pastry.

212. New York Baked Cheesecake

Serving: 10 | Prep: 120mins | Cook: 360mins | Ready in: 480mins

Ingredients

- 15 crackers crushed
- 2 tbs butter melted
- 250 g cream cheese
- 1 1/2 cup white sugar
- 3/4 cup milk
- 3 egg beaten
- 250 g plain yoghurt
- 1 tbs vanilla extract
- 1/4 cup self-raising flour

Direction

- Preheat oven to 175C and grease a 23 cm springform pan.
- Mix in a medium bowl, the crushed crackers with the butter until no butter lumps remain.
- Press onto the bottom of the springform pan. Place in freezer to set.
- In a large bowl, mix cream cheese with the sugar until smooth.
- Blend in the milk and then the eggs. Mix in the yoghurt, vanilla extract and flour until mixture is smooth.
- Pour the batter onto the crust, and bake for 1 hour. Switch off the oven and let the

cheesecake cool in the oven for 5-6 hours with the door closed.
- Chill in the refrigerator and serve cool.

213. No Spread Lemon Sugar Cookies Recipe

Serving: 0 | Prep: 20mins | Cook: 20mins | Ready in: 40mins

Ingredients

- 125 g unsalted butter
- 1/2 cup white granulated sugar
- 2 cups plain flour
- 1 tsp baking powder
- 1 tsp salt
- 1 lemon rind
- 1 egg
- 1/2 lemon juiced

Direction

- Preheat your oven to 180C.
- Line two baking trays and set aside.
- Cream 125g butter, lemon rind and 1/2 cup of sugar together with electric beaters until light in colour and smooth in texture. Add your lemon juice and 1 egg to mixing bowl and continue to mix until well combined.
- Sift 1tsp baking powder, 1tsp salt and 2 cups of flour to the bowl, return to the electric beaters and bring together on a low speed.
- Remove your dough from the mixing bowl, need together into a neat ball and cover tightly in cling wrap. Place in the fridge while you prepare your workspace for the next step.
- For rustic rock cookies: If you wish to make rustic little cookies like mine, all you will need to set up is a 2tsp capacity cookie scoop or pair of teaspoons and a shallow bowl containing 2tbs of icing sugar. Retrieve your baking trays and your cookie dough, create roughly 2tsp balls of cookie dough, roll in the icing sugar and set on your baking tray. Repeat until all cookie dough has been used. Place trays in the oven to bake for 18-20 minutes.
- For cookie cutter cookies: If you wish to make cookie cutter cookies, you will need a rolling pin, your cutters and ensure your bench space is coated with a thin layer of icing sugar to prevent your dough from sticking when you roll it out. Retrieve your cookie dough from the fridge and roll it out to roughly 6mm-1cm thick depending on how you like your cookies. Using your cookie cutters, cut as many cookies from your dough as you can, move them to your baking trays and repeat the process until all your dough has been used. Sift a layer of icing sugar over your cookies on the baking tray, and place in the oven to bake for 8-10 minutes.

214. No Bake Bliss Cake Recipe

Serving: 12 | Prep: 360mins | Cook: 10mins | Ready in: 370mins

Ingredients

- 500 g chocolate ripple biscuits
- 250 g butternut snap biscuits
- 600 ml pure cream whipped
- 250 g frozen raspberries crushed thawed
- 100 g frozen raspberries *to decorate
- Chocolate ganache
- 200 g dark chocolate finely chopped
- 170 g pure cream

Direction

- Line a deep, 20 cm round spring form cake tin with baking paper.
- Place a layer of chocolate biscuits in the tin. Cover with firmly whipped cream, ensuring biscuits are well-covered.
- Add a layer of butternut snaps, and then a layer of raspberries. Cover with cream.

- Add another layer of chocolate biscuits and then cream.
- Top with any remaining biscuits.
- Cover well with cling wrap, place a smaller tin on top and weigh down to compress the cake. Refrigerate overnight or up to 12 hours.
- Chocolate ganache: Bring cream to a scald, do not boil, and pour over the chopped chocolate. Leave to sit for at least 5 minutes.
- Starting in the centre of the bowl, slowly stir, being careful not to incorporate any air. Continue to stir until the chocolate combines with the cream.
- Leave to cool completely then cover and leave overnight.
- When ready to serve, place the ganache into a mixer and beat until fluffy and light. Pipe ganache onto the top of the cake.
- Remove cake from tin carefully and decorate with the fresh raspberries.

215. No Bake Brownies Recipe

Serving: 0 | Prep: 10mins | Cook: 10mins | Ready in: 20mins

Ingredients

- 1 cup walnuts
- 1 cup pitted dates
- 1/4 cup raw cacao powder
- 1 tbs maple syrup

Direction

- Blend all ingredients in a blender till mixture takes on a crumb consistency.
- Spoon out and roll into balls.
- Put in mini cupcake holders and serve.

216. No Bake Caramel Cheesecake Recipe

Serving: 8 | Prep: 15mins | Cook: 0S | Ready in: 15mins

Ingredients

- 250 g butternut snap biscuits crushed
- 125 g butter melted
- Filling
- 2 x 250 g cream cheese
- 380 g NESTLE Top n Fill Caramel
- 3 tsp gelatine powder

Direction

- Base: Combine biscuit crumbs and butter.
- Press into the base of springform pan.
- Refrigerate to set.
- Filling: Mix using an electric mixer, the cream cheese and Top 'n' Fill Caramel.
- Dissolve gelatine in 1 tablespoon of water, stir with fork or whisk until fully dissolved.
- Add to cream cheese mixture and beat until well combined.
- Pour into prepared biscuit base and refrigerate to set.

217. No Bake Carrot Cake Bliss Balls Recipe

Serving: 0 | Prep: 15mins | Cook: 0S | Ready in: 15mins

Ingredients

- 3/4 cup oat flour
- 3/4 cup cashew nuts
- 3/4 cup walnuts
- 3/4 cup almonds
- 3/4 cup desiccated coconut
- 1 tsp ginger powder
- 1 tsp cinnamon
- 6 medjool dates
- 2 tbs coconut oil
- 2 carrots, peeled and grated

- A pinch of nutmeg
- A pinch of salt

Direction

- Remove the stones from the medjool dates and soak them in warm water for around 30 - 40 mins.
- Place the desiccated coconut and nuts in a food processor with the ginger powder, flour, cinnamon, salt and nutmeg and blitz until the nuts are chopped into small pieces.
- Add coconut oil, medjool dates with 1 tbs of the soaked date water to the nut mixture. Blend again on high speed until the ingredients start to stick together.
- Add the grated carrots and blitz until mixed well.
- Scoop a tsp of the mixture and roll into bite-sized balls.

218. No Bake Cheesecake Recipe

Serving: 12 | Prep: 25mins | Cook: 360mins | Ready in: 385mins

Ingredients

- 250 g sweet plain biscuits
- 125 g unsalted butter, melted
- 375 g cream cheese softened
- 1 lemon zested
- 2 tsp vanilla essence
- 1/3 cup lemon juice
- 400 g NESTLE Sweetened Condensed Milk

Direction

- Process biscuits until finely crushed. Add butter and mix well.
- Press half of the biscuit mixture into the base of a greased and lined 20 cm springform tin.
- Use a glass or spoon to push the remainder of the mixture around the sides of the tin.
- Refrigerate for 15 minutes.
- Beat the cream cheese until smooth and creamy.
- Add lemon zest and vanilla and beat well.
- Gradually add the condensed milk and lemon juice, and continue to beat until smooth.
- Pour into the prepared tin and refrigerate overnight.

219. No Bake Cheesecake Recipe

Serving: 0 | Prep: 285mins | Cook: 0S | Ready in: 285mins

Ingredients

- Base
- 220 g biscuits
- 60 g butter melted
- Filling
- 1/4 cup boiling water
- 3 tsp gelatine powder
- 300 ml thickened cream
- 500 g cream cheese softened
- 2/3 cup caster sugar
- 170 g Violet Crumble chocolate honeycomb bar cut into pieces

Direction

- Crush half the biscuits in a food processor to create fine crumbs. Combine with melted butter.
- Press into a greased tin and refrigerate for at least 30 minutes.
- Filling: Sprinkle gelatine over boiling water and whisk until dissolved. Set aside to cool slightly.
- Break up the remaining biscuits and set aside.
- Beat cream cheese with sugar until smooth. Stir gelatine through to combine.
- Fold through cream, biscuit pieces and chocolate.

- Spoon mixture over biscuit base and smooth surface. Cover with plastic wrap and refrigerate for at least 4 hours.

220. No Bake Choc Orange Fudge Cake Recipe

Serving: 0 | Prep: 45mins | Cook: 0S | Ready in: 45mins

Ingredients

- 3 cup almond meal
- 1/2 cup walnuts
- 0.6 cup raw cacao powder
- 1 cup medjool dates pitted
- 1 pinch sea salt
- 1/2 orange rind
- 2 tsp orange juice
- 1 tsp agave syrup
- Icing
- 1/3 cup medjool dates pitted
- 1/3 cup raw cacao powder
- 1/2 orange rind
- 1/2 avocado ripe
- 30 ml agave syrup
- 30 ml honey
- 1 tsp orange juice

Direction

- Cake: Place almond meal, walnuts, cacao powder and salt in a food processor.
- Ensure the lid is on, blend until combined, pause to scrape the sides to assist in the mixing.
- Add dates and orange rind, blend until combined.
- While processor is running, add juice and syrup through the opening.
- Remove mixture and place onto a plate.
- Mould your cake mixture into the shape of a normal baked cake. Apply pressure to ensure the mixture is tightly held together, if it crumbles at all, press harder.

- Move the cake onto a clean plate, cover lightly and refrigerate while icing is made.
- Icing: Combine all icing ingredients in the processor.
- Mix until a well combined, smooth consistency. Scrape the sides of the processor to combine all ingredients well.
- Refrigerate, lightly covered with foil until required.

221. No Bake Choc Raisin Slice Recipe

Serving: 0 | Prep: 140mins | Cook: 0S | Ready in: 140mins

Ingredients

- 200 g plain biscuits
- 125 g butter
- 4 tbs golden syrup
- 2 tbs cocoa
- 50 g raisins
- 200 g milk chocolate

Direction

- Line a 20 x 20cm square tin with baking paper. Make sure you leave paper hanging over the edge to help you remove the slice once it has set. Crush the biscuits into small pieces and place in a bowl until needed.
- Put the butter and golden syrup into a large saucepan and cook over a medium heat for 3 minutes, stirring regularly until melted and combined.
- Remove the saucepan from the heat and add the cocoa and raisins and stir to combine.
- Add the crushed biscuits and stir to combine before pouring the mixture into the prepared slice tin and pushing down with the back of a spoon to smooth the surface. Place the slice into the fridge.
- In the meantime, break the milk chocolate into pieces and place it into a microwave-safe

bowl. Cook for 30 seconds on a high heat before giving it a good stir and cook for a further 30 seconds or until the chocolate has just melted. Pour the melted milk chocolate over the slice and place it back into the fridge for 2 hours to set. Cut the set slice into pieces and store in a covered container in the fridge for up to a week.

222. No Bake Chocolate Almond Slice Recipe

Serving: 20 | Prep: 10mins | Cook: 0S | Ready in: 10mins

Ingredients

- 1 packet sweet plain biscuits
- 250 g roast almond chocolate
- 125 g butter chopped
- 1/2 cup desiccated coconut
- 2 tbs cocoa
- 395 g sweetened condensed milk

Direction

- Line a slice tin with baking paper, leaving extra on each side to lift slice out.
- With a food processor, process biscuits until crushed.
- Combine chocolate and butter in a medium saucepan and stir over a low heat without boiling until chocolate is melted and mixture is smooth.
- Stir in biscuits, coconut, cocoa and condensed milk, and mix until well combined.
- Press mixture evenly into prepared tin. Cover and refrigerate for several hours until firm.
- Cut into small squares.

223. No Bake Chocolate Biscuit Cake

Serving: 8 | Prep: 15mins | Cook: 375mins | Ready in: 390mins

Ingredients

- 250 g chocolate biscuits
- 500 ml thickened cream
- 1/3 cup icing sugar mixture
- 1 tsp vanilla essence
- 2 x 50 g Crunchie chocolate honeycomb bar

Direction

- Whip cream, icing mixture and vanilla until thick and fluffy.
- Crush one Crunchie bar and stir into cream mixture.
- Join biscuits together with cream mixture. Continue this to make a log.
- With a knife, spread the rest of the cream over the log to cover all the biscuits.
- Cover with cling wrap and place in fridge overnight.
- Before serving, chop remaining Crunchie bar and sprinkle on top. Cut cake on an angle to get a rippled effect.

224. No Bake Chocolate Hazelnut Slice

Serving: 12 | Prep: 20mins | Cook: 120mins | Ready in: 140mins

Ingredients

- 250 g sweet plain biscuits crushed
- 3 tbs golden syrup
- 1/2 can condensed milk
- 90 g butter
- 30 g copha
- 250 g hazelnut chocolate
- 50 g slivered almonds toasted

Direction

- Line 18 x 28cm slice tin with alfoil.
- Heat milk, butter and syrup over low heat until caramel colour. (I usually bring to boil in microwave and then beat with whisk until smooth)
- Mix in biscuit crumbs and slivered almonds. Press into slice tin and smooth top.
- Melt Copha and chocolate over hot water or in microwave and pour over slice.
- Shake tin to even out hazelnuts. Refrigerate 2 hours then cut into small slices with hot knife.

225. No Bake Chocolate Log

Serving: 20 | Prep: 0S | Cook: 30mins | Ready in: 30mins

Ingredients

- 250 g wheatmeal biscuit crushed
- 1 cup coconut
- 1 handful coconut *to serve
- 395 g sweetened condensed milk
- 1 1/2 tbs cocoa powder
- 1 tbs brandy
- 2 tbs sultanas chopped
- 2 tbs cherries chopped

Direction

- Mix all ingredients, except coconut (to serve), together.
- Roll into two logs 5 cm in diameter.
- Roll in leftover coconut.
- Cover in plastic wrap.
- Refrigerate until firm enough to slice.
- Slice into 1½-2 cm thick rounds.

226. No Bake Chocolate Rum Slice

Serving: 0 | Prep: 30mins | Cook: 0S | Ready in: 30mins

Ingredients

- 250 g chocolate biscuits crushed
- 1/2 cup raisins chopped
- 60 g cream cheese softened
- 2 tsp rum
- 1/2 cup coconut
- 1/2 cup condensed milk
- 1 tsp vanilla essence
- 125 g milk chocolate melted *to dress

Direction

- Combine crushed biscuits, walnuts, raisins and coconut in bowl.
- Beat cream cheese with condensed milk and vanilla until blended.
- Add to dry ingredients.
- Spread in slab tin that has been lined with greaseproof paper. Chill.
- If desired, ice using 125 g plain chocolate, melted and then spread over top.
- Cut into bars and keep in refrigerator until required.

227. No Bake Chocolate Slice Recipe

Serving: 0 | Prep: 30mins | Cook: 5mins | Ready in: 35mins

Ingredients

- 9 Weet-Bix crushed
- 1 1/2 cup coconut
- 1/4 cup cocoa powder
- 100 g milk chocolate chips
- 400 g condensed milk
- 125 g butter melted
- 2 drops mint essence

- 100 g milk chocolate melted

Direction

- Combine Weet-Bix, cocoa, coconut and choc chips.
- Add butter, condensed milk and essence.
- Press into an 18 cm x 28 cm slice pan lined with baking paper.
- Place in fridge whilst melting chocolate.
- Spread melted chocolate over slice. Allow to cool.
- Cut into slices.

228. No Bake Christmas Cakes

Serving: 30 | Prep: 360mins | Cook: 0S | Ready in: 360mins

Ingredients

- 800 g fruit cake
- 1/2 cup sherry
- 40 g slivered almonds toasted
- 50 g dried cranberries
- 50 g dried blueberries
- 150 g milk chocolate
- 100 g white chocolate
- 2 tbs cachous

Direction

- Crumble fruit cake and mix with cranberries, blueberries and alcohol. Leave to marinate for up to two weeks, stirring occasionally.
- Add almonds and, using clean wet, hands, form mixture into walnut size balls. These can be placed in paper patty holders.
- Melt milk chocolate and spread on top of cakes. Melt white chocolate and dribble over milk chocolate to represent snow.
- Before white chocolate sets sprinkle with decorations.

229. No Bake Coconut Snowballs Recipe

Serving: 0 | Prep: 15mins | Cook: 0S | Ready in: 15mins

Ingredients

- 1 1/2 cups desiccated coconut
- 2 tbs coconut oil
- 1 tbs caster sugar
- 1 tsp vanilla extract
- 100 g white chocolate buttons
- 1/4 cup cream
- 1 cup desiccated coconut *extra
- 1 pinch salt

Direction

- Place coconut and coconut oil in the bowl of a food processor, and process for 2-3 minutes until it becomes a thick paste. Add sugar, vanilla and a pinch of salt, and blitz to combine.
- Form into small balls and place in the fridge.
- Meanwhile, make ganache by melting the white chocolate with the cream in a bowl over a saucepan of simmering water. Alternatively, you can use the microwave. Allow to cool slightly.
- Remove coconut balls from fridge and dip in ganache, then roll immediately in extra coconut. Refrigerate to set completely.

230. No Bake Coconut And Date Balls Recipe

Serving: 0 | Prep: 10mins | Cook: 0S | Ready in: 10mins

Ingredients

- 3 cups desiccated coconut
- 2 cups pitted dates

Direction

- Place 2 cups of coconut and the dates into a blender or food processor.
- Process on high speed for 3-4 minutes, pausing to scrape down sides as needed.
- Remove from processor and roll teaspoon-sized balls. Roll in remaining 1 cup of coconut.
- Pack in portions for snacks, to put in lunch boxes and keep on hand to satisfy a sweet tooth in a healthy way.

231. No Bake Cookies

Serving: 0 | Prep: 10mins | Cook: 5mins | Ready in: 15mins

Ingredients

- 2 cup icing sugar
- 100 g butter
- 1/2 cup milk
- 1/2 cup peanut butter
- 1 tsp vanilla essence
- 3 tbs cocoa powder
- 2 cup oats

Direction

- Heat the butter and sugar over high heat, and stir until light and fluffy.
- Add the vanilla essence and milk.
- Add the cocoa powder to the mixture. Bring to the boil over high heat and boil for 1 minute and 15 seconds. Remove from stove.
- Add the peanut butter and combine well.
- Add the oats and combine.
- While mixture is still warm, quickly place spoonfuls of mixture onto a tray and leave to cool.

232. No Bake Creamy Cheesecake Recipe

Serving: 12 | Prep: 15mins | Cook: 30mins | Ready in: 45mins

Ingredients

- 250 g biscuits crushed
- 1/2 cup butter melted
- 500 g cream cheese
- 1 cup caster sugar
- 1 cup whipped cream
- 1 tsp gelatine powder
- 180 g white chocolate melted
- 2 tbs lemon juice

Direction

- Combine butter and biscuit crumbs. Press into a springform tin.
- Beat cream cheese with caster sugar until creamy and smooth. Dissolve gelatine in 1/4 cup hot water.
- Add whipped cream, gelatine, melted chocolate and lemon juice, and mix well.
- Pour into biscuit base and refrigerate until set.

233. No Bake Creamy Rice Pudding Recipe

Serving: 4 | Prep: 5mins | Cook: 45mins | Ready in: 50mins

Ingredients

- 2 cup milk
- 2 tbs sugar
- 1/4 cup white rice
- 1/4 tsp salt
- 1/4 cup cream
- 1/4 tsp vanilla extract
- 1/3 cup sultanas
- 1 pinch ground cinnamon *to serve

Direction

- In saucepan gradually heat milk to a simmer.
- Stir in sugar, rice and salt.
- Simmer uncovered 45 minutes, stirring occasionally.
- Remove from heat.
- Stir in cream, vanilla and sultanas.
- Pour into serving dishes.
- Cool at room temperature.
- Sprinkle with cinnamon.

234. No Bake Dream Slice Recipe

Serving: 0 | Prep: 30mins | Cook: 0S | Ready in: 30mins

Ingredients

- 250 g Granita biscuits crushed
- 1 cup dried cranberries chopped
- 1 1/2 cup desiccated coconut
- 395 g sweetened condensed milk
- 125 g butter
- 1 1/4 cup milk chocolate melts

Direction

- Mix together biscuits, cranberries and coconut.
- In a saucepan, melt together butter and condensed milk. Add to dry ingredients. Mix well.
- Press mixture into a baking paper lined slice pan, then refrigerate.
- Once mixture has set, melt chocolate and cover slice.
- Refrigerate to set.

235. No Bake Fruit Tart Recipe

Serving: 8 | Prep: 40mins | Cook: 0S | Ready in: 40mins

Ingredients

- 150 g Scotch Finger biscuits crushed
- 6 tbs butter melted
- 250 g light cream cheese
- 1/4 cup low-fat vanilla yoghurt
- 100 g white chocolate
- 1 cup mixed berries *to decorate

Direction

- Combine biscuit crumbs and melted butter, and press into a tart tin with a removable base. Place in the fridge to chill.
- Melt the white chocolate and set to one side.
- Beat the cream cheese until fluffy. Add the melted chocolate and yoghurt and continue beating until creamy and smooth.
- Spoon into the tart shell and refrigerate until firm.
- Garnish with berries or other fruit and serve.

236. No Bake Ginger Caramel Slice Recipe

Serving: 0 | Prep: 30mins | Cook: 0S | Ready in: 30mins

Ingredients

- 1 x 250 g packet gingernut biscuits
- 115 g butter, melted
- Caramel Topping
- 1 x 400 g can sweetened condensed milk
- 50 g butter
- 1/2 cup brown sugar, firmly packed

Direction

- Grease and line a slice tin.
- Base: Process biscuits. Add melted butter to biscuits and process to combine.
- Press mixture into tin and refrigerate while making caramel topping.
- Topping: Place butter, brown sugar and sweetened condensed milk in a saucepan over

medium-low heat. Cook, stirring constantly for approximately 10 minutes, until sugar has dissolved. Be careful not to burn.
- Increase heat slightly and cook, stirring constantly for approximately 10 minutes or until mixture is thick and golden.
- Pour over base. Refrigerate until set.

237. No Bake Hazelnut Slice Recipe

Serving: 12 | Prep: 30mins | Cook: 5mins | Ready in: 35mins

Ingredients

- 125 g butter
- 3/4 cup condensed milk
- 2 tbs golden syrup
- 250 g milk arrowroot biscuits crushed
- 1 cup flaked almonds toasted
- Topping
- 250 g hazelnut chocolate
- 60 g copha

Direction

- Place butter, condensed milk and syrup into a small saucepan.
- Stir over low heat until melted, and simmer for 2 minutes.
- Combine biscuits and almonds, add butter mixture and combine well.
- Grease and line an 18 cm x 28 cm slab pan.
- Press mixture evenly into base.
- Refrigerate while preparing topping.
- For the topping, combine chocolate and copha in a small saucepan. Stir over low heat until smooth.
- Pour over biscuit base and refrigerate until set.

238. No Bake Lattice Lemon Cheesecake Slice Recipe

Serving: 0 | Prep: 15mins | Cook: 0S | Ready in: 15mins

Ingredients

- 2 tsp gelatine
- 1/4 cup boiling water
- 1 pkt Lattice biscuits
- 250g cream cheese
- 100g butter, softened
- 1/2 cup caster sugar
- 1/2 cup thickened cream
- 1 tbs lemon zest, finely grated
- 1/4 cup lemon juice

Direction

- Combine gelatine and boiling water in a small bowl and whisk until gelatine has dissolved. Set aside to cool slightly.
- Line a square cake tin with baking paper, leaving plenty of overhang. Place Lattice biscuits shiny side in a single layer in the base of the tin.
- Using hand-held beaters or a stand mixer, beat cream cheese, butter, caster sugar and cream for 4 minutes until smooth and thick. Add lemon zest, juice and gelatine mixture, and beat for a further 4 minutes.
- Spread cream cheese mixture over Lattice biscuits in tin in a smooth layer. Arrange more biscuits shiny side up on top. Refrigerate for 4 hours or overnight to set. Cut into squares to serve.

239. No Bake Lemon Cheesecake Recipe

Serving: 10 | Prep: 30mins | Cook: 0S | Ready in: 30mins

Ingredients

- 250 g Arnott's Nice biscuits

- 125 g butter melted
- 500 g cream cheese
- 1/3 cup lemon juice *to taste
- 1 cup cream whipped
- 1 cup NESTLE Sweetened Condensed Milk
- 2 tsp white vinegar
- 1 cup cream whipped *extra

Direction

- Crush biscuits finely, then mix with the melted butter.
- Line a 20cm cake tin, then add the biscuit crumb, pressing down to create the base, then place in the fridge to set.
- In a large mixing bowl, sieve the cream cheese.
- Add condensed milk, lemon juice and vinegar and beat until creamy. Fold in whipped cream.
- Pour on top of the crumb crust base and refrigerate overnight.
- Top with extra whipped cream and sprinkle with nutmeg.

240. No Bake Lemon Cheesecake Slice

Serving: 0 | Prep: 40mins | Cook: 0S | Ready in: 40mins

Ingredients

- 2 packets Lattice biscuits
- 250 g unsalted butter
- 250 g caster sugar
- 250 g cream cheese
- 1 sachet gelatine powder
- 1/3 cup lemon juice

Direction

- Cream the butter, sugar and cream cheese.
- Heat the lemon juice (microwave is fine) and stir in gelatine. Add to creamed mix and mix until completely smooth.
- Line a rectangle baking tray with grease-proof paper, leaving some flapping out the sides of the tray so you can lift the slice out once set.
- Lay Lattice biscuits in bottom of tray (shiny side down), cutting biscuits to fit right to the sides.
- Spread the creamed mix evenly over the layer of biscuits. Add another layer of biscuits to finish (shiny side up this time). Refrigerate until set. Cut into slices.

241. No Bake Lemon Cheesecake Recipe

Serving: 10 | Prep: 15mins | Cook: 370mins | Ready in: 385mins

Ingredients

- 250 g sweet plain biscuits crumbed
- 175 g butter melted
- 500 g cream cheese softened
- 400 g sweetened condensed milk
- 300 ml thickened cream
- 3 tsp gelatine powder
- 1/4 cup boiling water
- 1/4 cup lemon juice

Direction

- Combine biscuit crumbs and butter and press into the base of a 25 cm springform pan. Refrigerate.
- Beat cream cheese using an electric mixer until smooth.
- Dissolve the gelatine in the boiling water. Beat in condensed milk, cream and gelatine mixture until smooth, then add lemon juice and beat until combined.
- Pour mixture into prepared base and refrigerate 3 hours or overnight.

242. No Bake Lemon Coconut Slice Recipe

Serving: 10 | Prep: 30mins | Cook: 0S | Ready in: 30mins

Ingredients

- Base
- 2 x 250g sweet plain biscuits crushed
- 1 cup desiccated coconut
- 395g sweetened condensed milk
- 200g unsalted butter melted
- 1/3 cup lemon juice
- 2 lemons, rinds and seeds removed
- Icing
- 3 tbs lemon juice
- 50g unsalted butter melted
- 2 cups icing sugar

Direction

- Line a 20 x 30cm plastic airtight container with baking paper, leaving 5cm overhang on edges.
- Mix biscuits and coconut in a large bowl. Add all other base ingredients and combine well.
- Press mixture evenly into container and refrigerate.
- Icing: Combine all ingredients and mix until smooth.
- Spread evenly over slice and refrigerate until firm.
- Cut into squares to serve.

243. No Bake Licorice Allsorts Slice Recipe

Serving: 0 | Prep: 30mins | Cook: 0S | Ready in: 30mins

Ingredients

- 3 1/2 cups desiccated coconut
- 1 cup icing sugar
- 395 g condensed milk
- 1 splash pink food colouring
- 1 splash green food colouring
- 150 g Arnott's Marie biscuits
- 50 g butter melted
- 3 tbs condensed milk *extra
- 200 g dark chocolate
- 1 tbs coconut oil
- 1 packet licorice allsorts *optional

Direction

- Line an 18x25cm slice tin with baking paper.
- Combine coconut and icing sugar in a bowl, then add condensed milk and stir to combine. Remove half of the mixture to a second bowl. Add a few drops of pink food colouring to one bowl and mix well. Add a few drops of green food colouring to the second bowl and mix well.
- In a food processor, crush biscuits into a fine crumb. Add butter and extra condensed milk and blitz until well combined.
- Press pink coconut mixture into the base of the prepared tin and smooth evenly. Top with biscuit mixture, followed by green coconut mixture, smoothing down each layer evenly.
- Melt chocolate with coconut oil in a bowl over a saucepan of simmering water. Pour over slice in tin and spread out evenly. If using licorice allsorts, cut into three or four slices and press into the chocolate. Refrigerate until set.
- Slice into bite-sized pieces to serve.

244. No Bake Lindt Ball Cheesecake Recipe

Serving: 10 | Prep: 20mins | Cook: 6mins | Ready in: 26mins

Ingredients

- 250 g plain sweet biscuits
- 150 g unsalted butter melted
- 250 g Lindt Lindor Strawberries & Cream balls
- 125 g Lindt Lindor Strawberries & Cream balls *to serve *extra

- 2 tbs warm water
- 1 tsp gelatine powder
- 500 g cream cheese brought to room temperature chopped into pieces
- 100 g caster sugar
- 300 g sour cream
- 200 g white chocolate cooled melted
- 1 packet Lindt Lindor Mango & Cream balls *to serve
- 1 punnet fresh strawberries *to serve
- 1 mango fresh thinly sliced *to serve

Direction

- Line the base of a 7cm-deep, 20cm springform pan with baking paper. Lightly grease the side. Process the biscuits in a food processor until fine crumbs form. Add the butter and pulse to combine. Transfer the mixture to the prepared pan and press firmly into the base and up the side. Place in the fridge until required.
- Place the strawberry Lindor balls in a heatproof bowl. Place over a pan of simmering water (don't let the bowl touch the water), stirring occasionally, for 5 minutes or until melted.
- Place the warm water in a small microwave-safe bowl. Sprinkle over the gelatine and stir until well combined. Microwave for 30 seconds, then use a fork to dissolve the gelatine. Set aside to cool slightly.
- Use electric beaters to beat the cream cheese and sugar until smooth. Add the sour cream and beat to combine. Add the white chocolate and gelatine mixture. Beat to combine.
- Pour half the cream cheese mixture into the pan. Pour half the melted strawberry mixture over the top and use a flat-bladed knife to swirl into the cream cheese mixture. Add the remaining cream cheese mixture and remaining melted strawberry mixture and swirl again. Smooth the surface. Place in the fridge for 4 hours or overnight to set.
- Remove the cheesecake from the pan. Decorate with the mango balls, extra strawberry balls and fresh strawberries and mango.

245. No Bake Marshmallow Slice Recipe

Serving: 10 | Prep: 180mins | Cook: 0S | Ready in: 180mins

Ingredients

- 250 g plain biscuits crushed
- 1 cup desiccated coconut
- 1/2 cup chocolate drops
- 150 g marshmallows cut in half
- 395 g sweetened condensed milk

Direction

- Grease an 18 cm x 28 cm slice pan. Line base and sides with baking paper, extending 2 cm above pan edges.
- Place biscuit crumbs in a large bowl. Add coconut, milk chocolate drops, condensed milk and marshmallows.
- Stir until mixed well and press into the pan. Cover and refrigerate until firm.
- Lift slice from pan and cut into rectangles.

246. No Bake Mock Cheesecake Recipe

Serving: 10 | Prep: 15mins | Cook: 0S | Ready in: 15mins

Ingredients

- 250g sweet plain biscuits, crushed
- 120g butter, melted
- Filling
- 350ml evaporated milk, chilled
- 125ml condensed milk *optional
- 1 large lemon, juiced
- 85g lemon jelly
- 1 cup hot water

- 1 lemon rind

Direction

- Combine butter and crushed biscuits, mix well and press into the base of a 26cm springform pan. Refrigerate.
- Beat evaporated milk until doubled in volume. Dilute jelly in hot water, cooled but not set.
- Add condensed milk and continue beating for about two minutes.
- Add jelly and continue to beat for another two minutes.
- Add rind and juice of lemon and beat until mixture thickens for about three minutes. Spread over biscuit base and chill for about three hours before serving.

247. No Bake Muesli Bars Recipe

Serving: 0 | Prep: 240mins | Cook: 10mins | Ready in: 250mins

Ingredients

- 1/4 cup honey
- 1/4 cup sunflower butter
- 1/2 tsp vanilla extract
- 1 1/4 cup traditional rolled oats
- 1/2 cup dried apricots
- 2 tbs sunflower seeds raw
- 2 tbs pepitas
- 2 tbs sesame seeds

Direction

- Toast seeds in an 180C oven for about 5 minutes or until lightly golden.
- Place honey, vanilla extract and sunflower butter together in a microwave safe bowl. Melt in microwave on high for 45 seconds, stir.
- Mix remaining ingredients together in a separate bowl.
- Stir honey butter mixture into dry ingredients. Mix to combine, making sure all dry ingredients are coated.
- Press mixture firmly into bar moulds, plastic containers or into a non-greased 20 cm square pan.
- Refrigerate for 3-4 hours. Invert moulds and tap out bars.

248. No Bake Muesli Slice Recipe

Serving: 0 | Prep: 20mins | Cook: 10mins | Ready in: 30mins

Ingredients

- 1 cup rolled oats
- 1 cup Kellogg's Rice Bubbles
- 4 Sanitarium Weet-Bix crushed
- 1 cup desiccated coconut
- 1/2 cup mixed dried fruit
- 1/4 cup sesame seeds
- 1/2 cup brown sugar firmly packed
- 1/2 cup honey
- 1/2 cup peanut butter
- 125 g butter melted

Direction

- Grease a 19cm x 29cm slice pan.
- Combine first 6 ingredients in large bowl.
- Combine sugar, honey, peanut butter and butter in saucepan, stirring constantly over low heat until butter is melted and sugar is dissolved.
- Bring to the boil, reduce heat and simmer for 5 minutes. Stir constantly.
- Cool slightly and stir into dry mix.
- Press into slice pan and refrigerate until set.

249. No Bake Neapolitan Coconut Ice Slice Recipe

Serving: 20 | Prep: 10mins | Cook: 0S | Ready in: 10mins

Ingredients

- 2 x 137g pkts Oreo Original biscuits
- 60g butter, melted, cooled
- 395g can sweetened condensed milk
- 2 cups desiccated coconut
- 1 cup shredded coconut
- 2 cups pure icing sugar
- Pink food colouring
- Icing sugar, to dust (optional)

Direction

- Grease and line the base of a 20cm square cake pan, allowing 2 long sides to overhang.
- Process the Oreo biscuits in a food processor until finely chopped. Add the butter and process until combined. Press firmly into the base of the prepared pan. Place in the fridge for 15 minutes to firm.
- Place the condensed milk, coconuts and sugar in a bowl. Stir well to combine. Transfer half of the mixture to the pan. Use wet fingers to push down evenly.
- Add the food colouring to the remaining coconut mixture. Stir well to combine. Transfer to the pan and use wet fingers to press down firmly. Place in the fridge for 1 hour or until firm. Cut into squares and dust with icing sugar, if desired.

250. No Bake Nutella Bars Recipe

Serving: 0 | Prep: 0S | Cook: 0S | Ready in:

Ingredients

- 120 g butter
- 2 cups caster sugar
- 2 tbs cocoa sifted
- 1/2 cup milk
- 1/2 cup Nutella
- 1 tbs vanilla essence
- 2 1/2 cups rolled oats
- 2 1/2 cups Kellogg's Rice Bubbles
- 1/4 cup sprinkles *to taste

Direction

- Line a slice pan with baking paper and set aside.
- In a large saucepan melt the butter then add sugar, cocoa and milk. Whisk together and bring to the boil. Boil for one minute. Remove from heat.
- Add the Nutella, vanilla, rolled oats and rice bubbles to the pan and combine well.
- Pour into slice pan and smooth flat with the back of a metal spoon. Scatter over your choice of sprinkles. (I used coated chocolate chips.)
- Refrigerate until set. This will take about 3 hours. Cut into squares with a sharp knife.

251. No Bake Pavlova Recipe

Serving: 6 | Prep: 20mins | Cook: 5mins | Ready in: 25mins

Ingredients

- 2 egg whites
- 1 cup caster sugar
- 3 tsp gelatine powder
- 1 cup boiling water
- 500 ml thickened cream
- 1 cup fresh strawberries *to decorate

Direction

- Dissolve gelatine in boiling water and place in fridge to cool.
- Beat together egg whites, caster sugar and the dissolved gelatine and water. Mix with an

electric mixer for about 10 minutes or until very stiff.
- Place in large bowl and refrigerate for at least 2 hours or until set.
- Whip up cream and place on top of pavlova. Decorate with sliced strawberries or kiwifruit.

252. No Bake Pineapple Pudding Recipe

Serving: 0 | Prep: 20mins | Cook: 20mins | Ready in: 40mins

Ingredients

- 290 g sweetened condensed milk
- 100 g pineapple crush
- 250 ml sour cream
- 250 ml cream

Direction

- With an electric mixer beat sour cream and fresh cream until peaks form - do not over beat it.
- Add condensed milk slowly to your mixture using electric mixer on level one.
- Slowly fold in pineapple crush with spatula and dish into small glass bowls or one big one.
- Leave it in the fridge to set for 20-30 min. If you want it to set faster put it in the freezer for 15-20 min. Serve.

253. No Bake Strawberry Cheesecake Recipe

Serving: 6 | Prep: 30mins | Cook: 0S | Ready in: 30mins

Ingredients

- 200 g digestive biscuits
- 50 g butter
- 1 tbs honey
- 200 ml double cream
- 100 g cream cheese
- 200 g fresh strawberries finely chopped

Direction

- Process the biscuits into crumbs.
- Melt the butter and honey in a saucepan over a low heat and pour into the biscuit crumbs.
- Mix thoroughly and press the mixture into a greased tin. Refrigerate.
- Whip the double cream until it is stiff, then beat in the cream cheese.
- Spread over the biscuit base and pile the chopped strawberries on top.
- Refrigerate until ready to serve.

254. No Bake Strawberry Milkshake Cheesecake Recipe

Serving: 12 | Prep: 15mins | Cook: 0S | Ready in: 15mins

Ingredients

- 2 packets Strawberry Cream Oreo biscuits
- 70 g butter melted
- 750 g cream cheese
- 1/2 cup sugar
- 1 cup Nestle Strawberry Nesquik
- 1 tbs milk
- 250 ml thickened cream whipped

Direction

- Lightly grease a 24cm (9 inch) springform tin.
- Blitz or finely crush the biscuits.
- Stir the butter into the biscuit crumb, then press the crumbs across the bottom and 1/2 way up the sides of the tin. Refrigerate.
- Using an electric mixer, beat the cream cheese until smooth. Then add in the sugar, Nesquik and milk beating until well combined.
- Stir in the cream.
- Pour into the base, then cover with plastic wrap and refrigerate for at least 6 hours.

- Decorate with whipped cream, strawberries, mini Oreos and sprinkles.

255. No Bake Strawberry Slice Recipe

Serving: 0 | Prep: 40mins | Cook: 0S | Ready in: 40mins

Ingredients

- 250 g unsalted butter softened
- 250 g cream cheese
- 1 cup caster sugar
- 3 tsp vanilla essence
- 2 tsp gelatine powder
- 1 tbs boiling water
- 250 g fresh strawberries sliced
- 200 g Lattice biscuits

Direction

- Cream softened butter, cream cheese and caster sugar until light and fluffy. Add vanilla essence and dissolved gelatine and beat well.
- Fold in a few sliced strawberries.
- Line base of 30 cm x 25 cm pan with non-stick paper.
- Cover base with the lattice biscuits, flat side facing down.
- Cover biscuits with half of the creamed mixture and then arrange the remaining strawberries over the top. Push strawberries down into mixture.
- Spoon remaining creamed mixture over the top, making sure the strawberries are covered.
- Refrigerate to set. Cut into slices to serve.
- Store in covered container in fridge.

256. No Bake Trail Mix Cookies Recipe

Serving: 12 | Prep: 15mins | Cook: 0S | Ready in: 15mins

Ingredients

- 1 cup dried figs
- 1/2 cup raisins
- 1 cup quick oats
- 1/2 cup shredded coconut
- 1/2 cup shredded coconut *extra
- 1/2 cup sunflower seeds

Direction

- Place figs, raisins, oats and 1/2 cup coconut into a food processor. Process until mixture lifts away from the edges of the bowl.
- Remove from bowl and knead the sunflower seeds into the mixture. Form a log and slice into 12 even slices.
- Roll each slice in remaining coconut.

257. No Bake Walnut Cookie Recipe

Serving: 0 | Prep: 10mins | Cook: 20mins | Ready in: 30mins

Ingredients

- 1 cup walnuts
- 1/2 cup Unsweetened Shredded Coconut
- 1 tbs vanilla extract
- 2 tbs honey
- 1 tbs dark chocolate chips heaped
- 1 tbs Craisins dried cranberries heaped

Direction

- Use a food processor to blend the walnuts into a fine crumb.
- Get a large mixing bowl and place all the ingredients. Use your hands to mix, it's easier and more fun!
- Roll into small little dough balls onto baking/parchment paper. Squish down with a fork or the back of a spoon.
- Freeze for 20 mins then enjoy!

258. No Bake Weet Bix Slice

Serving: 20 | Prep: 25mins | Cook: 135mins | Ready in: 160mins

Ingredients

- 205 g skim sweetened condensed milk
- 10 Weet-Bix crushed
- 125 g butter
- 1/2 cup coconut
- 1 tbs cocoa
- 1/2 cup mixed fruit
- 1/2 cup mixed nuts
- Icing
- 1 tbs butter
- 1 tbs cocoa
- 1 1/2 cup icing sugar
- 2 tsp boiling water

Direction

- Melt the butter and add the condensed milk, stir to combine.
- In a bowl mix the Weet-Bix, coconut, cocoa, dried fruit and nuts.
- Pour over the butter mixture and stir to combine.
- Press the mixture into a slice tin lined with baking paper.
- Combine all the icing ingredients together and spread over the top of the slice.
- Chill and store in the refrigerator.
- Cut into squares to serve.

259. No Bake White Chocolate Cheesecake Recipe

Serving: 0 | Prep: 30mins | Cook: 240mins | Ready in: 270mins

Ingredients

- 2 x 250 g Arnott's Nice biscuits
- 100 g butter melted
- 2 x 500 g cream cheese room temperature
- 1 cup sugar
- 1 tsp vanilla extract
- 1 cup thickened cream
- 200 g white chocolate melts melted
- 2 sachet gelatine powder
- 1/4 cup water hot
- 1/2 cup chocolate chips

Direction

- Line a slice tin with baking paper and set aside.
- Process the biscuits and melted butter in a food processor until you have fine crumbs. Press into the base of the slice tin and refrigerate while you are making the topping.
- In the food processor, combine the cream cheese, sugar, vanilla extract, thickened cream and melted chocolate until smooth.
- Dissolve the gelatine in the hot water and add to the cream cheese mixture and combine well.
- Pour the mixture over the biscuit base and sprinkle chocolate chips over the top.
- Refrigerate for 3 hours or overnight. Slice into squares taking care to wipe the knife in between cuts.

260. No Bake Fruit Tart Recipe

Serving: 8 | Prep: 15mins | Cook: 0S | Ready in: 15mins

Ingredients

- 250 g milk arrowroot biscuits crushed
- 150 g butter melted
- 150 g pudding mix
- 750 ml milk
- 250 g fresh strawberries
- 2 passionfruit pulp

Direction

- In a large bowl mix together the crushed biscuits and melted butter until it forms a wet, crumbly cookie dough consistency. You should be able to ball it together in your fist without it breaking apart.
- Press the biscuit base mix into a fluted tart tin with removable base. Use the base of a glass to press the mixture into the sides of the tin.
- Put the base into the fridge while you make the custard.
- Pour the milk into a large bowl, then sprinkle the pudding mix over, whisking briskly and continuously until the pudding mix starts to set.
- Pour the custard into the tin and put it in the fridge to set for about 15 minutes.
- Hull and halve the strawberries and spread them over the top of the tart. Drizzle with passionfruit pulp.

261. No Bake Mini Cheesecakes Recipe

Serving: 0 | Prep: 60mins | Cook: 10mins | Ready in: 70mins

Ingredients

- 250 g cream cheese
- 1/2 cup condensed milk
- 2 tbs lemon juice
- 1/2 cup whipped cream
- 500 g butternut snap biscuits
- 1 tbs cinnamon sugar *to dress

Direction

- Preheat oven to 140C.
- Divide biscuits over two 12-hole shallow patty pans.
- Bake for five minutes or until soft to touch.
- Using the back of a teaspoon, gently press biscuits into pan holes. Cool in pans. Repeat until all biscuits are used.
- Beat cream cheese, lemon juice and condensed milk until smooth.
- Fold in whipped cream.
- When biscuits have cooled into shape, spoon approximately 2 teaspoons of mixture into each biscuit.
- Dust tops of the mini cheesecakes with cinnamon or cinnamon sugar.
- Place in refrigerator until mixture has cooled and set.

262. No Bake Peach Tart

Serving: 8 | Prep: 360mins | Cook: 0S | Ready in: 360mins

Ingredients

- 250g ginger biscuit
- 1 tsp mixed spice
- 100g butter, melted
- 425g peach, sliced
- 85g jelly
- 1 cup boiling water
- 300ml cream
- 1 cup coconut optional toasted *to decorate

Direction

- Process or crush biscuits and mix with melted butter and mixed spice.
- Press into a greased 28 cm flan tray, making sure to line the sides and chill for half an hour.
- Drain peaches and reserve juice. Arrange peaches on chilled base.
- Make up jelly with minimal boiling water and add peach juice, to make approximately 1.5 cups.
- Cool in fridge until luke warm.
- Whip cream until it starts to thicken, then slowly add jelly mix and whip for several minutes until combined.
- Pour cream/jelly mix over chilled peaches and base, sprinkle with toasted coconut (if using).
- Allow to set for several hours.

263. Nut Free Chocolate Bliss Slice Recipe

Serving: 0 | Prep: 30mins | Cook: 0S | Ready in: 30mins

Ingredients

- 1 tbs chia seeds
- 12 medjool dates pitted
- 1 cup quinoa cooked cooled
- 1/2 cup raw cacao powder
- 1 tbs coconut oil
- 1 tbs raw cacao nibs
- 1 tbs chia seeds
- 1 tsp ground cinnamon
- 1 tsp vanilla essence
- 1/2 tsp salt
- 1 tsp chia seeds

Direction

- Line a loaf pan with greaseproof paper and sprinkle with 1 tablespoon of chia seeds.
- Blend all ingredients in a food processor.
- Press mixture into loaf pan. Evenly sprinkle with 1 tablespoon of chia seeds.
- Refrigerate for at least 1 hour and cut into 12 pieces.

264. Old Fashioned Slow Cooker Rice Pudding Recipe

Serving: 6 | Prep: 5mins | Cook: 180mins | Ready in: 185mins

Ingredients

- 3/4 cup long-grain white rice
- 3 cups milk
- 1/2 cup granulated sugar
- 1/4 tsp ground cinnamon
- 1 pinch salt
- 2 tbs butter diced

Direction

- In a colander, rinse rice thoroughly under cold water.
- Put into a lightly greased slow cooker.
- Add remaining ingredients, except for butter and stir to combine.
- Sprinkle butter over rice mixture.
- Cover and cook on high for 2½-3 hours, until rice has absorbed the liquid.
- Serve warm.

265. Oma's Gingerbread Recipe

Serving: 0 | Prep: 15mins | Cook: 15mins | Ready in: 30mins

Ingredients

- 250 g butter
- 1 1/4 cups brown sugar
- 3 tsp bicarbonate of soda
- 1/4 cup lukewarm water
- 6 tbs golden syrup
- 5 cups plain flour
- 1 tbs ground ginger
- 2 tbs ground cinnamon
- 1/2 tsp ground cloves

Direction

- Cream together the butter and brown sugar.
- Add the bicarbonate of soda dissolved in a little warm water. Add the golden syrup and stir well.
- Combine the spices and flour one cup at a time.
- When the dough is soft, but firm in to touch, don't add any more flour.

- Roll out half of the mixture on a floured work surface to approximately 0.5 cm thick. Cut out shapes and place on papered tray.
- Bake at 180C for approximately 15 minutes until golden.
- Remove from oven, allow to cool before decorating.

266. Oreo Cheesecake

Serving: 16 | Prep: 45mins | Cook: 330mins | Ready in: 375mins

Ingredients

- 570 g Oreo biscuits crushed
- 1/3 cup unsalted butter melted
- 3 x 250 g cream cheese brought to room temperature
- 3/4 cup sugar
- 4 egg brought to room temperature
- 1 cup sour cream brought to room temperature
- 1 tsp vanilla extract
- 6 Oreo biscuits halved

Direction

- Reserve some cookie crumbs for the filling.
- Add melted butter to the cookie crumbs and mix well.
- Press mixture into a 23 cm spring form pan and press mixture 5 cm up the sides of the tin.
- Beat cream cheese and sugar with an electric mixer on medium until creamy. Add lightly beaten eggs, one at a time, mixing by hand.
- Stir in sour cream and vanilla. Fold in reserved cookie crumbs.
- Pour mixture onto the prepared cookie crust.
- Bake at 170C for 55-60 minutes or until set.
- Cool on a wire rack at room temperature for 15 minutes.
- Use a flat blade knife to cut around the edge of the cake to help it slide out of the pan. Don't cut into the cake.
- When cooled to room temperature, put it in the fridge for at least 4 hours.
- Remove side from pan and garnish with cream, cookie halves or cookie crumbs.

267. Pancakes Recipe

Serving: 0 | Prep: 10mins | Cook: 10mins | Ready in: 20mins

Ingredients

- 1 1/2 cups full cream milk
- 2 tsp fresh lemon juice
- 2 tbs sugar
- 1 1/2 cups self-raising flour
- 1/4 tsp bicarbonate of soda
- 1 extra large egg
- 1 1/2 tbs butter melted

Direction

- Stir milk, lemon juice and sugar together in a bowl, and set aside for at least 5 minutes. Mixture will have a curdled effect.
- Sift flour and bicarbonate of soda into a large bowl,
- Combine egg and melted butter with milk mixture and add to flour. Whisk until almost smooth. There may still be a few small lumps, but be careful not to over-mix as this will toughen the pancake.
- Leave the batter to stand for at least 2 minutes.
- Heat a large frying pan and lightly grease.
- Pour in mixture to form pancakes of desired size. Cook one side until bubbles appear and pop, flip pancake and cook until golden.

268. Passionfruit Cheese Lova Recipe

Serving: 0 | Prep: 40mins | Cook: 90mins | Ready in: 130mins

Ingredients

- 4 egg whites
- 1 cup caster sugar
- 1 tsp cornflour
- 1/2 tsp lemon juice
- 1 tsp vanilla extract
- 1 tub cream whipped *extra
- 1 cup mixed berries *to serve
- 1 cup passionfruit *to serve
- 1 mango *to serve
- For filling
- 300 ml cream
- 2 tsp gelatine
- 500 g cream cheese
- 3/4 cup caster sugar
- 170 g tinned passionfruit pulp seeds removed

Direction

- Preheat oven to 140C (120C fan-forced). Remove the base from a 22-24cm springform tin and set aside. Line the sides with baking paper, coming up a few centimetres above the edge. Place on a flat oven tray lined with paper.
- Whip egg whites until soft peaks form. With the beaters running, add caster sugar one spoonful at a time, mixing well in between each addition. This will take some time, but is important for the finished result. Add the cornflour in with the last spoonful of sugar. Continue mixing for 5-10 minutes until the sugar has dissolved completely. You can test this by rubbing a little of the mixture between a finger and thumb - it should be completely smooth. Add lemon juice and vanilla and continue mixing for another minute.
- Spoon into prepared tin (the meringue will be sitting directly on the lined tray), smoothing down the top evenly. Place in the oven and bake for 1.5 hours. Without removing pavlova, turn off oven, open the door slightly and allow to cool for a couple of hours or overnight.
- To make filling: beat cream until thick. Set aside. Dissolve gelatine in 1/4 cup boiling water. Set aside. Whip together cream cheese with caster sugar until smooth. Add dissolved gelatine and strained passionfruit and beat well. Fold through whipped cream.
- Spoon filling into tin on top of pavlova base, pushing it right to the edges and smoothing out evenly on top. Refrigerate for 4 hours to set completely.
- Just prior to serving, remove from fridge. Tilt tin and carefully remove paper from base, then place on serving platter. Unlock spring and carefully remove tin - you may need to first slide a knife around between tin and paper to unstick it. Pull off paper. Spread extra whipped cream around the sides to cover any imperfections. Top with fruit and serve.

269. Passionfruit Delicious Pudding Recipe

Serving: 4 | Prep: 15mins | Cook: 40mins | Ready in: 55mins

Ingredients

- 2 tbs butter
- 3/4 cup sugar
- 2 tbs self-raising flour sifted
- 1 pinch salt sifted
- 2 eggs separated
- 4 passionfruit
- 1 cup milk

Direction

- Cream butter and sugar.
- Add sifted flour and salt.
- Add passionfruit, egg yolks and milk.
- Beat egg whites until stiff and fold into mixture.

- Pour into a greased ovenproof dish and stand in a dish of cold water.
- Bake at 180-200C for 40 minutes.

270. Passionfruit Summer Snowcake Recipe

Serving: 10 | Prep: 15mins | Cook: 0S | Ready in: 15mins

Ingredients

- 1 can Carnation evaporated milk chilled
- 3 tbs caster sugar
- 5 tsp gelatine powder
- 3 passionfruit
- 1/4 cup boiling water
- 600 ml whipped cream

Direction

- Dissolve gelatine in boiling water. Allow to cool.
- Whip carnation milk until fluffy then add sugar slowly.
- Mix cooled gelatine into fluffy milk mixture.
- Fold in the passionfruit.
- Lightly grease cake tins and pour in the cake mixture.
- Refrigerate and once ready to serve cover with whipped cream and sprinkle a layer of coconut on top.

271. Passionfruit Vanilla Yoghurt Bars Recipe

Serving: 0 | Prep: 10mins | Cook: 0S | Ready in: 10mins

Ingredients

- 2 cups Greek yoghurt
- 1/4 cup shredded coconut
- 1 tsp vanilla paste
- 2 tsp maple syrup
- 1/4 cup fresh passionfruit pulp
- 1 tbs fresh passionfruit pulp extra
- 2 cups pureed mango
- 1 tsp lime juice

Direction

- Line a 20cm cake tin with baking paper.
- In a medium bowl, combine yoghurt, coconut, vanilla and maple syrup. Spread yoghurt mixture evenly across the base of the prepared tin and freeze for 1-2 hours, until just firm to the touch.
- Combine mango puree, lime juice and 1/4 cup passionfruit pulp. Spread over yoghurt layer and smooth top. Drizzle with remaining passionfruit and return to freezer until solid – approximately 4 hours, or overnight.
- Remove pan from freezer and set on bench for 5 minutes. Use baking paper to lift slice onto a cutting board and leave 5-10 minutes to thaw slightly. Cut into 12 bars, serve immediately or store in the freezer for a handy snack.

272. Pavlova

Serving: 12 | Prep: 20mins | Cook: 60mins | Ready in: 80mins

Ingredients

- 6 egg whites
- 4 1/2 cup caster sugar
- 1 1/2 tsp vanilla essence
- 3 tsp white vinegar
- 3 tsp cornflour
- 12 tbs boiling water
- 600 ml thickened cream
- 2 handfuls mixed berries *to decorate
- 1 tsp cornflour

Direction

- Preheat oven to 190C.

- Using an electric mixer place all the ingredients (except the 1 teaspoon of additional cornflour) into the bowl and beat on a high speed until very stiff. This will take approximately 15minutes.
- Line a baking tray with greaseproof paper and then sift 1 teaspoon of cornflour over the area.
- Heap the pav mix into the centre of the tray and then spread out shaping a round circle, heap it high in the middle allowing for it to settle down in the oven.
- Bake for 10 minutes and then reduce the oven temperature to 150c and continue to bake for a further 45 minutes. Then turn off the oven leaving the pav inside, open the oven door a small amount and wedge the door open with a wooden spoon if necessary. Keep the pav in the oven and let it cool down completely before removing it.
- To decorate place whipped cream on top and then your favourite selection of in season berries and fruit.

273. Pavlova Recipe

Serving: 12 | Prep: 10mins | Cook: 90mins | Ready in: 100mins

Ingredients

- 4 egg whites
- 1 cup caster sugar
- 1 tsp lemon juice
- 2 tsp cornflour

Direction

- In a small electric mixer bowl, beat egg whites until soft peaks form.
- Add sugar, lemon juice and sifted cornflour, and beat until stiff and glossy (at least 10 minutes).
- Cover a baking tray with baking paper.
- Pile meringue onto paper and shape into a large circle, leaving the centre slightly hollowed.
- Bake in at 130C for 1½ hours or until crisp on the outside.
- Turn oven off and leave pavlova to cool in oven with door ajar.
- Decorate with whipped cream and fruit in season.

274. Peanut Butter Cookies Recipe

Serving: 0 | Prep: 10mins | Cook: 15mins | Ready in: 25mins

Ingredients

- 1/2 cup brown sugar
- 1/2 cup caster sugar
- 1/2 cup unsalted butter, melted
- 1/2 cup peanut butter
- 1 egg
- 1 1/2 cups self-raising flour
- 1 tsp vanilla essence

Direction

- Combine sugars.
- Add melted butter and lightly beaten egg. Mix well.
- Gradually add sifted flour and remaining ingredients, mixing thoroughly.
- Place teaspoonfuls of mixture onto a greased tray, flattening with a fork.
- Bake for about 12-15 minutes at 160C.

275. Peanut Butter And Papaya Cream Protein Bars Recipe

Serving: 4 | Prep: 10mins | Cook: 5mins | Ready in: 15mins

Ingredients

- Base
- 1 1/2 cups rolled oats blended into a flour
- 1/2 cup vegan protein powder
- 1/2 cup hemp seeds
- 1/4 tsp salt
- 1/2 cup natural peanut butter
- 1/4 cup pure maple syrup
- 1/4 cup coconut oil softened or melted
- 1 tsp vanilla extract
- Topping
- 1 cup raw cashews soaked in water 4 hours then drained
- 1/2 Ruby Rise Red Papaya flesh only
- 1/4 cup lemon juice
- 1/4 cup coconut oil
- 2 tbs cacao butter
- 5 drops grapefruit essential oil (optional)

Direction

- To make the base, add base ingredients to a mixing bowl and combine well. Turn dough into a lined tin (I used 20cm square) or a silicone mould. Set aside.
- To make the topping, add coconut oil and cacao butter to a heatproof bowl. Set over a pot of gently simmering water and allow to melt. Once liquid, remove from heat and set aside to cool for 5 minutes.
- Add all ingredients to a high-speed blender. Blitz until very smooth. Pour this over the base and set in the freezer for a few hours.
- To finish, remove bars from freezer and cake tin. Allow to defrost a little before cutting into serving sizes. Store in an airtight container in the fridge or freezer.

276. Peppermint Chocolate Shapes

Serving: 0 | Prep: 40mins | Cook: 5mins | Ready in: 45mins

Ingredients

- 375 g dark chocolate melts
- 4 drops peppermint extract
- 185 g white chocolate melts
- 1 tsp green liquid food colouring

Direction

- Line base and sides of a 20 cm square cake tin.
- Place half the dark chocolate melts in a microwave safe bowl and microwave on high for 2 minutes stirring every 30 seconds with a metal spoon until smooth. Mix in 2 drops of essence.
- Pout into base of tin. Tap tin on bench to rid the mix of air bubbles.
- Refrigerate for 5 minutes until set.
- Place white melts in bowl and repeat above remembering to stir. Mix until smooth. Add green colour and pour over first layer. Refrigerate 5 minutes.
- Melt the second half of dark chocolate following the same procedure, add essence and pour over green layer. Tap to clear bubbles and refrigerate for 10-15 minutes.
- Use cutters to make desired shapes and place in airtight container in fridge or freezer.

277. Peppermint Crisp Cheesecake Recipe

Serving: 8 | Prep: 30mins | Cook: 205mins | Ready in: 235mins

Ingredients

- 170g Arnott's Nice biscuits crushed
- 85g butter melted
- 250g cream cheese
- 395g condensed milk
- 1/3 cup lemon juice
- 1 tsp gelatine powder dissolved
- 1 tbs hot water
- 1 Nestle* Peppermint Crisp chocolate bars grated
- 2 drops peppermint essence

Direction

- Add melted butter to crushed biscuits.
- Press into foil lined tart plate.
- Place in fridge to set.
- Mix all other ingredients together and pour into chilled biscuit base.
- Decorate with grated chocolate.

278. Peppermint No Bake Cheesecake

Serving: 12 | Prep: 15mins | Cook: 205mins | Ready in: 220mins

Ingredients

- 100 g butter melted
- 250 g chocolate ripple biscuits crushed
- 400 g condensed milk
- 250 g cream cheese brought to room temperature
- 1/3 cup lemon juice
- 1/2 tsp creme de menthe
- 2 drops green liquid food colouring

Direction

- Line a cheesecake tin with baking paper.
- Mix together melted butter and biscuit crumbs.
- Spread onto bottom of tin and press down until firm. Refrigerate.
- Beat cream cheese until soft. Add condensed milk and beat until smooth.
- Add flavouring and food dye to meet desired flavour and colour combination.
- Add lemon juice and beat until well mixed and thickened.
- Spread cream cheese mix on top of biscuit base and smooth. Refrigerate until set.

279. Pie Maker Vanilla Slices Recipe

Serving: 0 | Prep: 15mins | Cook: 20mins | Ready in: 35mins

Ingredients

- 1 cup caster sugar
- 1/2 cup custard powder
- 1/3 cup cornflour
- 3 cups milk
- 1 tsp vanilla essence
- 4 sheets frozen puff pastry, defrosted
- Icing sugar, to serve

Direction

- In a medium saucepan, whisk together sugar, custard powder and cornflour. Whisk in milk and vanilla. Stir over low heat until mixture thickens. Remove to a bowl and allow to cool.
- Preheat pie maker according to manufacturer's instructions. Use pastry cutter to cut 8 bases and 8 tops (make the tops slightly smaller than the base) from the puff pastry.
- Line pie maker plates with larger circles. Fill with 1/3 of a cup of the custard. Top with smaller pastry.
- Cook for 8 minutes until golden. Repeat with remaining ingredients.
- Allow to cool. Dust with icing sugar and serve.

280. Pineapple Lumps Cheesecake Recipe

Serving: 12 | Prep: 25mins | Cook: 0S | Ready in: 25mins

Ingredients

- 250g pkt Choc Ripple biscuits
- 125g butter, melted
- 185g Pascall Pineapple Lumps
- 500g cream cheese
- 1/2 cup caster sugar
- 3 tsp gelatine powder
- 300ml thickened cream, whipped
- 240g pineapple flavoured jelly, diced
- 100g dark chocolate, chopped
- 2 tbs butter

Direction

- Prepare a 24cm springform cake tin by greasing lightly with butter and lining the base and sides with baking paper.
- In a food processor, blitz biscuits into a fine crumb. Add 125g butter and blitz until just combined. Remove to a bowl. Place 50g Pineapple Lumps into a food processor and blitz for a few seconds into small pieces. Add to the biscuit mixture and stir to combine.
- Place in a prepared tin and use a large spoon to press an even layer along the base, raising slightly along the edges. Refrigerate for 30 minutes.
- Using an electric mixer, beat cream cheese with sugar until smooth.
- Place 2 tbs boiling water in a small bowl and sprinkle over gelatine. Whisk with a fork until gelatine is completely dissolved. Add to cream cheese mixture and whipped cream and beat for a further minute to fully combine. Carefully fold through diced jelly. Pour into the biscuit base, smooth over the top and return to the fridge for at least an hour, or overnight, to set.
- Place chocolate and 2 tbs butter in a heatproof bowl over a saucepan of simmer water. Stir until melted and smooth. Drizzle over set cheesecake. Roughly chop remaining Pineapple Lumps and sprinkle over chocolate. Return to the fridge for 30 minutes to set.
- Release cheesecake from cake tin and carefully remove baking paper. Transfer to a serving plate, slice and serve.

281. Pineapple And Banana Loaf Recipe

Serving: 10 | Prep: 15mins | Cook: 60mins | Ready in: 75mins

Ingredients

- 2 cups wholemeal flour
- 1/2 cup desiccated coconut
- 1 tsp ground cinnamon
- 2 bananas mashed
- 1 tsp vanilla essence
- 1 cup pineapple finely diced
- 3/4 cup milk
- 2 eggs lightly beaten
- 1/4 cup honey
- 1/3 cup extra virgin olive oil
- desiccated coconut *to decorate
- ground cinnamon *to decorate
- pineapple pieces *to decorate

Direction

- Preheat the oven to 180C fan-forced. Line a medium size loaf tin with baking paper.
- Combine flour, coconut and cinnamon in a bowl.
- In a separate bowl, combine mashed bananas, vanilla essence, pineapple, milk, eggs, honey and extra virgin olive oil.
- Add the pineapple mixture to the dry ingredients and gently mix until just combine. Do not overmix.
- Pour the batter into the loaf tin, top with the slices of pineapple, a sprinkle of cinnamon and a sprinkle of desiccated coconut.

- Bake in the oven for 50-60 minutes, or until cooked through.

282. Pink Lemonade Jelly Slice Recipe

Serving: 12 | Prep: 30mins | Cook: 10mins | Ready in: 40mins

Ingredients

- 250g butternut snap biscuits crushed
- 100g butter melted
- Filling
- 2 tsp gelatine powder
- 1 1/2 tbs water
- 375 g cream cheese softened
- 1 cup condensed milk
- 2 tbs lemon juice
- Jelly
- 3 tsp gelatine powder
- 2 tbs water
- 2 1/2 cups lemonade room temperature
- 1 tbs lemon juice
- 1 splash pink food colouring

Direction

- Line a 20cm square cake pan with plastic wrap. Combine crushed biscuits and melted butter in a bowl. Stir to combine. Press over base of pan. Refrigerate for 30 minutes or until firm.
- Filling: Sprinkle gelatine over water in a heatproof cup. Stand cup in a pan of simmering water, until dissolved and then cool slightly. Using electric beaters, beat cream cheese until smooth. Beat in condensed milk, lemon juice and then gelatine mixture. Spread mixture into pan and smooth the surface. Refrigerate for 3 hours or until just set.
- Jelly: Sprinkle gelatine over water in a heatproof cup. Stand cup in a pan of simmering water, until dissolved. Combine lemonade and lemon juice in a bowl. Tint with food colour. Whisk in gelatine mixture until combined. Pour jelly over filling. Refrigerate for 3 hours or until set. Serve slice cut into squares.

283. Poached Pear And Pomegranate Sponge Cake Recipe

Serving: 0 | Prep: 40mins | Cook: 60mins | Ready in: 100mins

Ingredients

- 4 eggs room temperature separated
- 2/3 cup caster sugar
- 2/3 cup self-raising flour
- 1/3 cup cornflour
- 1 tsp cream of tartar
- 1 tsp vanilla essence
- Cream
- 300 ml thickened cream
- 1/2 pomegranate juiced *to decorate
- 3/4 cup icing sugar
- Pears
- 3 pears
- 1/2 cup water
- 2 tsp white sugar
- Glaze
- 1/4 cup chardonnay
- 2 tsp white sugar

Direction

- Preheat your oven to 160C.
- Grease and line the base of a 20cm diameter non-stick spring form tin. Don't grease the edges, this may go against every baking instinct you have, but to get the maximum rise from your cake, it needs to be able to grip the sides a little.
- Separate your eggs, place your yolks in one mixing bowl, the whites in another and 1/3 a cup of sugar in with each.

- Beat your egg whites on high speed with an electric mixer until it holds soft peaks and is of a meringue texture (smooth, glossy, and thick).
- Beat your egg yolks on high speed with an electric mixer until egg yolks have doubled in size.
- Into a separate bowl, sift together your self-raising flour, cornflour, and cream of tartar.
- Pour egg yolks into your whites and sift your dry ingredients for a second time into the bowl on top.
- Fold together gently with a spatula until well combined.
- Pour mixture into pre-prepared tin. Avoid filling your cake tin more than half way, or you risk it spilling over in the oven.
- Place in your preheated oven for 25 minutes, or until a skewer inserted into the centre of your cake is removed clean.
- Place cake in the refrigerator to cool.
- Cut your pears into roughly 1cm x 1cm cubes, skin on or off, it's up to you (I've left it on.)
- Place 1/2 cup water and 1tbs caster sugar into a small saucepan, and place over a low heat.
- Toss your pears through the liquid and allow to simmer until the pears are soft and the liquid has thickened slightly, roughly 10 - 15 minutes. Set aside to cool.
- Once your cake has cooled completely, you can start working on your whipped cream icing.
- Place the seeds of half a pomegranate into a food processor and blitz until it forms a thick paste (the seed centres will remain whole).
- Place a sieve over a medium sized mixing bowl, and place your pomegranate paste into the sieve. Set aside, allowing the pomegranate juice to drip into the bowl.
- Retrieve your bowl from underneath your sieve, and add 300ml cream and 1/2 a cup of icing sugar, and beat together on high with electric beaters until cream hold stiff peaks. Set aside.
- Place 1/4 cup of chardonnay and 2 tsp sugar into a saucepan over a low heat.
- Allow to simmer softly until the sugar has dissolved into the chardonnay (roughly 5 minutes.) Remove from the heat and set aside.
- Retrieve your cake from the fridge, carefully slice the top 1cm off your cake.
- Pour your chardonnay over your separated cake top and set aside for a moment to soak in.
- Cut chardonnay sponge into 1cm x 1cm cubes.
- Apply a layer of pomegranate cream on top of the bottom slice of cake (save some for decoration on top).
- Arrange sponge cubes and pears on top of your cream, pipe small dots of cream on top and sprinkle with whole pomegranate seeds.

284. Portuguese Custard Tarts Recipe

Serving: 0 | Prep: 20mins | Cook: 50mins | Ready in: 70mins

Ingredients

- 4 egg yolks
- 115g caster sugar
- 2 tbs cornflour
- 400ml light milk
- 2 tsp vanilla extract
- 2 sheets puff pastry

Direction

- Lightly grease a 12-hole 80ml muffin tray.
- Whisk egg yolks, sugar and cornflour together in a saucepan until fully combined. Gradually whisk in milk until smooth.
- Over medium heat, cook, stirring, until the mixture thickens and comes to the boil. Immediately remove from the heat and stir in vanilla extract.
- Transfer custard to a bowl, cover surface with cling wrap and leave to cool.
- Preheat oven to 200C.

- Cut pastry dough sheet in half, place one half on top of the other. Do the same with the other sheet. Set aside to rest for 5 minutes.
- From the short end, roll up pastry tightly and cut the 'log' into 2cm rounds (six per pastry sheet). Lay each pastry round on a lightly floured surface and using a rolling pin, roll out to 10 cm circle.
- Press pastry rounds into the muffin tins and spoon in cooled custard.
- Bake for 20-25 minutes or until pastry and custard are golden.
- Leave the tarts in muffin tins for 5 minutes, then transfer to a wire rack to cool completely, or if serving hot, serve immediately with ice cream.

285. Pumpkin Scones Recipe

Serving: 0 | Prep: 15mins | Cook: 40mins | Ready in: 55mins

Ingredients

- 2 1/2 cups self-raising flour
- 1 cup pumpkin mashed
- 55 g butter
- 1 egg
- 1/2 cup sugar
- 1/2 cup milk

Direction

- Beat butter until soft, then add sugar.
- Mix in pumpkin and egg.
- Add milk, then slowly add flour.
- Turn dough onto a floured board and knead.
- Roll out and cut dough into small circles.
- Place onto a greased tray.
- Bake at 200C for 15 minutes.

286. Queenslander Truffles Recipe

Serving: 12 | Prep: 15mins | Cook: 0S | Ready in: 15mins

Ingredients

- 200g pkt dried pineapple pieces
- 1/3 cup desiccated coconut
- 1 tbs dark rum
- 180g pkt dark chocolate, chopped

Direction

- Line a plate with baking paper.
- Process the pineapple in a food processor until very finely chopped. Transfer to a bowl. Stir in the coconut and rum until well combined.
- Roll 2 tsp of the pineapple mixture into a ball. Transfer to the lined plate.
- Place the chocolate in a heatproof bowl over a saucepan of simmering water, making sure the base of the bowl doesn't touch the water. Stir until chocolate has melted. Remove the bowl from the pan.
- Working one at a time, use two forks to dip a ball into the melted chocolate. Allow excess chocolate to drain back into the bowl. Return to the lined plate. Repeat with the remaining balls. Place in the fridge for 2 hours or until the chocolate has set.

287. Quick And Easy Anzac Biscuits Recipe

Serving: 0 | Prep: 10mins | Cook: 20mins | Ready in: 30mins

Ingredients

- 1 cup plain flour
- 1 cup rolled oats
- 1 cup brown sugar
- 1/2 cup coconut
- 125g unsalted butter

- 2 tbs golden syrup
- 1 tbs water
- 1/2 tsp bicarbonate of soda

Direction

- Sift the flour into a bowl. Add the sugar, rolled oats and coconut.
- Melt the butter in a saucepan, then add golden syrup and water.
- Stir the bicarbonate of soda into the liquid mixture.
- Add the liquid to the dry ingredients and mix thoroughly.
- Place walnut-sized balls of mixture on a greased tray and bake at 175C for 15-20 minutes.
- Biscuits will harden when cool.

288. Quick And Easy Mango Fruit Cake Recipe

Serving: 0 | Prep: 0S | Cook: 0S | Ready in:

Ingredients

- 425 g canned mango in syrup
- 500 g mixed fruit
- 1/2 cup water
- 1 1/2 tsp bicarbonate of soda
- 2 eggs lightly beaten
- 1 1/2 cups wholemeal self-raising flour

Direction

- Grease a loaf pan and line with baking paper.
- Combine undrained mango, mixed fruit and water in a large pan, then bring to the boil for 1 minute, then allow to cool.
- Stir in combined flour, bicarb soda and eggs, and mix well, then pour mixture into pan.
- Cook in a moderately slow oven at 160C for about 1 hour, or until cooked. Cool in the pan.

289. Raspberry Jam Heart Palmiers Recipe

Serving: 0 | Prep: 10mins | Cook: 20mins | Ready in: 30mins

Ingredients

- 1 sheet puff pastry thawed
- 1 tbs white sugar
- 3 tsp raspberry jam

Direction

- Preheat oven to 220C degrees or 200C fan-forced. Line a baking tray with baking paper.
- Sprinkle puff pastry sheet with sugar. Press sugar into pastry with your fingers. Flip sheet over onto a clean board. Spread other side of puff pastry with jam.
- Starting on one side, roll half of the pastry towards the centre. Repeat, rolling from the opposite side to meet the first roll in the middle. Cut into 1cm slices. Pinch the base of each slice into a "Y" shape. Place on prepared tray, shaping pastries into hearts.
- Bake for 10 minutes. Turn and bake for another 6-8 minutes or until caramelised. Cool slightly on tray and serve warm.

290. Raspberry Meringue Trifle Recipe

Serving: 8 | Prep: 15mins | Cook: 15mins | Ready in: 30mins

Ingredients

- 300 g frozen raspberries
- 1 cup caster sugar
- 1 sponge cake
- 1/2 cup port
- 500 ml vanilla ice cream

- Meringue topping
- 2 egg whites
- 1/2 cup sugar

Direction

- Trifle: Place the berries and sugar in a small saucepan over low heat.
- Bring to the boil and simmer for 2 minutes, or until slightly syrupy. Set aside to cool.
- Slice sponge to fit an ovenproof/freezer-safe dish. Dip the slices of sponge into the port.
- Cover the base of the dish with the sponge, top with berries and ice cream.
- Freeze until ready to serve.
- Meringue topping: Preheat a griller until hot.
- Whisk the egg whites until soft peaks form. Gradually add the sugar and whisk until smooth and glossy.
- Remove dish from freezer and top with meringue.
- Grill the meringue for 1-2 minutes until golden brown.

291. Raspberry And White Chocolate Muffins Recipe

Serving: 0 | Prep: 15mins | Cook: 25mins | Ready in: 40mins

Ingredients

- 3 cups self-raising flour sifted
- 1 cup caster sugar
- 125 g white chocolate chips
- 125 g butter melted
- 1 egg
- 1 cup milk
- 1/2 cup cream
- 1 tsp vanilla essence
- 200 g frozen raspberries
- 12 fresh raspberries *to decorate

Direction

- Sift flour, then add dry ingredients.
- Melt butter, add all ingredients, except raspberries, and mix well.
- Add frozen raspberries and gently fold into mixture, be careful not to over mix.
- Spoon mixture into tray lined with cupcake liners.
- Bake at 200C for 22-25 minutes.

292. Raspberry, Orange And Almond Simnel Cake Recipe

Serving: 11 | Prep: 25mins | Cook: 60mins | Ready in: 85mins

Ingredients

- 1 orange large
- 1/2 cup sultanas
- 1/2 cup mixed peel
- 150 g unsalted butter room temperature
- 3/4 cup caster sugar
- 4 eggs
- 1 cup plain flour
- 1 1/2 cups almond meal
- 1 tbs baking powder
- 1 1/2 cups frozen raspberries defrosted
- 500 g marzipan
- 11 white chocolate truffles

Direction

- Preheat oven to 180C (160 degrees fan-forced). Grease and line the base and sides of a 20-22cm springform cake tin.
- Remove zest from the orange, then juice it to yield half a cup. Pour over sultanas and mixed peel in a bowl and allow to soak for 10 minutes.
- Meanwhile, cream butter and sugar until pale and fluffy. Add eggs one at a time, beating well between each addition. Fold through flour, almond meal and baking powder. Add soaked sultanas and mixed peel with the juice,

zest and raspberries, and fold until just combined.
- Roll out one packet of marzipan between two sheets of baking paper to form a circle the same size as your cake tin. Pour half the batter into prepared tin. Gently place marzipan circle onto batter, then pour over remaining batter and smooth the top. Bake for approximately 1 hour until a skewer inserted partially into the top comes out clean. Allow to cool in the tin.
- Roll out second packet of marzipan to the same diameter as the cake. Remove cake from tin and place on serving platter. Drape marzipan over the top of the cake and smooth down. Place truffles evenly around the edge of the cake. Decorate with extra Easter eggs as desired.

293. Raw Blueberry And Hemp Tarts Recipe

Serving: 0 | Prep: 20mins | Cook: 0S | Ready in: 20mins

Ingredients

- 1 tbs almonds
- 1/4 cup hemp flour
- 3 medjool dates
- 1/4 tsp sea salt
- Filling
- 3/4 cup cashews drained soaked in water
- 1/3 cup hemp flour
- 3/4 cup frozen blueberries
- 1 medjool date pitted
- Toppings
- 2 tbs desiccated coconut
- 1 tbs raw cacao nibs
- 1 tbs hemp seeds
- 1 handful fresh blueberries

Direction

- Grease 6 tart cases.

- Place all of the crust ingredients in a food processor and process until the mixture sticks together when pinched.
- Press the mixture into the base and sides of the greased tart cases. Place in the freezer for 20 minutes.
- Place the filling ingredients in a food processor or blend and process until smooth. Spoon the filling into the tart shells.
- Top with coconut, cacao nibs and blueberries. Refrigerate for at least 30 minutes before serving.

294. Raw Muddled Raspberry Cheesecakes

Serving: 0 | Prep: 20mins | Cook: 360mins | Ready in: 380mins

Ingredients

- Base
- 1 cup macadamias
- 1/4 cup coconut
- 6 medjool dates
- 1 g sea salt
- Cheesecake Filling
- 2 cup raw cashews soaked
- 1/2 cup raw organic honey
- 1/2 cup filtered water
- 3 tbs lemon juice
- 1 tsp vanilla essence
- 1/4 cup coconut oil melted
- 2 tbs lecithin powder
- Muddled Berry Jam
- 1 cup frozen raspberries
- 1 tbs raw organic honey
- 2 tbs chia seeds

Direction

- For the base place all ingredients in food processor. Process until mixture comes together. Press into ramekins and place in fridge

- For filling: place first 5 ingredients into the blender. Blend until smooth. Add lecithin and coconut oil, and blend until just mixed. Pour onto the base and place in freezer.
- For berry jam, muddle the 3 ingredients together with a fork. Then pour on top of cheesecake.

295. Reindeer Poop Recipe

Serving: 0 | Prep: 30mins | Cook: 5mins | Ready in: 35mins

Ingredients

- 30 marshmallows
- 660 g dark chocolate
- 100 g macadamias
- 225 g moist coconut flakes

Direction

- Have adequate bench space available and set out cooking trays lined with baking paper.
- Place coconut flakes on a flat plate. Put macadamias in one bowl and marshmallows in another.
- In a microwave safe bowl, melt 1 block of chocolate (or chocolate buttons) on medium heat for 1 minute, stir and return to microwave for a further minute.
- Dip marshmallows into melted chocolate and then place onto coconut flakes to make the bottom look like snow.
- Placed dipped mallows onto baking paper and continue to do the same with nuts, then repeat from step 3.
- Place onto trays and return to fridge to set for about 30 minutes.
- Once set, Place 4-6 marshmallows and a scattering of nuts onto a 30cm square of plastic gift wrap and tie up with ribbon. Add "Reindeer Poop" labels.

296. Rhubarb, Pear And Almond Cake Recipe

Serving: 8 | Prep: 10mins | Cook: 40mins | Ready in: 50mins

Ingredients

- 80 g butter
- 3/4 cup caster sugar
- 1 tsp vanilla essence
- 2 eggs
- 2 pears mashed ripe
- 1 1/3 cup self-raising flour
- 1 tbs milk
- 1 1/2 tsp ground cinnamon
- 4 stalks rhubarb chopped into pieces
- 1 tsp sugar
- 1/3 cup flaked almonds

Direction

- Beat together butter, caster sugar and vanilla until fluffy.
- Add eggs one at a time, beating fully in between.
- Add mashed pear, milk, flour cinnamon and mix until combined.
- Line bottom of a high sided cake tin with GLAD Bake and then pour in the cake mixture.
- Combine rhubarb with sugar in a GLAD bag, give it a shake, then press lightly into the top of the cake mix
- Sprinkle flaked almonds over the top and bake 40 minutes at 180C (170C fan forced). Enjoy.

297. Ricotta Tiramisu Recipe

Serving: 10 | Prep: 10mins | Cook: 70mins | Ready in: 80mins

Ingredients

- 1 cup thickened cream
- 1 cup coffee (liquid)
- 1/2 cup caster sugar
- 200 g Savoiardi sponge finger biscuits
- 2 tsp cocoa powder
- 2 tbs Tia Maria
- 500 g ricotta drained

Direction

- Blend ricotta, cream, sugar and approximately ⅓ cup of coffee until smooth. Don't add all the coffee, taste to see if enough.
- Dip biscuits in remaining coffee and lay in base of a 32 cm deep rectangular, ensuring the base is fully covered.
- Pour one to two tablespoons of Tia Maria over biscuits and then top with the ricotta mix.
- Refrigerate for at least an hour before serving.
- Dust the top with cocoa or shavings of dark chocolate just before serving.

298. Rocky Road Christmas Pudding Recipe

Serving: 0 | Prep: 15mins | Cook: 0S | Ready in: 15mins

Ingredients

- 290g pkt dark chocolate melts
- 100g white marshmallows
- 1 cup shredded coconut
- 1 cup unsalted peanuts
- 150g glace cherries
- 50g white chocolate melts
- 3 spearmint leaf lollies

Direction

- Line a small 3-cup capacity pudding bowl with a few layers of plastic wrap, leaving some overhanging.
- Melt dark chocolate in 30-second bursts in the microwave, stirring in between, until melted and smooth. Pour into a large bowl and add marshmallows, coconut, peanuts and glace cherries, reserving one cherry to garnish.
- Gently stir to combine and pour into prepared pudding dish. Cover with overhanging plastic wrap. Refrigerate for an hour to set.
- Melt white chocolate in 30-second bursts in the microwave, stirring in between, until melted and smooth. Removing pudding from the fridge and gently pull on the plastic wrap to release. Turn out onto a serving dish. Drizzle over with white chocolate and garnish with reserved cherry and spearmint leaves. When white chocolate has set, slice and serve.

299. Rocky Road Recipe

Serving: 10 | Prep: 15mins | Cook: 60mins | Ready in: 75mins

Ingredients

- 500 g milk chocolate melted
- 200 g marshmallows chopped
- 1/4 cup desiccated coconut
- 110 g Turkish delight chopped
- 1/2 cup peanuts chopped

Direction

- Combine all ingredients in a large bowl and mix well.
- Pour mixture into a lined slice tin and refrigerate until set.
- Use a warm knife to cut the slice into small squares.

300. Rocky Road Skillet Cookie

Serving: 8 | Prep: 30mins | Cook: 20mins | Ready in: 50mins

Ingredients

- 125 g butter
- 1/3 cup brown sugar
- 1/3 cup caster sugar
- 1 egg
- 1 cup plain flour
- 1/2 tsp bicarbonate of soda
- 1/4 cup desiccated coconut
- 1/4 cup roasted salted peanuts chopped
- 100 g marshmallows cut in half
- 1 tbs shredded coconut
- 40 g 70% cocoa dark chocolate melted cooled slightly

Direction

- Over medium heat, melt butter in a large skillet or oven-proof frying pan (approximately 22cm base and 28cm top). Stand for 10 minutes to cool slightly.
- Preheat oven to 180C or 160C fan-forced.
- Add sugars to skillet and whisk until combined. Add egg and whisk to combine.
- Sift flour and bicarbonate of soda over pan. Stir until combined.
- Add desiccated coconut and peanuts. Stir until combined. Press down with spatula to level dough.
- Bake for 17 minutes, or until skewer inserted in centre comes out clean.
- Take cookie out of the oven and top with marshmallows. Sprinkle with shredded coconut.
- Place under hot grill for 1 to 1 1/2 minutes, or until marshmallows are golden.
- Drizzle melted chocolate over top. Best served warm. You can cut into individual wedges or give each person a spoon to eat straight from the warm pan.

301. Rocky Road White Christmas Recipe

Serving: 10 | Prep: 15mins | Cook: 10mins | Ready in: 25mins

Ingredients

- 1 cup coconut
- 1 cup milk powder
- 1 cup icing sugar mixture
- 1 1/2 cup Rice Bubbles
- 50 g walnuts chopped
- 90 g red glace cherries chopped
- 125 g pink marshmallows chopped
- 250 g copha melted
- 250 g dark cooking chocolate melted
- 30 g margarine melted

Direction

- Line a lamington tin with baking paper.
- Combine coconut, powdered milk, icing sugar mixture, Rice Bubbles, walnuts, cherries and pink marshmallows in large bowl, mixing well.
- Add melted copha and mix well.
- Turn mixture into lamington tin, smooth the top and refrigerate until set.
- Combine dark cooking chocolate and margarine, and pour on top of mixture.
- Refrigerate until set.
- Cut into squares and store in refrigerator.

302. Rum Balls Recipe

Serving: 10 | Prep: 15mins | Cook: 0S | Ready in: 15mins

Ingredients

- 250 g Arnott's Milk Arrowroot biscuits crushed
- 395 g NESTLE Sweetened Condensed Milk
- 1 cup coconut
- 1/4 cup cocoa
- 1 1/2 tbs rum *to taste
- 1 cup coconut *to decorate *extra

Direction

- Combine all ingredients.

- Wet hands and roll mixture into small balls then coat in coconut.
- Refrigerate or freeze for later.

303. Sam Wood's Choc Mint Slice Recipe

Serving: 12 | Prep: 15mins | Cook: 0S | Ready in: 15mins

Ingredients

- 1 cup almonds raw unsalted
- 1/2 cup desiccated coconut
- 1/2 tbs cacao powder
- 1 pinch salt
- 2 tbs extra virgin coconut oil
- Filling and icing
- 1/4 cup cashews raw soaked overnight
- 1/4 cup coconut cream
- 10 drops peppermint oil
- 6 medjool dates pitted
- 150 g 85% dark chocolate melted *to decorate

Direction

- Line a square baking tray with baking paper.
- Blitz base ingredients together in a food processor. Transfer to lined tray and push down firmly and evenly to cover base. Refrigerate or freeze.
- Meanwhile to make the filling, drain and rinse cashews and put into a clean blender or food processor along with all second set of ingredients. Blitz to a butter.
- Remove base from refrigerator and spoon mixture over the top. Smooth out the top evenly. Refrigerate or freeze for a further 10-15 minutes.
- Drizzle with melted dark chocolate, return to freezer to set for a few minutes.
- Slice and serve.

304. Self Saucing Chocolate Pudding

Serving: 6 | Prep: 25mins | Cook: 50mins | Ready in: 75mins

Ingredients

- 1 cup self-raising flour
- 2 tbs cocoa powder
- 1/2 cup caster sugar
- 1/2 cup milk
- 1 tsp vanilla essence
- 1 egg
- 60g butter melted
- Topping
- 1 cup brown sugar lightly packed
- 1 tbs cocoa powder
- 1 3/4 cup boiling water

Direction

- Preheat oven to 180C. Butter a casserole dish with a 5-cup capacity.
- Sift flour and cocoa into a mixing bowl. Add sugar.
- Mix milk with vanilla, egg and butter.
- Make a well in the centre of dry ingredients and pour in milk mixture. Beat well with a wooden spoon for about 30 seconds.
- Spoon mixture into prepared dish.
- To make the topping, crush any lumps in sugar, sift cocoa over the top. Scatter over pudding mixture.
- Pour boiling water over pudding as evenly as possible.
- Bake for 45-50 minutes and serve.

305. Shortbread Biscuits Recipe

Serving: 12 | Prep: 10mins | Cook: 60mins | Ready in: 70mins

Ingredients

- 150 g plain flour
- 100 g butter
- 50 g sugar
- 1 tsp vanilla essence optional

Direction

- Chop flour and butter together and rub into small crumbs.
- Add sugar and work together to form a firm dough.
- Wrap in plastic and rest in fridge for 20 minutes.
- Roll out onto a sugared bench top.
- Cut shapes and bake on a dry baking tray for approximately 20 minutes at 180C.
- For chocolate shortbreads, replace 40 g of the flour with cocoa powder.

306. Shortbread Simple Recipe

Serving: 10 | Prep: 15mins | Cook: 25mins | Ready in: 40mins

Ingredients

- 2 cups plain flour
- 2 tbs rice flour
- 1/2 cup caster sugar
- 250 g butter

Direction

- Sift flours into a large bowl, then add sugar and rub in the butter.
- Roll mixture out on a floured surface to 1.5 cm thickness.
- Cut into desired shapes.
- Place on a baking tray and bake at 160C for 25 minutes.

307. Shortbread Recipe

Serving: 0 | Prep: 20mins | Cook: 35mins | Ready in: 55mins

Ingredients

- 225g butter softened
- 225g plain flour
- 115g rice flour
- 115g caster sugar
- 1 pinch salt
- 24 glace cherries

Direction

- Preheat oven to 150C. Sift dry ingredients together. Add softened butter and mix together with hands until well blended.
- Sprinkle some flour on a chopping board and flatten dough with hands until approximately 1cm thick.
- Cut dough with cookie cutters and place biscuits on a tray. Place a glazed cherry in the middle of each biscuit and bake in the oven for 35 minutes.
- Cool on tray for 10 minutes then place on wire rack until cold to touch.

308. Simple Banana Muffins Recipe

Serving: 0 | Prep: 15mins | Cook: 25mins | Ready in: 40mins

Ingredients

- 2 1/2 cups self-raising flour
- 3/4 cup brown sugar
- 1 cup milk
- 1 egg
- 2 tbs margarine
- 1 tsp vanilla extract
- 2 bananas ripe

Direction

- Combine milk, egg, margarine, vanilla and bananas, and blend in a mixing jug.
- Place flour and sugar in a large bowl. Mix in milk mixture.
- Pour mixture into a greased muffin tray.
- Bake for 20-25 minutes at 180C.

309. Simple Chocolate Cupcakes Recipe

Serving: 0 | Prep: 15mins | Cook: 20mins | Ready in: 35mins

Ingredients

- 3/4 cup plain flour
- 1/4 cup cocoa powder
- 1/2 cup caster sugar
- 2 tsp baking powder
- 1/2 tsp vanilla essence
- 80g unsalted butter
- 1/2 cup milk
- 2 eggs

Direction

- Preheat oven to 160C. Prepare 12 hole muffin tray or 24 hole mini muffin tray.
- Sift all dry ingredients into a mixing bowl.
- Make a small well in the middle of the bowl and then add remaining ingredients.
- Beat on low speed with electric mixer until just combined.
- Scrape down sides of bowl and beat on medium speed for a further two minutes.
- Place tablespoons of the mixture into 12 hole muffin tray until holes are half full. Heaped teaspoon of mixture for mini muffins.
- Place tray into oven for 15-18 minutes for 12 hole muffin pan or 10-12 minutes for mini muffin pan.
- Stand for 5 minutes and then turn out onto wire rack to cool.
- Ice or leave plain if preferred.

310. Slab Lova With Strawberry Curd Recipe

Serving: 8 | Prep: 15mins | Cook: 110mins | Ready in: 125mins

Ingredients

- 6 egg whites
- 1 1/2 cups caster sugar
- 1 tbs cornflour
- 1 tsp white vinegar
- Strawberry curd
- 250 g fresh strawberries hulled roughly chopped
- 3/4 cup caster sugar
- 125 g unsalted butter softened
- 1 tsp lemon zest grated
- 1 tbs lemon juice
- 5 egg yolks
- To serve
- 300 ml thickened cream
- 1 tsp caster sugar
- 1/4 tsp vanilla extract
- 1 punnet fresh raspberries
- 1 punnet fresh strawberries
- 20 g dark chocolate room temperature

Direction

- For the pavlova: Preheat oven to low 120C/100C fan-forced. Line a large baking tray (approx. 40cm x 30cm) with baking paper.
- Beat egg whites in a clean large bowl with an electric mixer until soft peaks form. Only then add caster sugar, a heaped tablespoon or so at a time, beating until dissolved (to test, rub some mixture between finger if too grainy, keep beating until glossy). Then fold in cornflour and vinegar.
- Turn out onto tray; using a palette knife or spatula, spread the mixture across the baking paper (approx. 30cm x 24cm), building up the

sides a little and creating a few tips and dips in the meringue as you go. (A wet spoon, spatula or palette knife helps.)
- Bake in very slow oven for about 1 ½ hours, or until set and dry (surface should be dry to touch). Turn oven off and prop door ajar with a wooden spoon and cool in oven.
- For the curd: Put the strawberries in a small saucepan with the sugar, butter, lemon zest and lemon juice. Stir over low heat until the butter has melted and the sugar dissolved.
- Simmer gently for 5 minutes, then remove from the heat.
- Lightly beat the egg yolks in a large bowl then, stirring constantly, slowly add the strawberry mixture in a thin stream. The mixture will thicken as you add it.
- Return to low heat and cook for 3 minutes, stirring constantly. Do not allow the mixture to boil or the curd will curdle.
- Test by running a finger across the back of the spoon to ensure the curd is thick and does not run.
- Put into a bowl and cover with plastic wrap to prevent a skin forming.
- To assemble: Whip cream with sugar and vanilla.
- Spread a small spoon of cream on a flat serving plate.
- Place pavlova on top then fill pavlova with curd, cream (ensuring you can still see some of the curd), then berries.
- Shave chocolate curls from a block of chocolate using a vegetable peeler.

311. Slow Cooker Christmas Cake Recipe

Serving: 0 | Prep: 10mins | Cook: 300mins | Ready in: 310mins

Ingredients

- 1kg mixed dried fruit
- 395g tin condensed milk
- 1 cup milk
- 1 cup Baileys Irish Cream
- 1 orange, zested and juiced
- 2 cups plain flour
- 2 tsp ground cinnamon
- 1/2 tsp ground nutmeg
- 1/2 tsp allspice

Direction

- Place dried fruit in a bowl with condensed milk, milk, Baileys and orange zest and juice. Stir well, cover and leave to soak overnight in the fridge.
- Remove from fridge and bring to room temperature. Stir well. Combine flour with spices, then fold through dried fruit mixture.
- Line base and sides of a slow cooker with 2 layers of baking paper, greasing the top layer with a little oil or butter. Pour in batter and smooth over the top. Place a tea towel over the top of the slow cooker just under the lid. Cook for 4 hours on low, until a skewer inserted into the centre comes out clean. Remove from slow cooker and allow to cool.

312. Snickers Slice: No Bake Recipe

Serving: 0 | Prep: 35mins | Cook: 0S | Ready in: 35mins

Ingredients

- 2 cups milk chocolate melts
- 145 g smooth peanut butter
- 200 g white marshmallows
- 1 1/2 cups icing sugar
- 400 g jersey caramels
- 1/2 cup thickened cream
- 1/2 cup peanuts

Direction

- Line a 28cm x 18cm slice tin with baking paper.
- Put 1 cup of the chocolate melts plus 3 tablespoons of the peanut butter into a heatproof bowl. Microwave for one minute, stir and heat again for another 20 seconds or until it's all smooth and melted.
- Pour the melted chocolate mixture into the base of the pan and put it in the freezer for about five minutes, or until it's set.
- In a clean bowl, place the marshmallows and microwave them for one minute (or until melted.) Stir in 1/4 cup of peanut butter and add the icing sugar.
- Stir the marshmallow mixture with a wooden spoon until it all combines to form a sticky dough. Press the dough onto the top of the first chocolate layer.
- Sprinkle that layer with peanuts and press them in with your fingers.
- Put the caramels and cream into a saucepan and melt over a medium heat until it is all smooth and combined. Pour the caramel layer on top of the sticky marshmallow dough layer.
- Put it in the freezer for about five minutes, or until set.
- In a heatproof bowl, melt the remaining 1 cup plus 3 tablespoons of peanut butter in the microwave. Pour the melted chocolate over the top of the set caramel layer.
- Refrigerate it for 10 - 15 minutes, or until set. Cut it into bars and eat it. (Not all at once, just have once piece every afternoon at 3pm.)

313. Snowballs Recipe

Serving: 24 | Prep: 5mins | Cook: 0S | Ready in: 5mins

Ingredients

- 9 Sanitarium Weet-Bix
- 1 cup desiccated coconut
- 1 cup sultanas
- 2 tbs cocoa
- 400 g condensed milk
- 1/2 cup desiccated coconut *to decorate

Direction

- Crush Weet-Bix finely in a large bowl.
- Add coconut, sultanas and cocoa and mix well.
- Add condensed milk and mix together well.
- Roll into walnut-sized balls, then roll in extra coconut.
- Place in fridge to firm up. Store in an airtight container in the fridge.

314. Soft Caramel Fudge Recipe

Serving: 0 | Prep: 15mins | Cook: 140mins | Ready in: 155mins

Ingredients

- 125 g butter
- 395 g NESTLE Sweetened Condensed Milk
- 2 tbs golden syrup
- 1 cup brown sugar
- 3/4 cup white chocolate chopped into pieces small

Direction

- Line a 7 cm x 25 cm bar tin with baking paper.
- Melt butter in a medium saucepan over a low heat. Add condensed milk, golden syrup and brown sugar.
- Stir over a low heat until it comes to the boil, then simmer for 10 minutes, stirring constantly.
- Remove from heat, stir in white chocolate and mix until smooth.
- Pour into prepared tin and allow to cool. Refrigerate for at least two hours. Serve cut into squares or slices.

315. Sour Cream Apple Slice Recipe

Serving: 12 | Prep: 15mins | Cook: 60mins | Ready in: 75mins

Ingredients

- 340g buttercake cake mix
- 125g butter melted
- 300g light sour cream
- 1 cup coconut
- 2 eggs beaten
- 440g canned pie apple
- 1 tsp ground cinnamon

Direction

- Combine cake mix, coconut and butter and press into greased 30cm x 20cm slice tin.
- Bake at 180C for 10-15 minutes or until golden brown.
- Spread apple over base while still warm, combine sour cream and beaten eggs then pour mix over base, sprinkle with cinnamon.
- Bake a further 15-20 minutes.
- Stand for 15 minutes until set. Keep refrigerated.

316. Speculaas And Coconut No Bake Cheesecake Recipe

Serving: 0 | Prep: 10mins | Cook: 240mins | Ready in: 250mins

Ingredients

- 150 g Speculaas biscuits
- 100 g butter
- 3 tbs brown sugar
- 1/2 cup desiccated coconut
- Filling
- 1 vanilla pod seeds removed
- 1/4 cup lime juice
- 1/4 cup water
- 4 tsp gelatine powder
- 680 g cream cheese
- 595 g sweetened condensed milk

Direction

- Line a 9 inch cake tin and set aside, don't just grease the base. As you're not cooking this cheesecake the butter won't melt beneath it to lubricate it, instead it will just act as glue and you won't be able to remove your cheesecake from the base once it's set.
- Place all ingredients for your base into a food processor and blitz until well combined.
- Scrape your base mix into your pre-prepared tin, and using the back of a spoon spread it out evenly, compacting it lightly as you go. Set aside.
- Place 1/4 cup of water into a saucepan and set on a cold stovetop. Sprinkle gelatine on the surface of the water and heat the water slowly, whisking gently with a fork until the gelatine has dissolved. Avoid allowing the mixture to boil as gelatine is sensitive to boiling temperatures and exposure to this sort of heat can cause it to lose it ability to set. Set aside to cool slightly.
- Place cream cheese and lime juice into a large mixing bowl and combine with an electric beater on a medium speed.
- Once loosely combined, add the seeds from your vanilla pod and gelatine, turn your mixer to full speed and gradually pour in your condensed milk. Continue to beat your cream cheese mixture until there are no lumps.
- Pour cream cheese mixture into your cake tin atop your base and set in the fridge to set for a minimum of 4 hours. Remove from tin and serve!

317. Sponge Flan With Cheesecake Cream And Strawberries

Serving: 8 | Prep: 20mins | Cook: 0S | Ready in: 20mins

Ingredients

- 200 g sweet flan pastry cases
- 80 ml orange juice to coat
- 125 g soft cream cheese
- 1 tbs orange rind, finely grated
- 2 tsp orange juice
- 2 tbs icing sugar mixture
- 250 ml thickened cream
- 250 g fresh strawberries thinly sliced
- 1/3 cup strawberry jam sieved warmed

Direction

- Place flan case on a serving plate and brush all over with the orange juice to soften.
- Beat cream cheese, orange rind, extra juice and icing sugar in a small bowl with an electric mixer until smooth.
- Beat the cream in a separate bowl until soft peaks form; fold into the cream cheese mixture.
- Fill the flan case with the cream mixture.
- Arrange sliced strawberries over the cream and brush strawberries with the jam.

318. Stay Fresh Scones Recipe

Serving: 0 | Prep: 15mins | Cook: 40mins | Ready in: 55mins

Ingredients

- 500g self-raising flour
- 1 egg
- 1 1/2 cup milk
- 1 tbs icing sugar
- 2 tsp baking powder
- 60g butter melted

Direction

- Sift dry ingredients into a bowl.
- Add beaten egg, milk and butter.
- Quickly combine all ingredients into a dough.
- Stand dough on a floured board for 20 minutes.
- Gently roll out to required thickness (about 2cm).
- Cut out circles using the rim of a glass dipped in flour.
- Stand scones close together on a lightly floured baking tray for a further 15 minutes.
- Bake at 210C for 10 minutes.

319. Stewed Rhubarb Recipe

Serving: 4 | Prep: 10mins | Cook: 20mins | Ready in: 30mins

Ingredients

- 1 bunch rhubarb dried trimmed washed
- 55 g raw sugar

Direction

- Cut rhubarb into 25 mm (approximately) chunks and weigh.
- Put rhubarb into a saucepan.
- Add raw sugar at the rate of ¼ (25%) of the weight of the rhubarb. Stir.
- Cover and cook over low heat until the rhubarb breaks down to desired consistency, approximately 10-15 minutes, stirring occasionally.

320. Sticky Mixed Fruit Puddings Recipe

Serving: 0 | Prep: 0S | Cook: 20mins | Ready in: 20mins

Ingredients

- Puddings
- 2 cup Sunbeam Gourmet Selection mixed fruit
- 3/4 cup boiling water
- 1/2 tsp bicarbonate of soda
- 60 g butter
- 1/2 cup brown sugar lightly packed
- 2 egg
- 1 1/2 cup self-raising flour
- 50 g butter
- 1/2 cup brown sugar
- 300 ml thickened cream
- 1 caramel sauce *to serve

Direction

- Preheat oven to 160°C. Grease 8 mini pudding moulds and line the bottom with baking paper.
- Place half the fruit, boiling water and bicarb into a bowl. Soak for 10minutes.
- Blend fruit mixture, butter, sugar, eggs and flour in a blender until combined. Stir in remaining fruit.
- Spoon mixture into moulds and bake for 20mins. Serve with sauce.
- Melt butter, sugar and cream in a saucepan over low heat. Stir until it starts to boil. Remove from heat.

321. Strawberries 'n' Cream Recipe

Serving: 4 | Prep: 20mins | Cook: 10mins | Ready in: 30mins

Ingredients

- 1/4 cup blanched almonds
- 1/4 cup caster sugar
- 5 filo pastry sheets thawed
- 50 g butter melted
- 250 g fresh strawberries cut in half hulled
- 1 tbs Grand Marnier
- 300 ml cream
- 1 tbs icing sugar
- 1 tsp vanilla essence
- 1 tbs icing sugar *to decorate

Direction

- Preheat oven to 180C degrees.
- Place almonds and caster sugar into a food processor and pulse until it resembles fine crumbs.
- Lay filo pastry out on workbench and brush one sheet with melted butter. Sprinkle 1 tablespoon of the sugar mixture onto the pastry sheet. Place second filo sheet on top and brush with melted butter and sprinkle with sugar. Repeat with all remaining sheets of pastry and sugar mixture. Trim edges from filo pastry to make smooth edges. Cut filo pastry into desired size, I used 6x7cm. Place cut pieces on a baking tray and bake in preheated oven for 8-10 mins, or until cooked and lightly golden. Allow to cool.
- Place strawberries in a bowl and pour over Grand Marnier.
- In a separate bowl, add cream, icing sugar and vanilla essence into a bowl and whip until stiff peaks form.
- To assemble, place some cream onto cooled filo square. Top with strawberries and then another filo square. Top with cream and strawberries and then a filo square. Continue until all filo has been used. To serve, dust with extra icing sugar.

322. Strawberry Cake Recipe

Serving: 8 | Prep: 20mins | Cook: 45mins | Ready in: 65mins

Ingredients

- 125 g butter
- 1/2 cup caster sugar
- 2 eggs
- 1 tsp vanilla essence
- 2 cups self-raising flour sifted

- 1/2 cup milk
- 1 cup fresh strawberries mashed
- 1 tsp strawberry essence optional *to taste
- Strawberry icing
- 3 fresh strawberries mashed medium
- 1 1/2 cups pure icing sugar

Direction

- Cake: Preheat oven to 180C (160C fan-forced).
- Lightly grease and line a 20cm cake pan.
- Beat the butter and sugar until light and fluffy.
- Add the eggs and vanilla, and beat until smooth.
- Fold in the flour and milk, mixing well.
- Add strawberries to the mix and fold together, add strawberry essence.
- Spoon mixture into the cake pan.
- Bake for 40-45 minutes, or until a skewer inserted comes out clean. Allow to cool.
- Strawberry icing: Add icing sugar to strawberries, mix until combined.
- Spread onto cold cake and serve.

323. Strawberry Cheesecake Recipe

Serving: 8 | Prep: 30mins | Cook: 0S | Ready in: 30mins

Ingredients

- 250 g Arnott's Marie biscuits crushed
- 125 g butter melted
- Filling
- 85 g jelly crystals
- 2 tsp gelatine powder
- 1 cup boiling water
- 175 ml CARNATION Light & Creamy Evaporated Milk
- 250 g cream cheese
- 2/3 cup sugar
- 1/2 cup fresh strawberries pureed
- 1 punnet fresh strawberries *to decorate

Direction

- Mix biscuit crumbs and butter.
- Line the base and sides of a large cheesecake pan with crumb mixture. Refrigerate until set.
- Combine jelly crystals, gelatine and boiling water and mix well. Place in fridge.
- Beat cream cheese and sugar until smooth. Add strawberry puree and strawberry jelly mixture. Mix well.
- In a clean bowl, beat milk until thick. Add jelly mixture and cream cheese, and combine well.
- Pour mixture into biscuit base and place in fridge to set.
- When firm, gently top with fresh strawberries.

324. Strawberry Pavlova Roll Recipe

Serving: 8 | Prep: 15mins | Cook: 1470mins | Ready in: 1485mins

Ingredients

- 4 egg whites
- 3/4 cup sugar
- 1 tsp white vinegar
- 1 tsp cornflour
- 1 tsp vanilla essence
- 300 ml whipped cream
- 250 g fresh strawberries
- 2 passionfruit optional

Direction

- Grease a Swiss roll tin and line with baking paper. Preheat oven to 170C.
- Beat egg whites until soft peaks form.
- Add sugar gradually and continue beating until mixture is stiff and glossy and all sugar is dissolved.
- Gently fold through vanilla, cornflour and vinegar.
- Spread meringue evenly into prepared tin. Bake for 12-15 minutes.

- Allow to cool completely before turning out onto sugared baking paper.
- Spread with whipped cream and top with sliced strawberries.
- Roll up from long side and place on serving plate, still covered with the baking paper.
- Refrigerate for 24 hours.
- Decorate top with strawberries and passionfruit if desired.

325. Strawberry Ripple Cheesecake Recipe

Serving: 8 | Prep: 180mins | Cook: 0S | Ready in: 180mins

Ingredients

- 250 g chocolate biscuits crushed
- 125 g butter melted
- 250 g fresh strawberries pureed
- 250 g fresh strawberries *to decorate *extra
- 1 cup whipped cream *to decorate
- Filling
- 3 tsp gelatine powder
- 1/3 cup water
- 250 g lite cream cheese
- 200 g low-fat strawberry yoghurt
- 1/2 cup caster sugar
- 300 g thickened cream whipped

Direction

- Combine biscuits and melted butter, then press into base and sides of a 22cm springform tin.
- Sprinkle gelatine over water in a cup.
- Stand cup in a pan of simmering water, until dissolved and then cool slightly.
- Beat cream cheese, yoghurt and sugar in a bowl until smooth.
- Gently fold in cream and gelatine.
- Pour half the filling over biscuit base and cover with half of the strawberry puree.

- Using a fork, gently swirl puree through filling.
- Repeat with remaining filling and puree, and swirl with a fork.
- Cover, then refrigerate for several hours, or until set.
- Serve decorated with extra whipped cream and strawberries.

326. Strawberry And White Choc Muffins Recipe

Serving: 0 | Prep: 5mins | Cook: 20mins | Ready in: 25mins

Ingredients

- 3 eggs
- 1 cup caster sugar
- 1 1/2 cups cream
- 2 cups self-raising flour
- 1 tsp vanilla essence
- 1 punnet fresh strawberries cut into pieces
- 300g white chocolate melts

Direction

- Beat eggs and sugar together. Add 1 cup of cream and vanilla.
- Fold in flour and strawberries.
- Melt white chocolate and add to mixture, mix until combined. Add remaining cream if mix is dry or not very smooth.
- Place into muffin trays and bake at 180C for 15-20 minutes.

327. Stuffed Strawberries

Serving: 4 | Prep: 15mins | Cook: 0S | Ready in: 15mins

Ingredients

- 1 punnet fresh strawberries large

- 150 g cream cheese
- 3/4 tsp vanilla extract
- 2 tsp icing sugar

Direction

- Beat cream cheese, vanilla and icing sugar until well combined.
- Wash strawberries and cut off the stalk end.
- Stand the strawberries on the cut end.
- Cut the pointed end to form a cross.
- Pipe or spoon cream cheese mixture into the cavity.
- Chill until ready to serve.

328. Sugar Free Mango Nice Ice Cream Recipe

Serving: 4 | Prep: 5mins | Cook: 0S | Ready in: 5mins

Ingredients

- 2 mangoes, peeled, pitted, cut into 2cm pieces, frozen
- 1 banana, roughly sliced, frozen
- 2 tbs milk

Direction

- Place mango, banana and 2 tbs of milk in a blender and blend until smooth. If the mixture still looks thick, gradually add more milk.
- Enjoy immediately or store in a container in the freezer to serve later.

329. Sugar Free Vanilla Cheesecake With Mango Topping Recipe

Serving: 0 | Prep: 200mins | Cook: 0S | Ready in: 200mins

Ingredients

- Base
- 250 g biscuits
- 70 g butter melted
- Filling
- 1/2 cup boiling water
- 2 tbs gelatine powder
- 500 g cream cheese room temperature
- 450 ml cream
- 1 tsp vanilla extract
- 1 tsp sugar substitute
- Topping (optional)
- 1/2 cup boiling water
- 2 tbs gelatine powder
- 40 g canned mango in syrup
- 3 drops orange liquid food colouring optional
- 1/2 tsp sugar substitute

Direction

- Line the bottom of a loose-based 25 cm cheesecake tin with baking paper.
- Crush or process the biscuits until they resemble fine breadcrumbs, then combine with the melted butter. Press into the base of the tin and refrigerate.
- Filling: Stir the gelatine into the boiling water until dissolved, then combine with the remaining filling ingredients in a blender or food processor. Blend until very smooth, and add more stevia if desired.
- Pour onto the base, and refrigerate until firm for at least 2 hours.
- Topping: Stir the gelatine into the boiling water until dissolved, then combine with the mango juice, food colouring (if using) and stevia.
- Slice the mango cheeks into thin strips and arrange over the filling, then carefully pour over the liquid mixture. Refrigerate until set for approximately 1 hour.
- To serve, run a fine knife around the edge of the tin before opening tin and carefully lifting it off the cheesecake. Transfer the cheesecake to a serving plate, loosening it first by inserting an egg-slide between the base and

the baking paper, and then using it to lever the base away as it slides onto the serving plate.

330. Summer Trifle With Pineapple Recipe

Serving: 3 | Prep: 15mins | Cook: 375mins | Ready in: 390mins

Ingredients

- 85 g jelly crystals
- 85 g jelly crystals
- 600 ml thickened cream
- 1 cup brandy *to taste
- 1 cup caster sugar
- 2 x 450 g Madeira
- 700 ml Midori
- 400 g (sliced) canned pineapple cut in half
- 400 g canned peaches quartered
- 1 L brandy custard
- 1 cup passionfruit juice

Direction

- Make jellies up to 500 mL each and allow to set overnight.
- Whip cream. Add brandy and caster sugar to taste.
- Cut sponge into 1½ cm slices and use to line the bottom of a very large clear bowl. Douse with Midori, Cointreau or juice.
- Line alternating pineapple and peach slices around the edges of the bowl.
- Pour over custard, then scatter jelly and passionfruit on top.
- Spread whipped cream evenly over the top.
- Repeat process from sponge layer until bowl is near full, then decorate with leftover cream, jelly, and fruit.
- Leave to set in fridge before serving.

331. Super Moist Chocolate Cupcakes Recipe

Serving: 24 | Prep: 45mins | Cook: 60mins | Ready in: 105mins

Ingredients

- 1 3/4 cups plain flour
- 1 3/4 cups caster sugar
- 1/4 cup dark brown sugar
- 1 1/2 tsp baking powder
- 3/4 cup cocoa powder
- 85 g instant pudding mix
- 1 tbs vanilla extract
- 1 cup buttermilk
- 125 g unsalted butter melted
- 1/4 cup vegetable oil
- 2 eggs
- 2 tsp coffee powder
- 1 cup boiling water
- Icing
- 600 g dark chocolate
- 225 g cream

Direction

- Preheat oven to 180C (160C fan-forced).
- Line 2 x 12 hole muffin trays with paper cases.
- Combine all dry ingredients apart from coffee in a large bowl of an electric mixer.
- Make a well in the centre of dry mix.
- Add eggs, buttermilk, vanilla, butter and vegetable oil into well, beat on high speed until smooth and well combined. The mixture will be very thick at this stage.
- Mix coffee powder with boiling water and add to mix, folding in with a spatula until well combined.
- Divide equally into paper cases.
- Bake on centre rack for 17-20 minutes or until a skewer inserted into centre comes out clean with just some moist crumbs clinging to it.
- Remove from oven, allow to cool slightly then remove from trays and place on wire cooling rack(s) until completely cool.
- Pipe with pre-prepared ganache icing.

- Icing: Break chocolate into squares and place with cream in a heat-proof bowl over a pot of simmering water.
- Stir occasionally until chocolate has melted and is completely combined with cream. The mixture will be thick, smooth and glossy.
- Remove from heat and allow to cool completely to room temperature. Refrigerate if desired.
- Beat well with electric beaters until thick and creamy but still holding its shape.
- Spread or pipe onto each cooled cupcake.

- Roll out pastry between two sheets of baking paper until 3mm thick. Use a round 6cm-diameter pastry cutter to cut 24 circles from the pastry. Line the base of 24-hole non-stick mini muffin pan (or use two 12-hole pans). Fill cases with fruit mince.
- Re-roll pastry and use a 4cm-diameter fluted pastry cutter to cut 24 circles for the lids. Brush the underside of lid lightly with water before gently pressing onto pie. Cut a small cross in the middle of each lid.
- Bake for 15 minutes or until golden. Allow to cool and dust with icing sugar before serving. Store in an airtight container for up to 1 week.

332. Sweet Petite Mince Tarts Recipe

Serving: 0 | Prep: 0S | Cook: 15mins | Ready in: 15mins

Ingredients

- Fruit mince
- 200 g Sunbeam mixed fruit chopped
- 2 tbs golden syrup
- 1 tsp lemon rind, finely grated
- 1 tsp mixed spice
- 1/4 cup brandy
- Pastry
- 1/2 cup Sunbeam almond meal
- 2 cup plain flour
- 1/2 cup caster sugar
- 200 g unsalted butter chilled diced
- 1 egg lightly beaten
- 1 tbs water lightly beaten
- 25 g icing sugar *to serve

Direction

- Preheat oven to 180°C
- Place all fruit mince ingredients in a saucepan. Simmer for 5 minutes, stirring occasionally. Allow to cool.
- Place almond meal, flour and sugar into a food processor and process until combined. Add butter and egg mixture and process until a ball forms. Wrap and refrigerate for 30 minutes.

333. Sweet Potato Marshmallow Pie Recipe

Serving: 10 | Prep: 180mins | Cook: 75mins | Ready in: 255mins

Ingredients

- Pastry
- 2 cups self-raising flour plus extra for dusting
- 125g unsalted butter cubed
- 2 tbs white granulated sugar
- 1 egg
- 2 tbs water
- Filling
- 1kg sweet potatoes
- 65g unsalted butter
- 3/4 cup brown sugar lightly packed
- 1/2 cup thickened cream
- 2 eggs
- Egg wash
- 1 egg
- 2 tbs milk
- Marshmallow
- 2/3 cup water
- 500g white granulated sugar
- Pinch of salt
- 6 1/2 tsp gelatin powder
- 1/2 cup boiled water

Direction

- Pre-heat your oven to 180C. Wrap sweet potatoes in foil and place in the oven until cooked through and the centre of the potatoes is soft.
- Meanwhile, grease your pie tin thoroughly and drop in 1tbsp of plain flour. Tilt and roll the tin around so as the flour coats all surfaces and tap the excess out into the bin.
- To make the pastry, combine self-raising flour, 2 tbs sugar and 125g butter in a food processor and blitz until the mixture resembles a crumble.
- Add egg and water to the food processor and blitz until your pastry forms into a ball.
- Remove your pastry from the food processor, press into a ball, wrap in glad wrap and place in the fridge for 30 minutes.
- Retrieve your pastry from the fridge, lightly flour your bench top, and using a rolling pin, roll your pastry out into a circle roughly 2mm - 3mm thick.
- Carefully drape your pastry over your pre-prepared pie tin, press it into the base and using a sharp knife, cut off any excess, overhanging pastry. Set aside.
- Once your potatoes are done, remove them from the oven, while hot, carefully peel off the skin and place the fleshy part of the potato into a large mixing bowl.
- Add butter to the mixing bowl and using a hand masher roughly mash your sweet potatoes.
- Pour in your thickened cream, brown sugar and 2 lightly whisked eggs. Combine roughly with your hand masher. Swap out your hand masher for a stick blender, and blend until smooth.
- Recover your pie dish, spoon your sweet potato mixture into the centre and (depending on the look you're going for) smooth the mixture flat with a spatula, or 'rustically' push your sweet potato mix out the edges.
- Crack an egg into a clean bowl, whisk roughly with a fork. Add 2 tbs milk and whisk with a fork until well combined.
- Paint egg mixture onto any visible pie pastry, and set in the oven to bake for 1 hour and 15 minutes. Once cooked through (a skewer inserted into the centre of your pie should be removed clean), set aside to come to room temperature.
- Once cooled completely, place 2/3 cup water and 500g sugar into a saucepan over a medium to high heat. Once the sugar has melted into the water, clip a candy thermometer onto the side of your saucepan, ensure the tip is immersed in the toffee, and allow it to come to roughly 116C.
- Meanwhile (as the temperature is nearing 116C), boil the kettle, pour 1/2 cup boiling water into your mixing bowl (of a stand mixer, if you have one) and sprinkle 6 1/2 tsp of gelatin powder across the water's surface. Let sit for a moment, then whisk the gelatin into the water until thoroughly combined. Add 1 tsp of vanilla essence and set aside.
- Once your toffee has reached temperature, remove it from the heat, and set it down on a cool part of the cook-top for roughly 2 minutes to cool slightly.
- Turn your electric beaters onto its lowest setting, and start mixing your gelatin as you pour your toffee down the side of your mixing bowl, allowing it to slowly drip into your gelatin.
- Once all the toffee has been incorporated, turn your beaters onto the highest setting and whisk until the mixture has roughly doubled in size and is smooth, glossy and holds stiff peaks (10-15 minutes).
- Spoon your marshmallow mixture into the centre of your sweet potato pie and slowly work it out towards the edges (I left mine just shy of the edge so you can see some of the pretty sweet potato filling).
- Let sit overnight to allow the marshmallow to set. Torch your marshmallow with a butane torch and serve.

334. TIFFXO: Tiffiny Hall's Spelt Chocolate And Zucchini Muffins Recipe

Serving: 12 | Prep: 15mins | Cook: 20mins | Ready in: 35mins

Ingredients

- 125 g coconut oil
- 120 g Capilano* Light & Smooth Honey
- 150 g wholemeal spelt flour
- 100 g LSA seed mix
- 1 tsp baking powder
- 1/4 cup cocoa powder
- 1/2 tsp salt
- 90 g Greek yoghurt
- 2 eggs lightly beaten
- 2 tsp vanilla extract
- 1 cup zucchini finely grated firmly packed squeezed
- 1 tbs coconut oil *extra for greasing

Direction

- Preheat oven to 160C and grease a 12-hole muffin tray with coconut oil.
- Place the coconut oil and honey in a small saucepan over medium heat until melted, set aside.
- In a large bowl, combine the flour, LSA, baking powder, cocoa powder, salt and whisk to combine. Add the yoghurt, eggs, vanilla, coconut oil and honey mixture, and mix well to combine, then fold through zucchini until evenly combined. Divide batter into 12 muffin holes and bake for 18 - 20 minutes until cooked through.
- Store muffins in an airtight container for up to 5 days. Muffins can also be frozen individually for up to 3 months.

335. Tim Tam Cheesecake Balls Recipe

Serving: 0 | Prep: 30mins | Cook: 0S | Ready in: 30mins

Ingredients

- 1 packet Arnott's Tim Tams
- 250 g cream cheese
- 300 g milk chocolate
- 100 g white chocolate optional *to decorate

Direction

- Crush Tim Tams in a food processor, then add cream cheese and mix well.
- Roll into small balls, then pop in the freezer for a minimum of 30 minutes.
- Melt the milk chocolate, then dip and coat each ball really well with chocolate while still frozen.
- Melt white chocolate, then drizzle over the balls to decorate.

336. Tim Tam Cheesecake With Salted Caramel Recipe

Serving: 12 | Prep: 360mins | Cook: 15mins | Ready in: 375mins

Ingredients

- 250 g Arnott's dark chocolate Tim Tams crushed
- 1/2 cup desiccated coconut
- 100 g butter melted
- Filling
- 500 g cream cheese brought to room temperature
- 1 cup icing sugar
- 200 ml double cream
- 1/2 cup salted caramel
- Ganache
- 115 g dark chocolate chopped
- 1/3 cup double cream

- 1 tsp butter
- Topping
- 1/2 cup salted caramel
- 3 Arnott's Tim Tams crushed

Direction

- To make the base - In a food processor, finely crush the Tim Tams. Add coconut and melted butter and pulse until combined. Press the biscuit mixture into a 23cm round spring form cake tin and put in the fridge to set.
- To make the filling - Place the cream cheese and icing sugar in a large mixing bowl and beat until smooth. Add in the double cream and beating until smooth and creamy. Pour the salted caramel over the top and use a skewer or chopstick to gently swirl through the cheesecake. Pour onto the cooled biscuit base and put in the fridge to set for at least 3 hours,
- To make the ganache - Bring the cream and butter to boil in a small saucepan over medium heat. Pour the hot cream mixture over the chocolate and stir until smooth and glossy. Pour the ganache over the cheesecake and return it to the fridge to set.
- To serve, release the cheesecake from its springform pan and serve on a cake stand or nice plate. It is best served at room temperature. Drizzle the remaining ½ cup of salted caramel over the top of the cheesecake, allowing it to drip over the edges, and finish off with some crushed Tim Tam shards.

337. Tim Tam Hedgehog Slice

Serving: 0 | Prep: 30mins | Cook: 10mins | Ready in: 40mins

Ingredients

- 200g milk chocolate Arnott's Tim Tams cut into 1cm pieces
- 200g white chocolate Arnott's Tim Tams cut into 1cm pieces
- 300g dark chocolate chopped
- 150g butter chopped
- 1/3 cup icing sugar
- 1 egg lightly beaten
- Chocolate icing
- 200g dark chocolate chopped
- 100g unsalted butter chopped

Direction

- Line a 19cm x 29cm (base measurement) slice pan with baking paper, allowing the 2 long sides to overhang. Reserve a quarter of the chopped biscuits for garnish. Place remaining biscuits in a large bowl.
- Heat the chocolate, butter and sugar in a saucepan over a low heat, stirring for 5 minutes or until the mixture is well combined and smooth. Remove from the heat. Whisk in the egg until well combined. Cool for 10 minutes.
- Pour the chocolate mixture over the biscuits and stir until well combined. Spoon into the prepared pan. Use the back of a spoon to press firmly into the pan. Place in the fridge for 2 hours or until firm.
- To make the icing, stir the chocolate and butter in a small saucepan over low heat until melted. Cool for 10 minutes. Spread over the slice. Sprinkle with the reserved chopped biscuit. Place in the fridge for 1 hour to set. Cut slice into squares or rectangles.

338. Tiramisu Recipe

Serving: 8 | Prep: 25mins | Cook: 150mins | Ready in: 175mins

Ingredients

- 6 eggs
- 6 tbs caster sugar
- 500 g mascarpone

- 2 cups espresso coffee (liquid)
- 20 Savoiardi sponge finger biscuits
- 100 ml Kahlua
- 100 g dark chocolate

Direction

- Separate the egg yolks from the whites.
- Cream the yolks with sugar until pale in colour.
- Mix through the mascarpone with a spoon, add half the Kahlua then set aside.
- Beat egg whites until stiff peaks form, then fold into the mascarpone mixture.
- Spread a layer of mascarpone mixture over the base of a rectangular baking dish or lasagna dish.
- Dip the Savoiardi biscuits one at a time in a bowl of cooled espresso coffee (can dilute with water) and the rest of the liqueur, taking care not to make them soggy.
- Place the biscuits side by side on the layer of mascarpone, then spread another layer of mascarpone across the biscuits.
- Repeat the process twice, finishing with a layer of mascarpone on top.
- Grate chocolate over the top and set aside for two hours before serving.

339. Toblerone Cheesecake Slice Recipe

Serving: 8 | Prep: 20mins | Cook: 0S | Ready in: 20mins

Ingredients

- 1 cup chocolate biscuits
- 1/3 cup butter melted
- 1/4 cup ground almonds
- 500g cream cheese
- 200g Toblerone chocolate bar melted
- 1/2 cup thickened cream
- 1/2 cup caster sugar

Direction

- Combined biscuit crumbs, butter and almonds, and press into the base of a lightly greased slice tin or spring form pan. Chill.
- Beat cream cheese for 2 minutes or until smooth. Add sugar, melted Toblerone chocolate and cream, continue beating until well combined.
- Pour onto the prepared base and refrigerate for 2-3 hours until set, or overnight.
- Serve topped with chocolate shavings.

340. Toblerone Mousse Recipe

Serving: 4 | Prep: 15mins | Cook: 135mins | Ready in: 150mins

Ingredients

- 4 egg whites
- 600 ml cream
- 2 x 100 g Toblerone chocolate bars
- 1 Cadbury Flake chocolate bar

Direction

- Beat egg whites until they are hard peaks.
- Whip the cream and separate into different bowls, one bowl is to have a bit more than the other.
- Gently fold egg whites into the larger amount of cream, until all mixed through.
- Melt the Toblerone bars, and fold into the same bowl as the combined egg whites, make sure all the chocolate is mixed through.
- Pour the combined chocolate, cream and egg whites into your serving bowl. Layer the remaining cream on top.
- Break up the flake and sprinkle over for decoration.
- Refrigerate until set.

341. Traditional Christmas Pudding Recipe

Serving: 8 | Prep: 40mins | Cook: 510mins | Ready in: 550mins

Ingredients

- 250 g butter chopped
- 1 cup brown sugar
- 4 egg
- 750 g mixed fruit
- 1/2 cup pitted prune chopped
- 3/4 cup dates chopped
- 1 cup brandy
- 1 1/2 cup plain flour
- 1 tsp mixed spice
- 1/2 tsp ground cinnamon
- 1/2 tsp ground nutmeg
- 1/2 tsp bicarbonate of soda
- 1/2 cup slivered almonds
- 1 cup fresh breadcrumbs
- 1 cup icing sugar *to serve

Direction

- Beat butter and sugar until light and creamy.
- Add eggs one at a time, beating well after each.
- Add fruit, brandy, sifted dry ingredients, almonds and breadcrumbs. Mix well.
- Spoon mixture into a greased 8-cup capacity pudding basin. Cover basin with baking paper, secure tightly with string. Cover with foil and basin lid.
- Place pudding in a large pan with enough boiling water to come halfway up the side of the basin. Cover pan, simmer for 6 hours making sure water level remains constant by adding more boiling water as necessary.
- Remove pudding from water, and allow to cool. Cover and refrigerate until ready to serve.
- On day of serving, re-boil pudding as above for 2½ hours. Turn out onto a serving platter and dust with icing sugar.

342. Tropical Cheesecake Log Recipe

Serving: 8 | Prep: 40mins | Cook: 0S | Ready in: 40mins

Ingredients

- 3 mangoes
- 250 g cream cheese room temperature
- 1/4 cup caster sugar
- 600 ml thickened cream
- 1/2 tsp vanilla essence
- 250 g Arnott's Granita biscuits
- 1/2 cup unsweetened orange juice
- 2 passionfruit
- 1 punnet fresh raspberries

Direction

- Slice cheeks from one mango and spoon out flesh into a food processor. Blitz to form a puree. Set aside. Reserve remaining two mangoes for garnish.
- Wipe out bowl of food processor. Add cream cheese, caster sugar and 1/2 cup of cream, and blitz until smooth and well combined. Remove to a bowl and fold through mango puree.
- In a separate bowl, whisk remaining cream with vanilla essence until thick.
- Spread a long, thick rectangle of whipped cream onto your serving platter. Dip a Granita biscuit in orange juice then spread with cream cheese mixture. Stand upright at one end of whipped cream. Repeat with remaining biscuits, sandwiching them together with the cream cheese filling to form a log. Cover the log with remaining whipped cream, then place in the fridge to set for 2 hours or overnight.
- When you are ready to serve, remove cheeks from remaining mangoes and use a large metal spoon to scoop out the flesh. Slice lengthwise into thin slithers. Drape over the top of the log and dot with raspberries. Drizzle over passionfruit pulp and serve.

343. Tropical Coconut Meringue Torte

Serving: 0 | Prep: 15mins | Cook: 40mins | Ready in: 55mins

Ingredients

- 125 g White Wings Pavlova Magic Dessert Mix
- 1/2 cup Home Brand desiccated coconut
- 600 ml thickened cream
- 2 mango sliced cheeks removed
- 4 passionfruit halved pulp removed
- 125 g fresh raspberries
- 1 tbs mint *to decorate
- 1 tbs shredded coconut toasted *to decorate

Direction

- Preheat oven to 170C.
- Line 3 baking trays with non-stick baking paper. Draw a 20 cm disc on each piece of paper.
- Prepare pavlova mix and fold in coconut.
- Spoon meringue mixture evenly among the prepared discs and smooth the surfaces.
- Bake, swapping the trays halfway through cooking, for 40 minutes or until the meringues are crisp and dry.
- Turn oven off. Leave meringues in oven, with door ajar, to cool completely.
- Place 1 meringue disc on a cake stand. Top with ⅓ of the cream and fruit, leaving a 2 cm border.
- Repeat with remaining meringue, cream and fruit.
- Garnish torte with mint and coconut.

344. Tuckshop Banana Cake Recipe

Serving: 8 | Prep: 15mins | Cook: 40mins | Ready in: 55mins

Ingredients

- 3 bananas large ripe
- 1 cup self-raising flour sifted
- 1 egg brought to room temperature
- 1/2 cup sugar
- 1/4 cup canola oil

Direction

- Preheat oven to 180C and lightly grease a loaf tin.
- Peel bananas, place in a mixing bowl and mash.
- Add the flour and then the remaining ingredients.
- Mix well until combined and pour into the loaf tin.
- Bake for 40 minutes until golden.

345. Turkish Delight Fridge Cake Recipe

Serving: 12 | Prep: 15mins | Cook: 20mins | Ready in: 35mins

Ingredients

- 400 g dark chocolate coarsely chopped good quality
- 1 cup thick cream
- 2 tbs Cointreau
- 250 g Arnott's Marie biscuits coarsely chopped
- 6 x 55 g Fry's Turkish Delight bars quartered
- 170 g Ocean Spray Craisins dried cranberries
- 1/2 cup icing sugar mixture for dusting
- 1 tbs double cream *to serve

Direction

- Line the base of a 20 cm springform pan with baking paper.
- Place chocolate and cream in a saucepan over low heat. Stir for 5 minutes or until chocolate melts and mixture is smooth.

- Remove from heat. Stir in Cointreau and set aside for 5 minutes to cool.
- Combine the biscuits, Turkish delight and craisins in a large bowl. Add the chocolate mixture and stir until well combined.
- Press firmly into the prepared pan. Place in the fridge for 6 hours or until firm.
- Dust the cake with icing sugar and cut into slices. Divide among serving plates and serve with cream.

346. Turmeric Mango Smoothie Bowl Recipe

Serving: 1 | Prep: 5mins | Cook: 0S | Ready in: 5mins

Ingredients

- 1 banana frozen
- 1/2 cup unsweetened plain yoghurt
- 1/2 cup frozen mango cubed
- 2 tbs nut butter
- 1/2 tsp ground turmeric
- 1 splash non-dairy milk
- 50 g Barley+ Freedom Foods pink lady & macadamia muesli *to garnish
- 1 tsp chia seeds *to garnish
- 1 sprinkle coconut flakes *to garnish

Direction

- Top with Barley+ Pink Lady & Macadamia muesli, coconut flakes and chia seeds and serve!

347. Vanilla Bean Panna Cotta With Mango And White Chocolate Macadamia Truffle Recipe

Serving: 6 | Prep: 15mins | Cook: 400mins | Ready in: 415mins

Ingredients

- 375 ml thickened cream
- 375 ml full cream milk
- 1 vanilla bean
- 1/2 cup caster sugar
- 2 tbs boiling water
- 1 packet gelatine powder
- 2 mango diced ripe
- 1/4 cup cream
- 200 g white chocolate
- 1 1/2 cup shredded coconut
- 1 cup macadamias whole

Direction

- Place the thickened cream and milk in a saucepan. Use a small sharp knife to split the vanilla bean lengthways, then scrape the seeds from inside the bean. Add the seeds and bean to the saucepan. Slowly bring to the boil over a medium heat. Remove from the heat and set aside for 10 minutes.
- Discard bean from cream mixture. Add sugar and return to a low heat. Cook, stirring, for 5 minutes, or until sugar dissolves.
- In a small heatproof bowl, place 2 tablespoons of boiling water. Sprinkle over gelatine.
- Bring a small saucepan of water to boil. Remove from heat. Sit the bowl of gelatine in the water and stir until dissolved. Cool slightly, then stir into the cream mixture.
- Lightly oil 6 x 1/2 cup (125ml) dariole moulds or ramekins. Place on a tray and pour in cream mixture. Refrigerate for 4 hours.
- In a pan simmer the cream over a gentle heat. Do not boil. Remove from heat.
- Remove from heat and whisk in the grated chocolate until melted and smooth. Stir in the

nuts then pour mix into a 20cm plastic lined square cake pan. Chill until firm (at least two hours).
- Invert firmed chocolate mixture on to a clean work surface and peel away the plastic. Cut into 2cm squares and roll each piece into a small ball. Roll in the coconut until thoroughly coated.
- Place truffles in small patty pans and store in an air tight container in the fridge.
- Chop mangoes and place on top of set panna cotta. Place 1 truffle above mango. Serve.

348. Vanilla Slice Recipe

Serving: 10 | Prep: 20mins | Cook: 30mins | Ready in: 50mins

Ingredients

- 2 sheets puff pastry
- 1/2 cup caster sugar
- 1/2 cup custard powder
- 1 1/2 cups cream
- 2 1/2 cups milk
- 1 tsp vanilla essence
- Icing
- 2 cups icing sugar
- 1 tsp butter
- 1 tsp vanilla essence
- 1/2 cup hot water

Direction

- Place puff pastry on lined oven tray. Prick with a fork and bake for 10-15 minutes at 220C.
- Put sugar, custard powder and cream into a saucepan and stir over a medium heat until it starts to thicken.
- Add milk ½ a cup at a time and whisk continuously until the custard is thick.
- Let everything cool slightly. Place in a 22 cm square tin, pastry, custard, pastry then icing.
- Icing: Place icing sugar, butter and vanilla in a bowl and add enough hot water to make thin to medium textured icing.

349. Vanilla Slice Recipe

Serving: 0 | Prep: 60mins | Cook: 10mins | Ready in: 70mins

Ingredients

- 2 sheets puff pastry
- 300 ml milk
- 600 ml thickened cream
- 2 packets Cottee's instant vanilla pudding mix
- 1/4 cup icing sugar sifted

Direction

- Preheat oven to 210°C. Line a baking tray with baking paper.
- Line a slice tin with baking paper and set aside.
- Bake pastry sheets for 10-15 minutes or until puffed and just golden. When you remove them from the oven, place a tray on top of the sheets to make them flat. Leave them to cool this way.
- In a bowl, using a mixer, add the milk, cream and pudding mix together and combine until thick.
- Cut one pastry sheet to fit the base of the slice tin and place in the tin.
- Pour the custard mixture into the slice tin and smooth out evenly.
- Cut the second sheet of pastry and place on top.
- Refrigerate until chilled through (about 3 hours) and sprinkle with sifted icing sugar before serving. Remove from tin and slice into squares or rectangles using a serrated knife.

350. Very Simple Banana Bread Recipe

Serving: 12 | Prep: 15mins | Cook: 40mins | Ready in: 55mins

Ingredients

- 2 1/2 cups self-raising flour
- 3/4 cup brown sugar
- 1 cup milk
- 2 tbs margarine
- 1 tsp vanilla essence
- 3 bananas mashed

Direction

- Preheat oven to 180C.
- Combine milk, margarine, vanilla, mashed bananas, flour and sugar in a bowl. Mix with a wooden spoon until mixture is completely moist.
- Pour into greased pan or muffin tray. Top with extra banana pieces.
- Bake for 30-40 minutes for a loaf.

351. Walnut Christmas Cookies

Serving: 30 | Prep: 15mins | Cook: 10mins | Ready in: 25mins

Ingredients

- 180 g ground walnuts
- 120 g caster sugar
- 200 g unsalted butter room temperature
- 260 g plain flour
- Filling
- 140 g ground walnuts
- 160 g caster sugar
- 160 g unsalted butter room temperature
- 2 egg
- 1 tbs rum essence
- Chocolate decoration
- 1/4 cup caster sugar
- 2 tbs water
- 1 tbs cocoa powder
- 80 g unsalted butter

Direction

- Preheat oven to 160C degrees.
- Sift flour into a bowl. Add butter, sugar and walnuts, and mix to make a dough.
- Using an aluminum walnut cookie mold, take small amounts of dough and using your thumb, press the dough into the mold. Don't push too hard - the dough should not be too thin.
- Place cookie molds on baking tray and bake for 10-15 minutes or until slightly brown. Allow cookies to cool slightly and then with your thumb, gently slide out from the shape. Store in a plastic container to add filling the next day.
- To make the filling; in a bowl combine walnuts with caster sugar, unsalted butter, eggs and rum essence. Keep in fridge until you need it.
- Take half (one piece) of the walnut shells and put a small amount of the filling inside. Add another to walnut shell and stick together. Store in a plastic container overnight. Dip in melted chocolate the next day.
- To make chocolate dip; in saucepan melt butter over medium heat. Add sugar and stir. Add water and cocoa and cook until smooth.

352. Warm Chocolate Brownies With Salted Caramel Sauce And Custard Recipe

Serving: 12 | Prep: 20mins | Cook: 40mins | Ready in: 60mins

Ingredients

- 350 g dark chocolate chips
- 95 g unsalted butter chopped
- 1 1/2 cups brown sugar

- 4 eggs lightly beaten
- 1/3 cup plain flour
- 2 tsp baking powder
- 1/4 cup cocoa powder
- 1/4 tsp sea salt
- 100 g sour cream
- 1/4 cup pecans chopped
- 1/4 cup hazelnuts chopped
- 1/4 cup coconut oil melted
- 1 cup dark chocolate chips *extra
- Salted caramel sauce
- 1 cup caster sugar
- 6 tbs butter chopped
- 1/2 tsp sea salt flakes
- 1 1/2 cups Pauls thick vanilla custard *to serve

Direction

- Preheat oven to 170C.
- Line a 4cm-deep, 20cm (base) rectangle baking dish with non-stick baking paper.
- Chocolate brownies: Heat butter, chocolate and sugar in a heatproof glass bowl over a saucepan of simmering water on low heat. Stir constantly, until melted and smooth. Take off the heat and set aside to cool slightly.
- Add eggs to the chocolate mixture. Mix well.
- Sift flour, baking powder and cocoa powder over chocolate mixture. Stir to combine.
- Add in sour cream and sea salt, and stir to combine.
- Fold in the nuts and coconut oil.
- Pour brownie mixture into dish. Sprinkle with extra dark chocolate pieces. Bake for 40 minutes or until just set. Set aside to cool slightly.
- Salted caramel sauce: Heat the sugar in a saucepan over a medium heat, stirring constantly with a wooden spoon.
- Sugar will eventually melt and darken, be careful not to burn. Once sugar is completely melted, add the butter. Stir the butter into the caramel until it is completely melted.
- Remove from the heat and allow to cool slightly. Add in the sea salt and custard, and stir until well combined.

- Cut brownie into squares while still warm. Dust with icing sugar, serve with salted caramel sauce and custard.

353. Weet Bix, Honey And Banana Loaf Recipe

Serving: 8 | Prep: 15mins | Cook: 40mins | Ready in: 55mins

Ingredients

- 2 cups of plain organic flour
- 4 Weet-Bix crushed
- 1/2 tsp baking soda
- 1/2 tsp baking powder
- 1 tsp cinnamon
- 4 bananas
- 2 eggs lightly beaten
- 1/4 cup coconut oil
- 1 tbs honey
- 1 cup coconut milk
- 2 tbs shredded coconut

Direction

- Preheat the oven to 180C. Lightly grease and line a 24cm x 14cm loaf dish.
- Combine the flour, Weet-Bix, baking soda, baking powder and cinnamon in a large bowl. Combine all 3 mashed bananas, eggs, coconut oil, honey and coconut milk in a separate bowl and whisk.
- Add the wet mixture to the dry mixture and mix until combined. Then pour into the prepared baking dish. Slice the remaining banana lengthways and add two halves on top with shredded coconut sprinkled on top.
- Cook on the bottom shelf of the oven for 40 minutes or until a skewer comes out clean.
- Let it rest for 10 minutes then serve with ricotta and honey.

354. Wendy's Easy Pavlova

Serving: 8 | Prep: 30mins | Cook: 40mins | Ready in: 70mins

Ingredients

- 2 egg whites
- 1 1/2 cup caster sugar
- 1 tsp cornflour
- 1 tsp white vinegar
- 3 tbs boiling water
- 300 ml whipped cream
- 1/2 cup fresh mixed fruit

Direction

- Preheat oven to 160C.
- Line a baking tray with a sheet of non-stick baking paper.
- Place the egg whites, sugar, cornflour, vinegar, vanilla essence and boiling water in a large bowl, and beat with electric beater for approximately 5 minutes until stiff peaks form.
- Place mixture onto the baking tray, and use a spatula or the back of a spoon to smooth out to about 22 cm diameter.
- Bake for 20 minutes, until lightly brown.
- Remove from oven and cool on the tray.
- Slide a large knife under the pavlova and carefully move it onto a serving plate.
- Whip the cream and spread over the pavlova, then top with fresh fruit.

355. White Chocolate Grand Marnier Truffles Recipe

Serving: 4 | Prep: 30mins | Cook: 60mins | Ready in: 90mins

Ingredients

- 375 g Nestle* white chocolate melts
- 395 g condensed milk
- 250 g Arnott's biscuits crushed
- 1/2 cup desiccated coconut
- 1 tsp vanilla essence
- 60 ml Grand Marnier
- 1 cup coconut to coat
- 1 cup sultanas chopped optional

Direction

- Combine all ingredients together until mixed.
- Place mixture in the fridge for half an hour.
- Roll mixture into small balls and place on a tray, put back in the fridge for 5 minutes.
- Melt the chocolate according to directions on the packet.
- Remove balls from refrigerator and using a skewer dip balls in the melted chocolate then roll in coconut.
- Place on baking paper in an airtight container then refrigerate or freeze.

356. White Chocolate Key Lime Pie Recipe

Serving: 12 | Prep: 20mins | Cook: 360mins | Ready in: 380mins

Ingredients

- 250 g ginger biscuit
- 1/2 cup butter melted
- 1/4 cup shredded coconut
- 310 g white chocolate
- 1 cup thickened cream
- 1/2 cup lime juice
- 1/2 lime zested
- 1 tbs sour cream
- 0.125 cup shredded coconut *to serve
- 1/2 lime sliced *to serve

Direction

- Grease a 24cm glass pie dish with cooking spray.

- Using a food processor, process the ginger biscuits until they are fine crumbs. Add the shredded coconut and melted butter and mix to combine.
- Press the biscuit mixture into the pie dish. Using your fingers, evenly distribute the biscuit mixture across the bottom and up the sides of the dish. You can use the bottom of a saucepan or plate to press bottom. Refrigerate biscuit mixture for at least an hour to allow the biscuit base to set.
- To make the filling – add white chocolate and cream to a small saucepan and heat gently over low heat until melted, stirring regularly. Take off the heat, add lime juice, zest and sour cream and mix well with spoon.
- Pour filling onto the biscuit base and return pie to the fridge to set for at least 6 hours or overnight.
- Take the pie out of the fridge just before you ready to serve and decorate with extra shredded coconut and lime wedges.

357. White Chocolate Malteser Cheesecake Recipe

Serving: 12 | Prep: 20mins | Cook: 0S | Ready in: 20mins

Ingredients

- 300 g chocolate biscuits
- 12 dates
- 1/2 cup coconut oil
- 180 g walnuts
- Filling
- 500 g cream cheese
- 3/4 cup caster sugar
- 200 ml thickened cream
- 400 g white chocolate
- 3 tsp gelatine powder
- 1/4 cup boiling water
- 250 g Maltesers

Direction

- Base: Process biscuits and walnuts until the mixture resembles breadcrumbs.
- Add the dates and butter/coconut oil. Process until well combined.
- Grease a springform pan. Firmly press mixture into the bottom of the pan and work up the sides. Cover and refrigerate.
- Filling: While the cream cheese softens, chop the Maltesers in half and set aside.
- Beat cream cheese and sugar with an electric mixer on medium speed until combined. Add the cream and mix until creamy.
- Combine gelatine with boiling water in a jug or mug. Add to the cream cheese mixture. Mix on medium speed until well combined.
- Melt white chocolate in a heatproof bowl over a small saucepan of boiling water. Do not allow the bowl to touch the water.
- Pour the melted chocolate and Maltesers into the bowl with the cream cheese mixture and mix until combined.
- Pour mixture over base. Add any extra maltesers for decoration if desired.
- Refrigerate for 5 hours or overnight.

358. White Chocolate And Mango Cheesecake Recipe

Serving: 8 | Prep: 30mins | Cook: 0S | Ready in: 30mins

Ingredients

- 200 g gingernut biscuits
- 100 g unsalted butter melted
- 50 g crystalized ginger optional
- Filling
- 250 g cream cheese brought to room temperature
- 200 ml condensed milk
- 150 g white chocolate melted
- 150 ml cream
- 3 1/2 tsp gelatine powder
- 125 ml boiling water
- Topping

- 2 mangoes medium
- 4 tbs caster sugar
- 2 tsp gelatine powder
- 100 ml boiling water

Direction

- Base: Blitz the biscuits in a food processor until they've been reduced to fine crumbs.
- Add the ginger, if using, and blitz until completely incorporated into the crumbs. With the machine switched on, pour the melted butter in until all combined.
- Press the crumbs into the base of a lined 24cm springform tin and refrigerate until firm.
- Filling: Add gelatine to the water and stir with a fork until all dissolved. Put aside to cool.
- Combine the cream cheese and condensed milk and beat until smooth and creamy. Stir in the melted chocolate and then pour in the cream.
- Pour in the cooled water and gelatine and stir until combined.
- Pour into the tin and put it into the fridge for at least an hour and a half to firm up.
- Topping: Puree the mango flesh. Add the sugar and blitz again. There should be approximately 350ml of puree.
- Combine water and gelatine.
- Combine with mango puree and pour carefully over top of the cheesecake.
- Refrigerate for 3 hours.
- Serve with some fresh mango, lychees and passionfruit, if desired.

359. White Chocolate And Strawberry Pavlova Recipe

Serving: 8 | Prep: 15mins | Cook: 0S | Ready in: 15mins

Ingredients

- 1 tbs icing sugar *to serve
- 1 cup fresh strawberries hulled quartered *to decorate
- 600 ml thickened cream whipped
- 110 g Woolworths Select white chocolate spread
- 500 g Woolworths Select classic pavlova base

Direction

- Place pavlova base on a large platter.
- Spoon white chocolate spread into a microwave-safe bowl and warm in microwave on medium for 30 seconds.
- Fold in whipped cream.
- Spoon over pavlova base and top with hulled and quartered strawberries
- Dust with icing sugar to serve.

360. White Christmas Peppermint Surprise

Serving: 0 | Prep: 30mins | Cook: 40mins | Ready in: 70mins

Ingredients

- 250 g copha
- 1 1/2 cup milk powder
- 1 1/2 cup Rice Bubbles
- 1 1/2 cup icing sugar
- 1 1/2 cup desiccated coconut
- Topping
- 35 g Peppermint Crisp chocolate bars crushed
- 15 raspberry lollies

Direction

- Melt copha over medium heat. Set aside to cool.
- Mix dry ingredients.
- Add melted copha to dry ingredients. Stir well until combined.
- Divide mix evenly between patty pans. Alternatively, press mixture into a tray.
- Sprinkle crushed chocolate bar over the patty pans.

- Using scissors, cut the raspberry lollies to a desired size and place on top.
- Refrigerate until firm.

361. White Christmas Pudding Balls Recipe

Serving: 30 | Prep: 15mins | Cook: 30mins | Ready in: 45mins

Ingredients

- 125 g sweet plain biscuits
- 400 g condensed milk
- 3 Peppermint Crisp chocolate bars roughly chopped
- 150 g white chocolate roughly chopped
- 1 cup coconut
- 1 tbs cocoa
- 1/2 cup coconut *to decorate
- Decoration
- 80 g white chocolate melts
- 1 packet spearmint leaf lollies cut into strips *to decorate
- 1 packet silver cachous *to decorate

Direction

- Blend biscuits to create crumbs, add cocoa, condensed milk, and coconut and mix until combined.
- Stir through peppermint bars and chocolate. Cover and refrigerate for 30 minutes to harden a little.
- Roll into balls and roll in coconut. Set aside.
- Decoration: Melt chocolate. Dip the top of each ball into melted chocolate.
- Top with spearmint leaves and cachous balls to resemble holly.

362. White Christmas Truffles Recipe

Serving: 0 | Prep: 25mins | Cook: 5mins | Ready in: 30mins

Ingredients

- 375g pkt white chocolate melts
- 295g can sweetened condensed milk
- 1 1/2 cups rice bubbles
- 1/2 cup shredded coconut, plus extra to roll
- 1/3 cup dried cranberries
- 1/4 cup pistachios, chopped

Direction

- Melt the chocolate in a medium heatproof bowl over a saucepan of simmering water (don't let the bowl touch the water). Fold in the remaining ingredients. Place in the fridge for 30 minutes or until firm enough to roll.
- Use a tablespoon to measure out the chocolate mixture and roll in a ball. Roll in extra coconut. Repeat with the remaining mixture to make 40 balls. Store in the fridge

363. White Christmas Recipe

Serving: 0 | Prep: 30mins | Cook: 5mins | Ready in: 35mins

Ingredients

- 1 1/2 cups Rice Bubbles
- 1 1/2 cups milk powder
- 1 1/2 cups coconut
- 1 1/2 cups icing sugar
- 250 g copha
- 3/4 cup glace cherries
- 3/4 cup sultanas

Direction

- Melt copha and combine with remaining ingredients in a bowl.

- Press into a tray and refrigerate.

364. Wholemeal Vegan Blueberry Pancakes Recipe

Serving: 3 | Prep: 5mins | Cook: 10mins | Ready in: 15mins

Ingredients

- 1 1/4 cups wholemeal plain flour
- 1 tsp bicarbonate of soda
- 1 no egg replacer
- 2 cups dairy-free milk
- 1/2 tsp vanilla essence
- 1 tbs brown sugar
- 1/2 cup fresh blueberries

Direction

- In a large bowl mix together ingredients. Batter will be thick.
- Heat a frying pan over medium heat. Pour batter onto pan and cook each side for about 2 minutes or until golden brown.
- Drizzle with syrup or serve with fresh blueberries, jam, or topping of choice!

365. Yo Yo Biscuits Recipe

Serving: 12 | Prep: 15mins | Cook: 30mins | Ready in: 45mins

Ingredients

- 185g butter
- 1/3 cup icing sugar
- 1 1/2 cups plain flour
- 1/3 cup custard powder
- Filling
- 1/2 cup icing sugar
- 2 tbs butter
- 2 tsp custard powder
- 1/2 tsp vanilla essence

Direction

- Biscuits: Cream butter and icing sugar, add sifted flour and custard powder. Mix well.
- Form into balls and place onto greased oven trays and press with a fork to form biscuits. Bake in a moderate oven for about 15 minutes.
- Filling: Cream ingredients together. Use as required for joining biscuits.

Index

A

Almond 3,5,6,10,96,123,125

Apple 3,4,6,10,52,133

Apricot 63

Arrowroot 25,127

B

Banana 3,4,5,6,7,14,15,21,28,52,60,76,118,129,146,149,150

Barley 147

Berry 5,88,124

Biscuits 4,5,6,7,38,50,54,75,121,122,128,155

Blueberry 3,6,7,23,124,155

Bran 31,146

Bread 3,4,7,14,31,52,53,149

Butter 3,4,5,6,17,24,31,38,39,52,53,58,61,65,75,115,116,128

C

Cake 3,4,5,6,7,8,11,15,17,20,21,23,26,33,34,42,43,47,50,52,54,55,57,58,59,60,70,72,74,75,76,78,83,85,87,89,92,93,95,96,98,119,122,123,125,131,135,136,146

Caramel 3,4,5,6,7,15,16,25,28,34,53,56,68,83,93,100,132,142,149

Carrot 3,5,35,93

Cheese 3,4,5,6,7,12,13,14,16,17,20,24,26,30,32,44,45,46,56,64,68,69,70,71,77,91,93,94,99,101,102,103,104,107,109,110,112,113,116,117,118,124,133,134,136,137,138,142,144,145,152

Cherry 3,23,26,27,30

Chocolate 3,4,5,6,7,29,30,31,32,33,34,40,45,48,49,52,53,59,60,64,65,92,93,96,97,109,111,116,123,128,130,139,142,143,147,149,150,151,152,153

Choux pastry 18

Christmas cake 74

Christmas pudding 86

Cinnamon 3,4,13,41

Coconut 4,5,6,7,42,70,82,83,98,103,106,108,133,146

Cranberry 4,45

Cream 3,4,5,6,8,9,11,12,13,16,35,36,40,44,46,51,61,67,76,78,79,83,89,91,92,99,102,103,104,107,108,111,113,116,119,131,133,134,135,136,138,144,155

Croissant 3,10

Crumble 4,35,62,87,94,98

Curd 4,5,6,70,76,130

Custard 3,4,6,7,10,13,19,31,40,43,47,48,120,149

D

Date 4,5,68,98

E

Egg 3,4,18,19,59,140

F

Fat 29

Fig 4,49,60

Flour 4,61

Fruit 3,4,5,6,23,31,37,54,55,60,62,63,65,74,78,88,100,109,122,134,140

Fudge 5,6,95,132

G

Gin 4,5,6,39,64,100,111

H

Hazelnut 5,96,101

Heart 6,122

Honey 3,4,7,38,67,80,142,150

I

Icing 3,4,9,13,23,34,35,41,42,43,50,57,71,72,87,95,103,106,109,117,139,140,148

J

Jam 4,6,51,122,124

Jelly 4,5,6,38,68,70,81,119

Jus 12,113

L

Lemon 4,5,6,55,61,69,70,71,72,73,89,92,101,102,103,119

Lime 7,151

M

Macadamia 5,7,74,147

Madeira 139

Mango 3,4,5,6,7,19,42,55,62,76,77,78,79,80,81,82,83,86,87,104,122,138,147,152

Marshmallow 5,7,85,104,140

Meringue 5,6,7,71,79,122,123,146

Milk 4,6,25,43,53,71,94,102,107,127,132,136

Mince 3,4,5,7,31,62,74,140

Mint 3,6,10,32,128

Morel 22

Muesli 5,105

Muffins 3,4,5,6,7,28,39,40,52,82,123,129,137,142

N

Nut 4,6,29,57,106,111

O

Orange 3,4,5,6,32,49,57,58,66,89,95,123

P

Pancakes 3,4,5,6,7,18,43,73,112,155

Papaya 6,116

Parfait 3,4,5,12,49,82,83

Pastry 3,10,35,91,140

Peach 6,110

Pear 3,6,13,119,125

Peel 10,11,15,20,77,83,84,146

Pepper 6,7,8,10,30,116,117,153,154

Pie 3,4,5,6,7,10,15,18,61,68,71,88,117,140,151

Pike 4,58

Pineapple 3,6,7,13,23,107,118,139

Pistachio 4,45

Pizza 3,24

Plum 4,40

Pomegranate 6,119

Popcorn 3,38

Port 6,120

Potato 7,140

Pulse 31

Pumpkin 6,121

R

Raspberry 3,5,6,14,33,83,122,123,124

Rhubarb 6,125,134

Rice 4,5,6,30,41,46,84,85,99,105,106,111,127,153,154

Ricotta 6,125

Royal icing 51

Rum 3,4,5,6,22,33,64,97,127

S

Salt 3,5,7,28,34,83,142,149,150

Shortbread 3,6,26,128,129

Shortcrust pastry 63

Spelt 7,142

Stew 6,134

Strawberry 3,4,6,7,20,24,48,107,108,130,135,136,137,153

Sugar 4,5,6,7,29,54,92,138,150

Syrup 87,89

T

Tea 33

Toffee 4,18,38,84

Truffle 4,5,6,7,53,74,121,147,151,154

Turkish delight 126,147

Turmeric 7,147

V

Vegan 7,155

W

Walnut 3,6,7,13,15,37,108,149

Wine 5,89

Y

Yoghurt 5,6,72,114

L

lasagna 144

Conclusion

Thank you again for downloading this book!

I hope you enjoyed reading about my book!

If you enjoyed this book, please take the time to share your thoughts and post a review on Amazon. It'd be greatly appreciated!

Write me an honest review about the book – I truly value your opinion and thoughts and I will incorporate them into my next book, which is already underway.

Thank you!

If you have any questions, **feel free to contact at:** *author@chardrecipes.com*

Michele Sova

chardrecipes.com

Printed in Great Britain
by Amazon